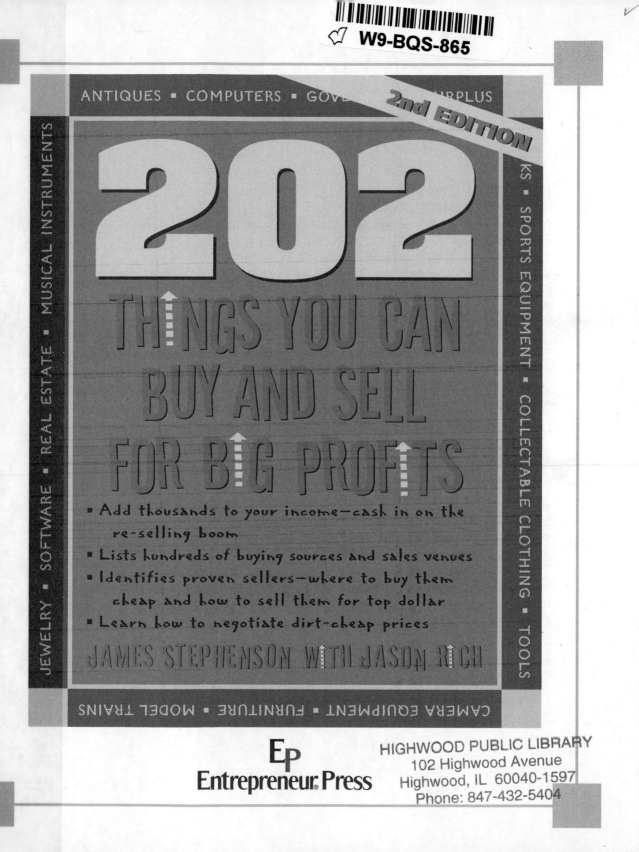

ANTIQUES ▪ COMPUTERS ▪ GOVE... ...URPLUS

2nd EDITION

MUSICAL INSTRUMENTS ▪ REAL ESTATE ▪ SOFTWARE ▪ JEWELRY

KS ▪ SPORTS EQUIPMENT ▪ COLLECTABLE CLOTHING ▪ TOOLS

202

THINGS YOU CAN BUY AND SELL FOR BIG PROFITS

- Add thousands to your income—cash in on the re-selling boom
- Lists hundreds of buying sources and sales venues
- Identifies proven sellers—where to buy them cheap and how to sell them for top dollar
- Learn how to negotiate dirt-cheap prices

JAMES STEPHENSON WITH JASON RICH

CAMERA EQUIPMENT ▪ FURNITURE ▪ MODEL TRAINS

EP
Entrepreneur Press

Publisher: Jere L. Calmes
Cover design: Beth Hansen-Winter
Production and Editorial Services: CWL Publishing Enterprises, Inc., Madison, WI,
www.cwlpub.com

This publication is designed to provide accurate and authoritative information in regard to the
subject matter covered. It is sold with the understanding that the publisher is not engaged in ren-
dering legal, accounting, or other professional services. If legal advice or other expert assistance is
required, the services of a competent professional person should be sought.

ISBN 13: 978-1-59918-184-4
      10: 1-59918-184-3

Library of Congress Cataloging-in-Publication Data

Stephenson, James, 1966-
   202 things you can buy and sell for big profits / by James
Stephenson with Jason R. Rich. — 2nd ed.
     p. cm. -- (202 series)
   ISBN 978-1-59918-184-4 (alk. paper)
   1. Purchasing. 2. Selling. 3. Home-based businesses—Management. 4. Small business—
Management. I. Rich, Jason. II. Title. III. Title: Two hundred two things you can buy and sell for
big profits.
   HF5437.S72 2004
   658.85—dc22

                                                                                    2008015781

Printed in Canada

12 11 10 09 08   10 9 8 7 6 5 4 3 2 1

CONTENTS

CHAPTER 4

Where You Can Buy Things Cheaply _ _ _ _ _ _ _ _ _ _ 105

CHAPTER 5

Where You Can Sell Things for Big Profits _____ 135

CHAPTER 6

The Mega-List: 202 Things You Can Buy and Sell for Big Profits _____ 165

Things You Can Buy and Sell for Big Profits

INTRODUCTION

Unless you're already a multimillionaire, chances are you're constantly worrying about money and the stability of your job. With the economy on shaky ground and employers constantly cutting back and laying off employees, job security is no longer available to most hardworking Americans.

Add to this the ever-rising costs of everyday living, and many people have trouble making ends meet. Even fewer people are able to regularly put money into their savings accounts, properly plan for retirement and/or somehow improve their current overall quality of life.

Most people would greatly appreciate and be able to make good use of a bit of extra cash each month, yet not everyone is able to pursue a promotion or pay raise at their current job, or has enough time in their day to take on a second job (working for another employer) in order to supplement their income.

By tapping your creativity and adopting an entrepreneurial attitude, however, it's possible to generate extra money by buying and selling items that are capable of generating profit. As you're about to learn from this book, not only are there countless items that can be bought and sold (and that are readily available to you for this purpose), there are also many different ways to sell items that can fit your lifestyle and schedule.

Becoming an entrepreneur who buys and sells items in order to generate profits is not a get-rich-quick scheme, nor is this typically something that can happen extremely quickly. If, however, you have a great idea about what you can sell, figure out whom to sell those products to, and you're able to market your business to the right audience, it is possible to establish a successful business on a part-time or even a full-time basis.

It's important, however, that as you continue reading this book, you develop a realistic understanding of what's possible and commit to investing the time, effort and money necessary to achieve success. First, you need to figure out what your goals and objectives are, and then you need to determine how much time and money you initially have to invest into a new business venture.

As you do this, you'll also want to carefully evaluate your professional skills, experience, knowledge, motivation and interests, plus learn how to identify potentially profitable opportunities. Simultaneously, you'll want to brush up on your internet and computer skills, since (as you'll discover in Chapter 3) there are amazing opportunities available to buy and sell all kinds of items online. For example, literally millions of people just like you have learned how to buy and sell items on eBay and other online auction websites. Countless others continue to generate profits operating their own e-commerce websites or by selling items on Craigslist.

The good news is that eBay is only the tip of the iceberg when it comes to potential opportunities to buy and sell items for a profit. People also use flea markets, trade shows, classified ads and additional online marketplaces to sell new and used goods—and earn big profits in the process! With the help of this book, so can you.

By picking up a copy of this book, you've already expressed an interest in learning how to effectively buy and sell items in order to make money. You already

Things You Can Buy and Sell for Big Profits

know that this objective is viable. To begin doing it yourself, you'll first need to understand your rationale or motivation behind pursuing this type of business venture. Ask yourself, "What are my primary financial goals or objectives?"

Some of your potential answers might be to:

- Pay off existing debt
- Change jobs and pursue something that allows you to earn more money on a full-time basis
- Set up your own business and become your own boss
- Begin working from home
- Pay your way through college or graduate school
- Pay down your mortgage faster
- Build up your savings or create a financial nest egg
- Establish or better fund your retirement account
- Give yourself something to do after your formal retirement
- Improve your current quality of life by supplementing your current income with a job that allows you to set your own hours and schedule

Any of these objectives can be within your reach and ultimately achieved by starting and operating your own buy-and-sell enterprise. People just like you are doing it right now, and many more are joining their ranks daily.

At this point, you may be asking yourself, "Do I have what it takes to do this?" Well, chances are, the answer is an unequivocal "Yes!" This book will provide the core knowledge you need to get started, plus help you generate ideas about what type of product(s) you can buy and sell in order to start generating profits.

People from all walks of life, regardless of their education level, age group, income level, or current personal situation, are discovering innovative ways to buy and sell their way to a better part-time or full-time income. Many people are discovering that after their business is established, they can work less, earn more, and be a lot happier in the process. They can also take control over their own lives by becoming their own boss.

This newly revised second edition of *202 Things You Can Buy and Sell For Big Profits* includes details about some of the very best products you can buy and sell, plus describes the very best places to do the buying and selling, based on your lifestyle, goals and available resources.

In addition to serving as a comprehensive resource that's chock full of ideas for items and products you can buy and sell, this book will cover important topics you'll need to understand in order to get started. Some of the business-related topics covered include the following items.

Legal Issues

You will discover answers for all of those tough legal questions, including:

- *Licenses and permits.* What business licenses, permits and sales tax ID numbers are required to start and run a buy-and-sell enterprise, and where do you get them?
- *Business structure.* What legal business structure is right for your needs and your new buy-and-sell enterprise: sole proprietorship, partnership, limited liability corporation or corporation? The advantages and disadvantages of each option are explained.
- *Insurance.* Do you need insurance to buy and sell? In some cases, yes. You will learn what property, inventory, and liability insurance are, why you may need them, and where you can secure the insurance coverage you need to protect your family, business and assets.

Financial Issues

You will find out how to deal with all of the financial issues pertaining to starting and operating a buy-and-sell venture, including:

- *Cash requirements.* How much money will be required to start your buy-and-sell enterprise, and what are the sources available to you in terms of obtaining the required startup capital? You will learn how to start your buy-and-sell venture for peanuts, and in some cases, get suppliers to fund your venture almost entirely.
- *Money management.* Learn how to set up your books, work with accountants and bookkeepers, and open commercial bank accounts. You will discover how to establish a credit card merchant account so you can provide your customers with convenient purchase payment options, including credit cards, debit cards, electronic money transfers, and retail financing and leasing options.
- *Pricing.* You will learn how to calculate fixed costs, direct costs, income and profit, so that you can establish a selling price that will leave you in the black, not seeing red.
- *Taxation.* What taxes are you required to pay on the money you earn buying and selling, and what are the tax advantages of a buy-and-sell operation? Both issues are explained.

Getting Started

You will learn the key steps for launching a buy-and-sell enterprise, including:

- *Setting up.* Learn how to set up and organize your work space, including equipment requirements, time management tips, storage needs and an inventory recording and tracking system.
- *Technology.* Discover the technologies that can be used to help increase sales and profits while saving you time and money.
- *Trade accounts.* Establish trade accounts with suppliers. Learn how to buy on terms and negotiate the lowest price, and learn about drop-shipping, delivery and order-fulfillment services.
- *Build an e-commerce website* (a website that allows you to sell items online and process credit card payments from your customers). What you need to know to get on the internet and start doing business there, such as building your site, selecting the right domain name, and registering with search engines.

Sales and Marketing

You will discover what is required to market your products like a seasoned pro, including:

- *Developing a marketing strategy.* Learn how to develop a marketing strategy that is right for your needs, enabling you to meet and exceed your objectives and goals. You will learn how to identify potential customers, provide great customer service, overcome challenges and grow your buy-and-sell enterprise into a profitable business venture.
- *Personal selling.* The information featured takes you through the entire sales cycle, from prospecting and presenting to closing the sale and negotiating the highest possible price for your goods.
- *Advertising.* Create great ads that sell, learn the sources for free and very inexpensive advertising, secure free publicity, and discover how to use promotional fliers and signs to increase your sales and profits.
- *Online marketing.* Consumers spend billions every month purchasing products online, and you will learn about online permission-based marketing and advertising to reach them so you can claim your portion of the very lucrative internet pie. This includes the use of search engine marketing (aka keyword advertising), which has become a powerful, cost-effective way to find and attract new customers using the web.

The Best Buying Sources

You will discover what the best buying sources are, including:

- *Wholesalers.* You will find the contact information for hundreds of national and international wholesalers of brand-name, highly salable merchandise that can be bought low and sold for as much as 10 times your cost.
- *Liquidators.* Every year retailers and manufacturers unload billions of dollars' worth of brand-name, top-quality merchandise directly to liquidators at insane rock-bottom prices. You will find out who these liquidators are, how to contact them and how to get the best deals on the best products for resale.
- *Manufacturers.* Find hundreds of manufacturing sources nationally and internationally, so you can skip the middleman markup and buy direct.
- *Craftspeople.* Often you can look no further than right in your local community to find great, highly salable crafts that you can buy low and sell high. Working with local craftspeople to market their goods can make you rich, and this book will show you how.
- *Sales agents.* Thousands of manufacturers nationally and internationally are represented by sales agents. You will learn where they are, how to contact them and how to negotiate great deals.
- *Classified advertisements.* One of the best sources for finding great second-hand products to resell for big profits is right in your local classified advertisements. Learn how to buy products from classified ads and resell the same products for huge profits.
- *Garage sales.* There is an endless supply of fantastic garage sale bargains in every community. You will learn how to be first in line, what types of used products to look for and how to negotiate rock-bottom prices.
- *Flea markets.* The majority of flea market vendors do not know the true value of their merchandise, and because of this, treasures can be found at every flea market, every time you go. You will learn how to separate the treasures from the junk, buy low, and resell directly to collectors and your customers for big profits.
- *Auctions.* Without question, auctions and government surplus sales represent some of the best opportunities to find products, equipment and merchandise at pennies on the dollar, which can be resold for huge profits. You will learn who organizes these auctions and how to find out what is being sold long before the sale.
- *Online marketplaces.* Go online and buy cheap merchandise, art, antiques, and more, all at the click of a mouse and at incredible prices. You will learn where the best sites are and how to find the best deals.

Things You Can Buy and Sell for Big Profits

The Best Selling Venues

You will discover what the best selling venues are, including:

- *Auctions.* The key to successful buying and selling is knowing where to buy and where to sell. It is possible to buy an item at one auction and sell the same item at another auction for huge profits, and this book will explain how to do it.
- *Classified advertisements.* Find out how to place advertisements in your local paper that will make the telephone ring off the hook with customers eager to buy your goods at top dollar. You need to learn what sells best, the best days to run your ads, the best categories to place an ad under, and what to tell people that will make them take action and buy.
- *Direct to collectors.* You can sell your goods at incredible profits directly to collectors or businesses. You will learn what equipment and products are best suited to accomplish this and how to get started.
- *eBay.* People just like you have struck it rich and continue to do so selling products using eBay. You will learn how to set up your own eBay seller's account, list products, market your goods, and start making money like thousands of people are already doing, all from the comfort of home.
- *E-Commerce websites.* Discover how you can market your products to a worldwide audience of potential consumers via your website and other online marketplaces.
- *Flea markets.* Find out where the best flea markets are, how to select the most visible vendor space, what products sell best, how to merchandise your goods, and how to sell hard, get your price and take no prisoners.
- *Garage sales.* Get the great tips you need to plan, organize and host profitable garage sales. Find out what sells best and how to advertise the event so hundreds of people show up, ready to buy.
- *Homebased showrooms.* You can set up a showroom right in your own home to showcase and sell your products. You will learn how to do this, what zoning requirements must be met, how to keep your neighbors happy, and, most importantly, how to generate sales and profits right from home.
- *Kiosks.* Find out how renting mall kiosks from which you can sell your goods can make you rich. You will learn what products sell best, how to merchandise them, and what time of year is best to rent kiosk retail space.
- *Trade and consumer shows.* The trade show sales environment can be a fast-paced, exciting and profitable one, and the information and tips in this book will show you how to find the best shows, display your merchandise and command top dollar on each sale.

202 Viable Products to Buy and Sell

Need an idea about what you can start buying and selling in order to achieve your financial objectives? You will discover ideas for 202 new and used products that are viable for generating impressive profits. Each product idea showcased in this book includes the details you need to learn more and get started, including:

- *Product description.* A complete product description explaining what it is used for, who buys it, and what makes it such a great product to buy and resell.
- *Buying sources.* Multiple buying sources are featured for each product, including contact information. However, this is meant to be just a sampling of the possible buying sources you can do business with.
- *Potential selling venues.* You will learn where to sell your products and for how much. Each product description features a sample list of the best places to sell your goods. Again, these are only suggestions. Many more possible opportunities will typically apply.
- *Resources.* Of course, one of the keys to success will be your ability to buy low and sell high. You have to know where you can purchase highly salable merchandise at the lowest possible price, and where the same merchandise can be sold at the highest possible price to maximize your return on investment and profits. After all, the entire premise of a buy-and-sell enterprise is to buy low and sell high. That is why you will find hundreds of valuable resources throughout this book. The resources featured include American, Canadian and international private corporations, business associations, government agencies, individuals, websites, publications, products, services and lots more.

If you want to track down additional buying sources or resources pertaining to a specific product or product category, look no further than Google or Yahoo! If you're looking for additional wholesale sources, for example, enter the search phrase, "Wholesale [insert product name]." You can also find industry associations and trade publications online that will provide a wealth of additional expertise pertaining to specific types of buy-and-sell opportunities, depending on the product(s) you're interested in.

To help you get the most out of each of the 202 product descriptions featured within this book, a handful of graphic icons are used, including:

🖰 A mouse icon represents an online resource, such as a website address.

☎ A telephone icon represents a resource's contact telephone number.

All of the resources featured were active links, telephone numbers and mailing addresses at the time of writing (March 2008). However, over time some information changes and becomes outdated. While every effort has been taken to ensure that all of the resources offered herein are for reputable businesses, organizations and publications, inclusion in this book does not constitute an endorsement for any specific companies, products or services.

Ultimately, it's up to you to do your own research to ensure that the products you opt to sell are of the highest quality possible, and that the companies and/or individuals you choose to do business with are indeed reputable. Resources such as the Better Business Bureau (**www.bbb.org**) or specific industry trade associations can be utilized to help you pinpoint reputable companies and individuals.

Plan On Making an Ongoing Time and Financial Investment

Some of the ongoing responsibilities involved with operating your own business include:

- Acquiring and maintaining inventory
- Processing and fulfilling orders
- Handling returns
- Managing your company's financial records (bookkeeping)
- Planning, designing, implementing and managing the marketing, advertising and public relations campaigns designed to promote your product(s) and business
- Handling customer service issues

Like starting any type of business, starting a buy-and-sell enterprise involves some level of risk. Thus, you'll typically want to start off on a smaller scale and gradually build up your business. Seriously think twice before quitting your current job and giving up your stable income in order to launch a new business.

A buy-and-sell enterprise can typically start off as a small, part-time project (where you work evenings or on weekends, for example), and slowly grow. Only when it becomes a stable and profitable business venture should you consider making this your full-time career.

Also, as you move forward, always have an exit strategy in place. If your business fails, how will you and your family handle the financial ramifications? You'll soon discover there are strategies you can implement to avoid unnecessary financial hardship or bankruptcy, should your business fail or take longer than expected to become successful.

Whether you're starting a traditional business or an online-based one, when you get right down to it, a business is a business. Thus, as you establish your buy-and-sell enterprise, you'll want to follow the same basic steps that you would for any type of business. This means starting off by creating a detailed and well-thought-out business plan that includes details about your business, its goals, financial projections, market research and other details that will provide a roadmap for you to follow as you move forward. This is an important step that should not be skipped!

For help creating a detailed business plan, check out the Business Plan Pro software from Palo Alto Software (**paloalto.com**). The $99.95 Standard Edition (for Windows) of this software offers an interactive, step-by-step business plan guide, plus more than 500 sample plans and a variety of other useful resources. The U.S. Small Business Administration offers free tools and advice for writing business plans. Point your web browser to s**ba.gov/smallbusinessplanner/plan/write-abusinessplan/index.html**.

A Comprehensive Resource Is Now in Your Hands

The primary goal of this new, second edition of *202 Things You Can Buy and Sell for Big Profits* is to be the most authoritative and comprehensive buy-and-sell book available.

The information within this book will give you the ability to identify the best products, where to buy them cheaply, and how to sell them for the most profit. While the core facts and information you'll need are now within your hands, you must find and harness the needed motivation, dedication and confidence within yourself to achieve success.

Achieving success will require hard work, proper planning, time, dedication and an initial financial investment on your part. The more knowledge and experience you already possess of business, marketing, advertising and bookkeeping, the bigger advantage you'll have as you get started.

If you determine that the internet will be your primary tool for selling products, for example, you'll need to learn all about e-commerce and how to profit from online auctions.

In addition to this book, two additional books written by bestselling author Jason R. Rich that might be helpful include *Design and Launch Your eCommerce Business in One Week* (Entrepreneur Press) and *The Unofficial Guide to Starting a Business Online*, 2nd Edition (Wiley), which are currently available from bookstores everywhere, or from the author's website at **JasonRich.com**.

Things You Can Buy and Sell for Big Profits

Unfortunately, as with any type of new business venture, there are no easy shortcuts to get started, and there are absolutely no guarantees of success. Even with all of the necessary tools at your disposal, not every business venture will ultimately become successful.

Performing the necessary research before you launch any business venture, and then developing a thorough understanding of what you're selling, whom you're selling to, the best ways to acquire and sell your product(s), how to manage your business's finances, and how to offer top-notch customer service will all dramatically improve your chances of success.

Now, if you're ready to get started, Chapter 1 begins with an explanation of what a buy-and-sell enterprise actually is, and will help you start thinking about how launching this type of business venue can benefit you personally, based on your needs, wants, expectations, knowledge, interests, experience and available resources—all of which must be carefully taken into consideration as you develop your initial business plan.

Additional Books Written by Jason R. Rich and Published by Entrepreneur Press

The following books are now or will soon be available wherever books are sold, or can be ordered from the EntrepreneurPress.com website. For more information about these and other books written by bestselling author Jason R. Rich, visit his website at **JasonRich.com.**

- *202 High-Paying Jobs You Can Land Without a College Degree*
- *Mac Migrate: The Business Person's Guide to Easily Switching From PC to Mac*
- *Smart Debt*

Entrepreneur Magazine's Personal Finance Pocket Guides

- *Buying or Leasing a Car: Without Being Taken For A Ride*
- *Dirty Little Secrets: What the Credit Bureaus Won't Tell You*
- *Get That Raise!*
- *Mortgages & Refinancing: Get The Best Rates*
- *Mutual Funds: A Quick Start Guide*
- *Why Rent? Own Your Dream Home*

Entrepreneur Magazine's Business Traveler Series

- *Entrepreneur Magazine's Business Traveler Guide to Chicago*
- *Entrepreneur Magazine's Business Traveler Guide to Las Vegas*
- *Entrepreneur Magazine's Business Traveler Guide to Los Angeles*
- *Entrepreneur Magazine's Business Traveler Guide to New York City*
- *Entrepreneur Magazine's Business Traveler Guide to Orlando*
- *Entrepreneur Magazine's Business Traveler Guide to Washington, DC*

CHAPTER

WHAT IS A BUY-AND-SELL ENTERPRISE?

F or entrepreneurs, the concept behind a buy-and-sell enterprise is based upon the concept of purchasing items/products inexpensively (at wholesale prices) and then reselling those same items at higher retail prices. The difference between what you pay and how much you sell the products for (after taking into account business operating expenses) is your profit.

Your goal as a buy-sell enterprise operator can be summed up in four words—"buy low, sell high." Of course, if it were really that easy, absolutely everyone would be doing it and we'd all be millionaires. Well, in reality, many people are doing it, and many of those people have in fact become millionaires, or at least supplemented their income enough to greatly improve their standard of living.

In addition to adhering to the "buy low, sell high" principle, to be successful operating this type of business venture, you'll need to find the perfect product(s) for you to buy and sell.

This "perfect product" will be based on a wide range of factors, including your:

- Knowledge
- Experience
- Interests
- Schedule
- Available resources
- Geographic location
- Economic conditions

You'll also need to take into account the following:

- Your ability to raise startup c apital
- When and where you'll sell your products (online or in the real world)
- Your ability to acquire the products cost-effectively
- Your ability to maintain ample inventory
- Your ability to identify and reach the target audience interested in what you'll be selling
- Your ability to efficiently m and sell your products

In reality, different people will excel and be successful buying and selling different types of items, so what works for you might not work for someone else (and vice versa). The trick is to find the right product(s) that you believe you can confidently and successfully buy and sell. Ideally, you should find a product you can be truly passionate about and that you wholeheartedly believe in.

Depending on what you'll be buying and selling, learning basic marketing, advertising, public relations and customer service skills will most likely be essential, as will developing a basic understanding of fundamental business skills, such as the ability to negotiate with suppliers, as well as bookkeeping and record keeping.

Buying and selling for profit is nothing new. It has been around for thousands of years. In recent times, however, one of the primary reasons why buying and selling has exploded, instead of being a closely guarded secret held by a few, is the proliferation of the internet in our culture and daily lives.

The Internet Makes It Easy to Buy and Sell

The proliferation of the internet gives entrepreneurs from every walk of life and from every geographic location access to a global audience of buying consumers, eager sellers, information and resources. It's an extremely powerful tool that has changed our buying habits, our social habits and how we communicate as a society.

The internet has made it easier to sell products in the global marketplace utilizing online sales venues, such as **eBay.com**, e-commerce websites and e-classifieds. It also provides a limitless source of in-demand products, which can be bought cheaply from domestic and overseas suppliers and then resold for potentially handsome profits. (Of course, other people have also caught on to this opportunity, so depending on what you plan to buy and sell, you'll most likely have to deal with fierce competition.)

Now, with a few clicks of a mouse, you can buy products cheaply from thousands of suppliers around the globe and then resell those same products to a potentially worldwide audience using several different online marketplaces, as well as through local community retailing opportunities such as flea markets or mall kiosks.

eBay Versus an E-Commerce Website

Launched in September 1995, eBay now boasts more than 276 million registered users worldwide (as of December 2007). During 2007, gross merchandise volume totaled more than $59 billion. This translates to worldwide users buying and selling more than $2,039 worth of goods on eBay every second.

Using an online auction business model (that also allows for items to be bought or sold for a fixed price), ordinary people can buy or sell virtually anything. This has created a massive marketplace for new and used items, which is categorized online into 50,000 unique categories. For many entrepreneurs, eBay has allowed them to launch a successful buy-and-sell business venture.

According to a June 2007 survey conducted by ACNielsen International Research, there are approximately 1.3 million sellers around the world who use eBay as their primary or secondary source of income. Depending on how you plan to buy and sell your products once you launch your buy-and-sell enterprise, you too could become one of these success stories.

So what's really selling on eBay? In a nutshell, almost anything and everything can potentially be bought or sold online using this service. For a small fee, eBay offers a marketplace research service, which allows you to track how well specific products and items are selling on eBay at any given time. For example, once you select a product, you can obtain the average sale price, the average price range, the number of successful sales, the average number of bids per auction, and a wide range of pertinent information that can help you as a buyer or seller. You can also determine what the top searches are in specific product categories, to help you pinpoint products that might be worth selling.

Marketplace research is available from eBay for $9.99 per month (other pricing and service tiers are also available) by visiting **http://pages.ebay.com/marketplace_research/index.html**.

In addition to using eBay to buy and sell products, many sellers have achieved success by launching their own e-commerce websites or online business ventures. Revenues generated by online businesses—including the online aspects of traditional retail businesses—during 2006 generated over $96 billion, which is up from $83 billion in 2004.

According to the U.S. Census Bureau, "Rapid growth in e-retail has been the norm. From 2000 to 2005, retail e-sales increased at an average annual growth rate of 27.3 percent, compared with 4.3 percent for total retail sales."

The Census Bureau also reported that "the estimate of U.S. retail e-commerce sales for the second quarter of 2007, adjusted for seasonal variation and holiday and trading-day differences, but not for price changes, was $33.6 billion, an increase of 6.4 percent from the first quarter of 2007."

When selling online, your potential audience is vast. By 2010, more than 1.8 billion people worldwide are expected to be using the internet, according to the *Computer Industry Almanac*.

Until recently, if you wanted to launch an e-commerce website to sell products online, you needed to be a computer guru with a thorough understanding of HTML programming, Java, Flash, and a wide range of other complex programming languages and software-based website design tools. You also needed to invest weeks, often months, to create a website from scratch capable of handling the functionality needed to securely sell products online. Of course, a team of programmers and graphic designers could also be hired (at a significant expense) to handle much of the programming for you, but as the website operator, you still needed a good understanding of website design and programming.

These days, however, a handful of well-known and established companies offer complete e-commerce turnkey solutions that allow ordinary people—with no programming or graphic design knowledge whatsoever—to utilize a set of easy-to-use tools and professionally designed templates to effortlessly design and publish awesome-looking and extremely powerful websites in a matter of hours, not days or months. Best of all, many of these turnkey solutions have a very low startup cost (often under $100). These solutions also include the tools needed to begin accepting orders and online credit card payments for those orders.

In other words, you don't necessarily need to set up a costly credit card merchant account with a local bank or financial institution to begin accepting Visa, MasterCard, American Express or Discover credit card or debit card payments. This alone eliminates a significant barrier to entry that until recently never existed.

Depending on your level of experience, your website design knowledge, what you're selling, and your personal preferences, you should be able to select and start using a turnkey e-commerce solution that meets your wants and needs.

Some of the powerful, popular, inexpensive and comprehensive turnkey solutions include:

- Yahoo! Stores, **http://smallbusiness.yahoo.com/ecommerce/index.php**
- eBay.com ProStores, **prostores.com**
- GoDaddy.com Quick Shopping Cart, **godaddy.com/gdshop**
- OSCommerce, **OSCommerce.com**

Even with the most advanced and powerful e-commerce turnkey solutions that utilize the best, most eye-catching website design templates, you'll still need to create professional-quality text and incorporate professional-looking photos and other graphic elements (referred to as assets) into your website to insure it's capable of helping you to achieve your goals. Basically, to compete effectively, your website will need to look and function as well, if not better, than what your competition offers. Of course, you must also offer products that your customers want or need.

The New Economy Is Buying and Selling

It is no secret that manufacturing, technology and middle-management jobs in the U.S. and Canada continue to disappear daily, swallowed up by overseas economies with cheaper labor, raw product and lower production costs. In fact, some studies suggest the job drain in these areas is occurring at an alarming rate, faster than most people—including politicians and policy makers—are aware of or care to admit.

If you're currently employed and working in a specific field or industry, you can learn about the long-term forecast for your industry or occupation by evaluating the ongoing research conducted by the U.S. Department of Labor. *The Occupational Outlook Handbook* is available online (**bls.gov/oco**) for free. The hard copy (book) edition can be found at most public libraries.

According to the U.S. Department of Labor, "Total employment is expected to increase from 150.6 million in 2006 to 166.2 million in 2016, or by 10 percent. The 15.6 million jobs that will be added by 2016 will not be evenly distributed across major industrial and occupational groups. Changes in consumer demand, technology, and many other factors will contribute to the continually changing employment structure in the U.S. economy."

In February 2008, The Associated Press reported, "With economic growth slowing, the Fed projected that the national jobless rate will rise to between 5.2 percent and 5.3 percent this year. That is higher than the central bank's old forecast for the rate to climb to as high as 4.9 percent. Last year, the unemployment rate averaged 4.6 percent."

Like so many people, you may discover that forecasts for your industry or occupation predict massive job reductions and cutbacks. This resulting fallout in North America has created a dramatic increase in the number of new small-business startups. Many people who have been or who will soon be affected by the new global economy have chosen self-employment as a way to keep in tune with changing times, make money and secure their long-term future.

Launching your own buy-and-sell enterprise is just one potential solution for helping yourself survive financially in these rough economic times, whether you choose to pursue this type of opportunity on a part-time, seasonal or full-time basis.

The Advantages of a Buy-and-Sell Enterprise

When you consider the advantages of a buy-and-sell enterprise over traditional retail or service-provider businesses, it quickly becomes apparent why many people have wisely elected to buy and sell, and why buying and selling will make up a large percentage of new business startups and the new economy.

Let's consider some of these reasons, which include:

- *Low Investment/Low Startup Costs:* The vast majority of buy-and-sell enterprises require only a minimal investment to start. Many require under $2,000 in initial inventory and under $10,000 in overall startup costs.
- *Minimal Financial Risk:* Because much the money you spend to get started goes into buying inventory and equipment needed to launch your business, there is limited financial risk involved. If you decide to quit, you can simply sell off stock and equipment in order to potentially recoup much of your investment.

- *Impressive Profit Potential:* This will depend on what you're selling and how you're selling it, plus your ability to "buy low, sell high." With proper planning and a great business idea, the income potential can be significantly better than working a traditional nine-to-five job.
- *Work From Home:* For people wanting to work from home, a buy-and-sell venture is a great choice, because most of these opportunities can be operated and managed from home.
- *Flexibility:* No other business opportunity or career choice offers as much flexibility, especially if you concentrate on online sales. Part-time, full-time or seasonally, you set your own schedule and level of commitment. You're your own boss and have the ability to control your professional and financial destiny.
- *Minimal Skill Requirements:* There are few skill requirements needed to get started, operate and prosper in a buy-and-sell enterprise. Most or all of the necessary skills can be self-taught and mastered by novice entrepreneurs over time. Depending on what you're selling, this is a rare opportunity where ambition and motivation are more important than special skills. However, the more business and sales knowledge and experience you already possess, the better off you'll be.
- *Tax Advantages:* Being your own boss and operating a home-based business and/or operating a legal buy-and-sell business has numerous tax advantages and business write-offs, which will leave more money in your pocket and less in Uncle Sam's. You definitely want to go over the potential tax benefits with your accountant as you get started operating this type of business venture, as the benefits will vary by state.
- *Growth Potential:* Once you become good at selling one type of product, it's easy to grow your business by taking on additional items or by expanding your target audience for the product(s) you're already selling.

Who Can Buy and Sell?

The answer is simple: anyone. One of the best aspects of starting and operating a buy-and-sell venture is that almost everyone is qualified. Buying and selling know no boundaries. Anyone with a need or desire to earn extra money or work from home, or who wants to start and own their own business, can buy and sell, regardless of their age, experience, education and financial resources.

Thus, this type of business venture is the ultimate self-employment option for the vast majority of people. In a nutshell, it's cheap, easy, quick, proven to work and allows people to generate huge profits.

Imagine the flexibility and opportunities that buying and selling offer to you right now, based on your current life situation. For example, you can start a buy-and-sell venture on a part-time basis to pay off debts, supplement your existing income, or pay your way through school.

Or you can buy and sell on a full-time basis to replace your current income and potentially earn more over time. Another option is to buy and sell seasonally, enabling you to pursue other interests, such as travel. Or you can buy and sell to help supplement your retirement income and stay active in your golden years. Many stay-at-home moms enjoy this type of opportunity, because it offers something exciting to do from home, while not compromising the amount of time you have available for your kids.

Much of what is discussed in this book is aimed at helping you capitalize on your existing knowledge, experiences, skills and interests, and channeling these into selecting the right things for you to buy and sell. Use the resources at your disposal, as well as your own creativity and business savvy, to help you pinpoint the best opportunities for you.

Buying and Selling Part Time

The first, and most logical, option for most people is to start buying and selling on a part-time basis; perhaps selling merchandise on eBay, renting a booth at a weekend flea market, or placing classified ads in your local newspaper. Starting small and part time enables you to eliminate risk by limiting your financial investment. It also allows you to test the waters to make sure buying and selling is something you enjoy and want to pursue.

If all goes well, you may decide to transition from your current job, devoting more time to your new buy-and-sell enterprise each week and decreasing the time at your current job until you are buying and selling on a full-time basis.

There are many advantages to starting off part time, including keeping income rolling in, taking advantage of health and employee benefits, and building your business over a longer period of time, which generally gives it a more stable foundation. If it turns out you are not the type of person who is comfortable with buying and selling, you have risked little and still have the security of your current job.

If you're currently employed, do not quit your job until you're 100 percent certain that your buy-and-sell enterprise can and will be successful and profitable. When starting any type of business venture, always have a fallback plan in place in case things go wrong. It might make sense for you to sit down with an accountant, for example, to help you create realistic financial projections or forecasts for your business, before you decide to pursue this on a full-time basis and give up your stable paycheck.

Buying and Selling Full Time

As the commitment would suggest, you can throw caution to the wind and buy and sell on a full-time basis. This option would appeal to people without a current job or business, or to people who want to start a full-time business, but not necessarily a traditional business, like fixed-location retailing or providing a service. It might also appeal to someone who is retired, or who wants to take time off from attending school.

There is nothing wrong with starting off full time, especially if you take the time required to conduct research, develop a detailed business and marketing plan, and have the necessary financial resources to start the business and pay for your living expenses until the business is profitable (which could take one month, three months, six months, 12 months or even longer, depending on what you're selling, whom you are selling to and where you're selling.)

The main downside to starting off full time is risk. If you jump ship and leave your current job, you risk loss of current employee benefits and have absolutely no guarantee of a steady income.

The upside to starting off full time is the potential rewards, including the opportunity to make more money than you can at your current job. You also gain control of your work schedule and your financial future and, therefore, your true potential to succeed. If you've never operated your own business, however, this can be a very daunting and frightening decision to make, as well as a challenging career path to pursue, especially if you don't have the drive and dedication to be your own boss and make important decisions on your own.

Your decision to operate your new buy-and-sell business on a full-time basis will largely be determined by your current financial situation, your own risk-reward assessment, and your goals and objectives for the future. Jumping in full time will appeal to those ultra-confident people with a true entrepreneurial mind-set.

Buying and Selling Seasonally

Seasonal buy-and-sell enterprises run during one specific season, although some— such as a roadside vegetable stand—can start in the summer and end in the fall.

A seasonal buy-and-sell venture can still be operated with a full- or part-time effort, but the majority are run full time to maximize revenues and profits over the normally short time span. Just about any product can be bought and sold seasonally or occasionally, but some are better suited to seasonal sales than others.

Examples of products you might buy and sell seasonally, depending on your geographic location, include vegetables, boats, landscape supplies, Christmas trees, patio furniture, vacation/tour packages and some types of sporting equipment (such as snow skis and fishing gear).

A seasonal venture will appeal to people with a special interest in a seasonal product or activity, and to people who want the ability to earn enough money during part of the year in order to do as they please with the remainder of the year, such as travel, pursue education or work at another job.

The potential to earn a very good living buying and selling for only part of the year is real, as proven by the thousands of people who are currently doing it.

Buying and Selling to Supplement Your Retirement Income

Another option is to buy and sell when and as needed, in order to supplement your regular income or retirement income. It's also a viable and potentially fun option for people who want to stay active in their golden years.

Retirement businesses have become extremely popular in the past decade for a number of reasons. First, the cost of living has dramatically increased, often outpacing wages, retirement benefits and retirement savings. The result is lots of people heading into retirement needing a little extra income to cover expenses and provide an adequate lifestyle, or to maintain their pre-retirement lifestyle.

Also, people are living longer and healthier now than in decades past. These same people are also seeking new challenges, because they have the spirit, drive and health to do so.

For some retired people, the concept of just sitting on a porch in a rocking chair and growing old is simply unacceptable. People want to be vibrant and active. Operating their own buy-and-sell businesses give them a way to stay active physically and mentally.

In fact, many innovative retired entrepreneurs have learned how to combine their buy-and-sell businesses with travel, and work their way across the country, buying, selling, traveling and enjoying their retirement—all at the same time. Stay awhile in any RV park, and you will soon discover many people who buy and sell at flea markets, online and through community events to fund their retirement and travel.

Capitalize on Your Knowledge

To help you determine what to sell, whom to sell to, and where you'll do the majority of your selling, first take a close look at yourself. Evaluate everything about yourself, including:

- Areas of Existing Expertise
- Availabilities
- Available Resources
- Current Financial Situation
- Education
- Experience
- Hobbies
- Interests
- Long-Term Goals
- Short-Term Goals
- Skills

Initially, do not fret if you lack important (and ultimately necessary) skills, such as person-to-person selling, negotiating, bookkeeping, time management, and creating effective advertisements. There's no question these are important skills to have, but at the same time, the majority of these skills can be self-taught or learned by attending adult-education classes, reading books, participating in online classes, watching videos, or hiring the experienced freelance experts necessary to help you out as you get started.

Right now, as you're formulating the idea for your business, the most important question to consider is what knowledge and experience you currently have that can be leveraged and used to your advantage in a buy-and-sell enterprise.

Knowledge is one of your biggest and most marketable assets. The more you know about a product, its value, the industry, and the people who are most likely to buy, the better off you will be and the shorter the road to profitability.

For instance, if you know how to repair small engines, that knowledge can be used to acquire (cheaply, or even for free) outdoor power equipment in need of repair that you can fix and resell for big profits.

Likewise, if you have knowledge of antiques, this can be applied to buying antiques at below-market prices and then reselling them for a profit. Or if you have been an avid boater for 20 years, this knowledge can be leveraged to your benefit to buy and sell boats or boating equipment.

Knowledge about a specific industry, product, product category or target customer will enable you to:

- Know how to fix something that is broken, and thereby greatly increase its value and marketability.

- Know how much a specific item(s) is worth and how much profit can be earned from buying and reselling it.
- Know the best places to buy items and the best places to resell.
- Know how many people buy this specific item, where they are located, and how this market can be accessed.

Choosing the Best Product(s) To Sell

While initially, the product(s) you have in mind to sell may seem extremely viable, after considering all of the necessary factors, you may discover that an opportunity you thought existed might not be as lucrative as you would have hoped. This, unfortunately, is extremely common. Thus, it could take you weeks, maybe months, to find the perfect products to buy and sell.

Consider Your Existing Competition

Don't kid yourself. You're not the first entrepreneur with the idea to start a buy-and-sell enterprise. In fact, if you do some research, chances are you'll find competition offering identical or similar products to what you're thinking about selling. Assuming this is the case, how will you set your business and its products apart? What added value will you offer? Think realistically about why people will become your customer and not do business with your competition.

One of the biggest mistakes you can make is focusing exclusively on offering the lowest price possible for your products. While you'll be able to undercut your competition in the short-term, there will always be a competitor who can offer even lower prices. This dramatically cuts your profit margin. With lower profits, you'll earn less money for yourself, plus you probably won't earn the funds needed to properly market and grow your business in the future.

While you'll always want your prices to be competitive, you don't necessary want or need to offer the absolute lowest prices. Depending on the product, people are often willing to pay extra if you offer superior customer service or if you somehow add value to what you're selling. People will also pay a premium for hard-to-find products or highly collectible items.

As you develop the plans for your business, pay careful attention to what your existing competition is doing. Focus on what you can do better, plus how you can better serve the wants and needs of your target customer base. Also, consider what competition is likely to appear in the near future.

Will you be able to complete with companies that are willing and able to spend more money than you on marketing and advertising, or that are able to purchase their inventory in much larger quantities in order to keep costs down?

Once you pinpoint a product you might be interested in selling, tap your internet skills and seek out websites and companies that are currently selling the same or similar products. Discover who your competition will be. Utilize search engines, like Google and Yahoo!, and enter a wide range of different search phrases (using product names, product categories, product descriptions and company names). Also, be sure to check shopping and price comparison websites, like **nextag.com**, as well as online-based mass-market retailers, like **Amazon.com**.

For new buy-and-sell business operators, the best products to offer are ones that are unique, customizable, collectible or hand-crafted, or that are not readily available through local retail stores, mall stores or mass-market retailers (such as Wal-Mart or Target). Ideally, the product(s) you choose to sell should also be hard to find online.

While Chapter 6 describes 202 products you can potentially buy and sell for big profits, here are a few preliminary suggestions.

Small online business operators have experienced success selling a wide range of products. Just a sampling of what items could be sold using an e-commerce website includes:

- Antiques
- Any products that are bundled together, modified or customized to provide added value to the customer
- Art
- Clothing and shoes (especially in hard-to-find sizes)
- Collectibles
- Crafts and handmade items
- Gift items (especially items that are customized, engraved or personalized)
- Hard-to-find tools, items, supplies and equipment for various hobbies, such as specialty photography equipment, fishing gear, sewing gear, scrapbook making supplies, knitting supplies, etc.
- Jewelry (new, antique, hand-crafted, one-of-a-kind, etc.)
- Specialty items for specific jobs or occupations
- Used books
- Used video and computer games
- Vintage or custom-made clothing

Calculate Your Costs

The ideal formula for a successful business is to be able to purchase or acquire your inventory for the absolute lowest cost per unit possible, and then resell those products at the highest retail price possible in order to generate a profit. No matter what quantity you're buying in, always know what your cost per unit is, and make sure there's enough profit margin to cover all of your operating expenses (including your own salary, the cost of operating your website, and your company's marketing/advertising, for example).

As you determine your costs, be sure to calculate appropriate shipping charges, sales taxes (if applicable), order processing fees, warehousing costs, packaging costs, insurance, finance charges (interest, etc.), and any other expenses that will diminish your potential profit margins.

You'll quickly discover that in most cases, when acquiring inventory, you'll receive the best prices when you seek out quantity discounts. Depending on the product, this might mean ordering dozens, hundreds or even thousands of the same product(s) at once in order to benefit from the savings offered by a manufacturer, wholesaler or distributor. When placing larger orders, shipping and warehousing costs go up, so be prepared to do some number crunching to determine what's best for your business.

Some business operators rely on credit to be able to acquire their initial inventory. Whether you utilize credit terms from your supplier or use a credit card to purchase inventory, chances are you'll need to pay finance charges and interest, so calculate these additional fees into your per-unit pricing.

Depending on what you'll be selling and from whom you're acquiring your inventory, don't be afraid to negotiate for the best pricing possible, especially if you're purchasing a significant quantity of an item.

Know the Demographics Related to Your Target Audience

One topic that has already been mentioned and that will be repeated multiple times within this book is the absolute need to understand and know your product(s), as well as your target customer. This is one of the keys to success that should not be ignored!

You must have a thorough understanding of who your target customer is, what they want, what they need, and how what you're offering addresses those wants and needs, or helps to solve a specific problem.

The majority of small but successful buy-and-sell business operators cater to a niche target audience with a specific product that is in demand by that audience.

Your target audience can be defined in many ways. Just some of the characteristics you can use to carefully define your target audience include:

- Age
- Club or Association Memberships
- Education Level
- Geographic Region
- Height
- Hobbies
- Income
- Investing Habits
- Marital Status
- Medical Necessities
- Occupation
- Religion
- Sex
- Sexual Orientation
- Special Interests
- Spending Habits
- Weight

It's common for a target audience to be defined by combining several of these factors. For example, you might determine that the product you'll be selling caters mainly to well educated, single women between the ages of 18 and 49 who earn at least $50,000 per year, and who live in a major city. You might determine that your target audience is comprised mainly of married, affluent men between the ages of 49 and 60 who enjoy playing golf.

Once you know exactly who your primary target audience is, it becomes easier to create an advertising, marketing, public relations and promotional campaign that works. Trying to sell a product to someone who doesn't want or need it is an absolute waste of your time, money and effort.

Likewise, you'll find it more difficult to sell products that cater to a mass-market audience (i.e., almost everybody), because you'll probably be competing head-on with mass-market retailers such as Wal-Mart or Target, plus major department stores, chain stores and other local retailers.

A key to success is to really get to know your target customer base, be able to get inside their heads, and understand their true wants and needs. Next, your objective should be to address those wants and needs with your products in a way that solves a problem or addresses an issue that they're facing.

Figure Out How You'll Reach Your Audience

Once you determine what you'll be selling and to whom your products will appeal, you can consider how you'll target that audience with your advertising, marketing, public relations and promotions. You'll also be able to determine if you'll be able to reach this audience cost-effectively, or if getting their attention will simply cost too much or require resources that are not at your disposal.

If you understand your audience, know what they're looking for, and can quickly and succinctly address their needs, wants and concerns, you're more apt to generate sales.

Forecast the Current and Future Demand for Your Product(s)

For your buy-and-sell business venture to have long-term success potential, you'll want to offer products that are in demand today, and that will continue to be in demand in the months and hopefully years to come. Through market research, you should be able to determine how quickly your target audience is growing (or shrinking), and whether or not your business will continue to be viable in six months, one year, three years, five years and over the long term.

Again, determining the future potential demand for your product will require a strong understanding of the product itself, as well as your target audience, your competition, and any changes that may happen in the marketplace over time. In the future, people's buying habits may change, as will their wants and needs. As a business operator, not only do you need to understand this concept, you must also be able to plan for it and transform your business accordingly to keep up with current and future trends.

If you determine that in one year, the demand for your proposed product will be diminished, that gives you a relatively small window during which to build up your business and generate a profit, before you'll need to abandon the business or dramatically change its focus. Establishing a business requires time, money and resources. You don't want to waste your investment by selecting products to sell that don't have the ongoing potential to generate the profits you're striving for.

Having a Passion for Your Products Is Very Helpful

As a general rule, you're more apt to achieve success if you wind up selling products that you truly believe in, that you're highly knowledgeable about, and that you have a passion for. For example, if you're an avid fisherman, selling specialty fishing gear to fellow enthusiasts will be more enjoyable for you than selling products you have little or no interest in.

One way to find the perfect product(s) to sell is to first focus on what interests you, and then consider what types of unique or hard-to-find (non-mass-market) items you personally tend to purchase.

How Much Money Can You Earn Buying and Selling?

So, how much money can you make buying and selling? As intriguing as the answer to that question could be, the question should really be: How much money do you need or want to earn from buying and selling?

If you work at a job for $20 per hour, calculating your maximum pretax income is easy: Multiply the number of hours your boss will let you work or you are capable of working each week by your hourly rate, and you'll know your maximum income potential.

Buying and selling is much different. While there are certainly upper limits in terms of income and profit potential, at the same time the measure of one's success is generally determined by ambition and motivation and not by a clock.

Once again, the income and profit you earn will largely depend on your financial needs, your goals and your personal motivation. Additional factors influencing profit potential include product costs, overhead costs, marketing costs, selling prices, competition and sales volumes.

With that said, if you follow the proven buy-and-sell concepts and ideas outlined in this book, and if you are prepared to work hard, there is a good chance you will earn more buying and selling than you do working in your current field.

Plan on Making an Ongoing Time and Financial Investment

You already know that starting and then operating a successful buy-and-sell business is not a get-rich-quick scheme. For your business venture to become truly profitable, you'll need to invest a significant amount of time, resources and money—on an ongoing basis—to build, establish, maintain and grow your business.

To find potential customers, plan on spending money on advertising, marketing and public relations efforts, and investing the time necessary to properly and cost-effectively implement these efforts while also handling the other day-to-day tasks associated with the operation of your business.

Some of your additional responsibilities may include:

- Acquiring and maintaining inventory
- Processing and shipping orders
- Handling returns
- Constantly updating and improving your website

- Working a booth or kiosk at a flea market, mall, trade show or event
- Managing your company's financial records (bookkeeping)
- Planning, designing, implementing and managing the marketing, advertising and public relations campaigns designed to promote your website and product(s)
- Handling customer service issues

Before getting started with this, or any other type of business venture, make sure you have the mindset, confidence and dedication to become your own boss and are willing to juggle a wide range of different responsibilities on an ongoing basis.

Once you're ready to proceed, Chapter 2 will help you establish your buy-and-sell business venture and choose what form it should take.

LEGAL AND FINANCIAL ISSUES OF A BUY-AND-SELL ENTERPRISE

Depending on what you'll be selling and where you'll be doing business, local laws and regulations will vary greatly. As you move forward, consider sitting down with an attorney who has experience helping local entrepreneurs establish their business ventures, and make sure all of the necessary licenses and permits are acquired and the necessary paperwork is completed correctly.

As you already know, starting a buy-and-sell enterprise is like starting any other type of business. To do this correctly, you have to follow the letter of the law. A few of the legal and financial issues that you will need to deal with include:

- Registering a business name
- Selecting a legal business structure
- Obtaining a business license
- Obtaining a sales tax ID number
- Acquiring appropriate insurance
- Establishing a company bank account
- Preparing and filing business and income tax returns

Investing the funds necessary to seek out professional legal and financial (accounting) advice will be money well spent, as the guidance you obtain from these people will not only help you avoid costly mistakes, but also assist you in properly establishing your business venture.

Lawyers with small business experience will be able to advise you on which legal business structure best meets your needs, as well as review with you related insurance and liability issues. Your lawyers will also draft necessary legal documents, create or review your supplier and vendor agreements, and help you address many other important legal issues.

The lawyer you hire, at least initially, will help you decipher the legalese associated with starting a new business and help you make sense of complicated matters pertaining to that business. Likewise, working with an accountant will help you decipher the sometimes complicated financial information you need to know in order to comply with state and federal tax regulations as you establish your business and begin to operate it within your state.

Depending on your level of expertise and previous experience operating a business, it may only be necessary to hire a lawyer and/or accountant for a few hours as you get your business up and running. Once your business is fully operational, however, you'll also want a lawyer and accountant at your disposal when a question or need for their services arises. Having established relationships with a lawyer and accountant will ultimately save you time, aggravation and money.

To obtain a referral for a competent and experienced lawyer, consider contacting the bar association of the state where you plan to do business. A referral for an accountant can be obtained by contacting your state's board of accountancy. You can find the appropriate listing by visiting the National Association of State Boards of Accountancy's (NASBA) website at **nasba.org**. If, however, you can obtain a personal referral from someone you know, that too may be a wise strategy.

Legal Business Structure Options

The starting point of the buy-and-sell enterprise (from a legal standpoint) is the selection of a business structure. Your primary choices for a business being established to earn a profit (as opposed to a nonprofit organization) include:

- Corporation
- Limited Liability Corporation
- Partnership
- Sole Proprietorship (or DBA)

Issues such as budget, tax implications and your personal liability as a business operator will be determining factors when selecting a business structure. Again, this is a decision your lawyer and accountant can help you make.

Initially, many people choose a sole proprietorship (also referred to as a "DBA" or "Doing Business As") if they are on a tight budget and comfortable with the liability issues associated with this type of business. This is the easiest and least expensive type of business to establish. However, a partnership is the right choice if you will be running your new business with a spouse, family member, friend or business partner.

A limited liability corporation (LLC) or corporation will be the appropriate choice if your plans include expansion and you want to minimize personal liability concerns. What you'll ultimately be selling may also be a determining factor. Again, there are also different tax liability issues associated with each of these business entities. Some of the advantages and disadvantages of each are discussed later in this chapter.

Regardless of the legal structure you adopt for your business venture, you will need to select and register a business name. The name you choose can incorporate your own name, such as "John Doe's Widgets For Less," or it can be a totally made-up name, such as "Acme Widget Wonderland." The key is to come up with a name that's unique and that does not violate another company's trademark or copyright.

Have two or three name options ready to go, in case another business is already using your first choice. Business registration costs vary by state and province, though generally this one-time fee is less than $200 if you're registering a sole proprietorship. Your lawyer can assist you with this process, or you can file the necessary forms yourself with local and/or state governments.

Normally, you have to show proof of business registration in order to establish a company bank account, be able to buy products wholesale, obtain a business loan, and/or secure a credit card merchant account.

RESOURCES
- American Bar Association, ☎ (202) 662-1000, ♂ **abanet.org**
- Canadian Bar Association, ☎ (800) 267-8860, ♂ **cba.org**
- Canadian Business Service Centers (Small-business registration services and information), ☎ (888) 576-4444, ♂ **cbsc.org**
- Canadian Corp. Online Filing, ♂ **canadiancorp.com**
- Small Business Administration (SBA), ☎ (800) U-ASK-SBA, ♂ **sba.gov**
- National Association of State Boards of Accountancy (NASBA), ♂ **nasba.org**

The Sole Proprietorship

A sole proprietorship is the most common type of legal business structure, mainly because it is the simplest and least expensive to start and maintain. A sole proprietorship means your business entity and your personal affairs are merged together as one. For example, you'll file single state and federal tax returns, and take on personal liability for all accrued business debts and actions (including legal actions). You personally also control all revenues and profits.

Even if you're operating a sole proprietorship, it's important to separate your business finances from your personal finances for record keeping and income tax purposes. For instance, interest payments on credit cards used for business purchases are tax-deductible, while interest payments on personal credit cards (used for personal purchases) are not tax-deductible.

Perhaps the biggest advantage of sole proprietorships is that they are very simple to form and can be started, altered, bought, sold or closed at any time, quickly and inexpensively. Also, other than obtaining routine business registrations, permits and licenses, there are few government regulations.

The biggest disadvantage of a sole proprietorship is that you are 100 percent legally and financially liable for any number of business activities that could go wrong. As a result, all of your personal assets—including investments and real estate—could be lost as a direct result of generating too much business-related debt or from a successful litigation against the business.

Partnership

A partnership is another low-cost legal business structure. It allows two or more people to start, operate and own a business, such as a buy-and-sell enterprise. If you opt to start a business with a family member, friend or business partner, make sure the partnership is based on a written partnership agreement, not just a verbal agreement. Again, this is a topic to discuss with your attorney.

Your partnership agreement should be a legally binding document that addresses a variety of issues, such as financial investment, profit distribution, the duties of each partner, and an exit strategy should one partner want out of the agreement later.

The absence of a formal agreement can be extremely problematic should disagreements arise that cannot be resolved—a very common occurrence—or if one of the partners unexpectedly dies or wants out of the business. As in a sole proprietorship, business profits are split among partners proportionate to their ownership and are treated as taxable personal income.

One potential advantage of a partnership is that all financial and legal risks, as well as the work associated with operating the business, are shared by more than one person. This allows each partner to take on specific tasks based on his or her own area of expertise, in order to benefit the collective team. Record keeping requirements are basic and on a par with a sole proprietorship.

Unfortunately, partnerships also have disadvantages. The most significant is that each partner is legally responsible and personally liable for the other partners' actions in the business. It's important to understand that a non-incorporated partnership offers no legal protection from liability or financial issues. All partners are equally responsible for the business's debts, liabilities and actions.

The Limited Liability Corporation (LLC)

A limited liability corporation combines many of the characteristics of a corporation with those of a partnership. Like a corporation, an LLC provides protection from personal liabilities, but the tax advantages of a partnership are associated with it.

An LLC can be formed by one or more people. These people, alone or together, organize a legal entity that's separate and distinct from each owner's personal affairs in most legal and financial respects.

There are multiple advantages of a limited liability corporation (over a corporation or partnership). For example, an LLC is less expensive to form and maintain than a corporation, plus this type of business entity offers protection from personal liability (which is something that partnerships do not provide). There are also simplified taxation and reporting rules associated with an LLC (compared to a corporation). Because of these advantages, limited liability corporations have become the fastest-growing form of business structure in the United States.

To determine if forming an LLC is appropriate for your business, seriously consider consulting with an attorney and/or accountant who specializes in these matters.

Corporation

The most complicated business structure option for a startup business is to establish a corporation. When you form a corporation, you create a legal entity that is totally separate and distinct from the shareholders of the corporation (as well as the business's owners/operators).

Because the corporation becomes its own entity, it pays taxes, assumes debt, can legally sue or be sued, and—as a tax paying entity—must pay taxes on its taxable income (profit) prior to paying any dividends to the shareholders. The corporation's finances and financial records are completely separate from the finances of its shareholders and operators.

The biggest advantage to incorporating your buy-and-sell business is that you can greatly reduce your own personal liability. Because a corporation is its own entity, it can legally borrow money and be held accountable in a number of matters from a legal standpoint.

In effect, this releases you from most personal and financial liability. The major disadvantage is double taxation. Corporation profits are taxed, and then the same profits are taxed again in the form of personal income tax when distributed to the shareholders as a dividend. Unfortunately, the same does not hold true if the corporation loses money. Financial losses cannot be used as a personal income tax deduction for shareholders.

Forming a corporation is a relatively quick process. However, this process varies by state. In addition to a filing fee, there are annual fees, as well as annual state and federal tax liabilities associated with operating a corporation, whether or not it is profitable. Your attorney will be able to help you establish a corporation if it's deemed appropriate, or you can file the paperwork yourself.

For a fee, several online services, such as Incorporate Fast (**incorporatefast. com)**, Legal Zoom (**legalzoom.com**), My Corporation (**mycorporation.com**) and The Company Corporation (**incorporate.com**) allow you to set up your own corporation in minutes.

Licenses Are Needed to Operate a Buy-and-Sell Enterprise

All businesses must be licensed. In fact, chances are you will to need to obtain several licenses and permits, depending on the type of product(s) you sell, how the product(s) will be sold, and where you'll be doing business.

At minimum, you will need a business license, vendor's permits, and a resale certificate or sales tax permit ID number. Additional permits and licenses may be needed, including a health permit if you sell food; a police clearance certificate if you sell home-security products, and an import and export certificate if you bring products into the country or ship products out. A home-occupation permit is required to work from home in some states, as is a building permit if you significantly alter your home to suit your new business venture. A tobacco vendor's permit is required if you sell any tobacco products.

Don't even think about skipping any of the required licenses and permits! At the very least, this could result in huge fines. Depending on what laws you break, it could also be a criminal offense and result in imprisonment.

You'll probably need a license or permit to buy wholesale, open commercial bank accounts, obtain credit card merchant accounts, sell products from home and/or import or export goods.

Business License

To legally operate a business in all municipalities of the United States and Canada, you will need to obtain a business license. Business license costs vary depending on your geographic location, expected sales, and the type of business or products you'll be selling.

Because these licenses are issued at the municipal level, contact your city/county clerk's or permits office for the full requirements for a business license. The Small Business Administration (SBA) also provides a directory, indexed by state, outlining where business licenses can be obtained. This directory is located at **sba.gov/hotlist/license.html**.

Additionally, in the United States and Canada, you can also contact your local Chamber of Commerce to inquire about business license requirements and fees. Check your local phone book or Yellow Pages for a listing.

Permits

What permits are called sometimes vary, based on your geographic location, but whatever you want to call it, you need a permit to collect and remit sales tax. Common terms used include "resale certificate," "sales tax permit," or "tax ID number." Almost all states and provinces now impose a sales tax on products sold directly to consumers or end users. It is the business owner's responsibility to collect and remit these sales taxes. The same sales tax permits are needed when purchasing goods for resale from manufacturers and wholesalers, so the goods can be bought tax-free. (Ultimately, the tax will be paid by the retail customers when the items are later resold.)

The SBA provides a directory, indexed by state, outlining where and how sales tax permits and/or ID numbers may be obtained, including information on completing and remitting sales tax forms. This directory is located at **sba.gov/ hotlist/license.html**. In Canada there are two levels of sales tax. The first is charged by most provinces on the sale of retail products to consumers, and the second is charged by the federal government. The latter is known as the goods and services tax and is charged on the retail sale of all goods and most services.

You can obtain a Federal Goods and Services Sales/Harmonized Sales Tax (GST/HST) number by contacting the Canada Customs and Revenue Agency (**ccra-adrc.gc.ca**).

Insurance

Just as people utilize health insurance, homeowner's insurance, automobile insurance, life insurance and dental insurance to help protect them financially, businesses also require insurance. As a business operator, what type of insurance you require will depend on several factors, including what you'll be selling, how and where you'll be storing your inventory, who you'll be selling to, and where you'll be conducting your business. The business insurance you acquire will also protect your personal assets.

In short, if you operate a business, you need the protection and peace of mind provided by business insurance. Many people operate their buy-and-sell enterprises primarily from their homes, but they often wrongly assume their current insurance coverage extends to cover these business activities. *This is a false assumption!*

From the insurance companies' perspective, they cannot take the risk of insuring what they do not know about. The vast majority of buy-and-sell businesses are registered as sole proprietorships, and if there is a successfully litigated claim made against such a business, the owner could be held personally liable. In all likelihood the plaintiff would attempt to seize personal assets, as well as business financial assets. So regardless of size, it is important to be fully insured as a business operator as well as an individual.

Invest the time to meet with an insurance company representative or broker to help you review your current personal insurance coverage and determine what additional business-related coverage is required. To further protect yourself personally, you might also investigate purchasing an umbrella insurance policy that offers at least $1 million of additional coverage.

Step one is to choose an insurance agent or broker who is familiar with the specific insurance needs of the small-business owner. Not only will the agent be able to translate insurance legalese into easily understandable, plain English for you, but he or she will also be able to find the best coverage for your individual needs and at the lowest cost. Be sure to shop around and get quotes from at least three different insurance providers.

There is a plethora of business insurances available for every imaginable contingency, but the coverage you'll definitely require as a buy-and-sell enterprise operator is property and liability insurance. Many sales venues, such as farmers' markets, public markets, flea markets and mall kiosks, require vendors to show proof of liability insurance as a condition of renting booth or table space.

RESOURCES
- The Independent Insurance Agents and Brokers of America offer a free online "find-an-agent" search service that is indexed geographically, ♂ **iiaa.org**
- The Insurance Brokers Association of Canada offers a free directory, listing more than 25,000 insurance agents and brokers, indexed geographically, ♂ **ibac.ca**

Property Insurance

Because most entrepreneurs operate or manage their buy-and-sell businesses from their homes, property insurance, which generally covers buildings and contents, is your first line of protection.

Depending on how extensive your property insurance is, often it will provide protection in the form of a cash settlement or paid repairs in the event of fire, theft, vandalism, flood, earthquake, wind damage, acts of God and malicious damage.

Property insurance is the starting point from which you should branch out to include specialized tools and equipment, inventory and other liability riders, depending on what you buy and sell. Contacting your insurance agent and asking questions specific to your business, equipment and inventory will quickly reveal what is or is not covered by your existing policy.

In most cases, you will want to increase the value of the contents' portion if you use expensive computer and office equipment. You also want to insure cash on hand, accounts receivable records and inventory, which will require a special rider added to your basic insurance policy.

Make sure your insurance covers all inventory, tools and equipment while in transit, as well as at selling venues you might utilize, such as flea markets, auctions and community events.

Liability Insurance

Most homeowners have some sort of liability protection built into their basic homeowner's insurance policy. This is also true of people who rent, because landlords are obligated by law in most places to carry property and liability insurance on rented buildings and land.

No matter how diligent you are in terms of taking all necessary precautions to protect any person or customer by removing potential hazards from your home, property, business and products, you could still be held legally responsible for events beyond your control. The best protection against this is liability insurance coverage.

This type of extended liability insurance is often referred to as general business liability or umbrella business liability. General business liability coverage insures a business against accidents and injury that might occur at the home, at a customer's location or at retailing venues, or other perils related to the products you sell.

It provides protection from the costs associated with successful litigation or claims against your business or you, depending on the legal entity of your business, and covers such things as medical expenses, recovery expenses, property damage, and other costs typically associated with liability situations.

Also, even if your business is not directly involved in manufacturing the products you sell, you still must be proactive in terms of product liability insurance concerns. In litigation situations, it is not uncommon for plaintiffs who have suffered damages as a result of product malfunction to name numerous defendants in their claim, including the product retailer.

Health & Long-Term Disability Insurance

If you'll be operating your buy-and-sell business venture on a full-time basis and it will represent your entire income, consider investing in health and long-term disability insurance. Health insurance will cover your medical bills if you become ill or get injured.

What happens, however, if—due to a long-term illness or injury—you're unable to work for three months, six months, one year or longer? What would happen to your personal financial situation if you no longer had an income and became unable to work? This is where long-term disability insurance kicks in. Obtaining this type of policy involves additional cost, but it can save you from total financial ruin if a medical emergency happens.

How Much Money Do You Need to Start Buying and Selling?

Another important consideration is how much money you need to start a buy-and-sell enterprise. The amount needed depends on the type of product(s) you will be buying and selling, as well as other factors such as transportation, marketing, advertising and equipment requirements.

Some people will already have many of the things needed to operate their business, while others will have to purchase or rent these items. The following worksheet (Figure 2.1) will help you calculate how much money will be needed to start your business. This is just one of the financial projections you'll ultimately want to incorporate into your comprehensive business plan.

If this is your first foray into the world of business ownership, you should know that in addition to startup capital, you will also need working capital. This is the money needed to keep the business operational until it becomes profitable. Again, depending on what you're selling and a variety of other factors, this could take several months or up to a year or longer.

Startup capital is needed to purchase equipment and office furniture, to meet legal requirements, to pay for training, and to purchase initial inventory. Working capital is needed to pay bills (for your company as well as for yourself) until the business generates revenues and profits and becomes self-sufficient.

You will also need working capital for other activities, such as renting flea market booth space or creating and launching an e-commerce website.

Acquiring The Funds You'll Need

Knowing you need funds to get started, the next logical question is, Where will this money come from? Well, you have several options, including:

- Personal Savings
- Loans From Family or Friends
- Bank Loans
- Government Loans (Small Business Loans)
- Credit Cards
- Finding an Investor or Investors
- Social Lending Services

Personal Savings

The fastest and simplest way to finance your buy-and-sell enterprise is right from your own bank account, especially if the investment is small and manageable. Self-financing means you do not have to worry about applying for a loan, accumulating unnecessary debt, or paying interest on borrowed money.

You can use your personal savings, cash in an investment certificate, or use retirement funds, mutual funds, stocks or insurance policies. Keep in mind, however, that money you remove from fixed certificates or retirement investments may be subject to additional personal income tax or specific penalties for early withdrawal or cancellation.

FIGURE 2.1: Startup Costs Worksheet

Use this handy worksheet to calculate how much money you will need to start your buy-and-sell business. Ignore items not relevant to your business, and add items as required.

Section A. Business Set-Up

Business registration	$ _____
Business license	$ _____
Vendor's permits	$ _____
Other permits	$ _____
Insurance	$ _____
Professional fees	$ _____
Training/education	$ _____
Bank account	$ _____
Merchant accounts	$ _____
Payment processing equipment	$ _____
Association fees	$ _____
Deposits	$ _____
Other _____	$ _____
Subtotal A	$ _____

Section B. Business Identity

Business cards	$ _____
Logo design	$ _____
Letterhead	$ _____
Envelopes	$ _____
Other _____	$ _____
Subtotal B	$ _____

Section C. Office

Computer hardware	$ _____
Communication equipment/devices	$ _____
Software	$ _____
Furniture	$ _____
Other office equipment	$ _____
Office supplies	$ _____
Office renovations	$ _____
Other _____	$ _____
Subtotal C	$ _____

Section D. Transportation

Upfront cost to buy/lease transportation $ _____

Registration $ _____

Insurance $ _____

Moving equipment $ _____

Shipping/delivery supplies $ _____

Other _____ $ _____

            Subtotal D $ _____

Section E. Website

Domain registration $ _____

Site development fees $ _____

Search engine/directory fees $ _____

Equipment $ _____

Software $ _____

Content creation $ _____

Website hosting (ISP) $ _____

E-commerce turnkey solution $ _____

Other _____ $ _____

            Subtotal E $ _____

Section F. Marketing

Research and planning costs $ _____

Signage $ _____

Brochures/fliers (design/printing) $ _____

Catalogs (design/printing) $ _____

Initial advertising budget $ _____

Initial online promotion budget $ _____

Search engine optimization budget $ _____

Search engine marketing budget $ _____

Public relations budget $ _____

Other _____ $ _____

            Subtotal F $ _____

Section G. Merchandising

Product samples $ _____

Pricing/value guides $ _____

Display racks/cases $ _____

Kiosks/carts $ _____

Portable booth $ _____

Section G. Merchandising

Other _____ $ _____

Subtotal G $ _____

Section H. Inventory

#1 _____ $ _____

#2 _____ $ _____

#3 _____ $ _____

#4 _____ $ _____

#5 _____ $ _____

Subtotal H $ _____

Adding Up the Costs

Business Set-Up $ _____

Business Identity $ _____

Office $ _____

Transportation $ _____

Website $ _____

Marketing $ _____

Merchandising $ _____

Inventory $ _____

Total startup costs $ _____

Working capital(*) $ _____

Total capital needed $ _____

(*) With the help of your accountant, perform financial projections based on 3, 6, 12, 18 and 24 months.

Be sure to consult with a financial planner before cashing, selling or redeeming any investments or certificates. Also, depending on the investment you want to liquidate, you might actually be earning a higher rate of return than the interest rate you can secure for a business startup loan.

One innovative way to fund your venture is to create a list of all personal items you no longer want or need and sell them by holding a garage sale, by using eBay or by renting a flea market booth. Not only can this raise the money needed to get started, but you also gain valuable sales experience in the process and clear your home of unwanted junk.

Borrowing From Family and Friends

If you don't have the necessary startup capital yourself, another potential source is to borrow money from friends or family. There is a potential downside to this, however. First, as an "investor," your friend or relative may feel entitled to offer you unsolicited advice and criticism about how you run your business.

Also, if the buy-and-sell business fails, will you be able to pay back the money you borrow? If not, the relationship could be damaged beyond repair. In reality, many extremely successful business ventures have been built on money borrowed from friends and family members. This type of funding is often referred to as a "love loan."

If you decide to borrow from friends or family to fund your buy-and-sell startup, treat the transaction as you would if you were borrowing the money from a bank. Have a promissory note drawn up and signed, noting all the details: principal loan amount, interest and repayment dates. Whatever you do, make sure you stick like glue to your repayment schedule to avoid disputes.

VirginMoney.com (800-805-2472) is a relatively new service that facilitates the borrowing (or lending) of money between friends and family members. Acting as an independent and unbiased middleman, for a small fee, VirginMoney.com helps establish the terms of the loan, then creates the necessary paperwork and manages the loan. Having this formal agreement in place protects both parties and eliminates the chance of confusion or misunderstandings.

Bank Loans (Small Business Loans)

If you have good credit (a personal FICO credit score higher than 650), you can apply for a small-business or startup loan from a bank or credit union. The loan can be secured, meaning it is guaranteed with some other type of investment, such as a guaranteed investment certificate, or it can be unsecured, with the funds advanced because of your creditworthiness.

Secured loans have lower interest rates, by as much as 5 percent. Another option is to talk to your banker about setting up a line of credit. Secured lines of credit also enjoy lower interest rates than unsecured credit lines. One advantage of a line of credit over a standard business loan is that most only require you to repay interest based on the account balance, and not on the entire principal and interest.

For example, a $10,000 line of credit fully extended with a per annum interest rate of 5 percent would require minimum monthly payments of $41.66 ($10,000 multiplied by 5 percent divided by 12 months = $41.66). Of course, this is interest repayment only, and you would not be paying down the principal amount. But this flexibility provides exactly the kind of breathing room new business ventures need to get rolling.

In addition to meeting with local banks, don't forget to compare interest rates and fees with credit unions and internet-based banks. Especially if you have an above-average credit score, you should definitely shop around for the best loan opportunities you can find.

According to the SBA, "When applying for a loan, you must prepare a written loan proposal. Make your best presentation in the initial loan proposal and application; you may not get a second opportunity. Always begin your proposal with a cover letter or executive summary. Clearly and briefly explain who you are, your business background, the nature of your business, the amount and purpose of your loan request, your requested terms of repayment, how the funds will benefit your business, and how you will repay the loan. Keep this cover page simple and direct. Many different loan proposal formats are possible. You may want to contact your commercial lender to determine which format is best for you. When writing your proposal, don't assume the reader is familiar with your industry or your individual business. Always include industry-specific details so your reader can understand how your particular business is run and what industry trends affect it."

The SBA's website offers plenty of additional information about how to apply for a small business loan. Some of this information can be found at **sba.gov/services/financialassistance/eligibility/applyLoan/index.html**.

Government Loans (SBA Loans)

Depending on your background, you may be eligible for a government loan or government-secured loan to help launch your business. For more information about SBA loans, visit **sba.gov/services/financialassistance/sbaloantopics/index.html**.

If you're a military veteran, you may also be eligible for a special type of small-business loan. According to the SBA, "The U.S. Small Business Administration has announced the SBA's Patriot Express Pilot Loan Initiative for veterans and members of the military community wanting to establish or expand small businesses." For additional information about loans for veterans, visit **sba.gov/patriotexpress/sba_patriot_expressloan.html**.

Eligible military community members include:

- Veterans
- Service-disabled veterans
- Active-duty service members eligible for the military's Transition Assistance Program

- Reservists and National Guard members
- Current spouses of any of the above
- The widowed spouse of a service member or veteran who died during service or of a service-connected disability

Credit Cards

The biggest drawback to using your credit cards to fund your business startup is that most have high annual interest rates, often in the 20 to 30 percent range. This makes them a less attractive financing option, especially if you cannot pay off the balance for an extended period.

They are, nonetheless, still a funding option, especially if you have no other funding options. If you are going to use your credit cards to fund your startup, try to pay off your balance as quickly as possible. This will leave you carrying less debt, with lower monthly obligations, and with the opportunity to borrow more money against the cards to buy valuable products for resale.

Shop around for credit cards with the lowest interest rates and no annual fees. Many banks and credit unions offer small business credit cards (such as the Visa Small Business Card) that offer special services such as travel insurance and lower interest rates. You can shop for credit card deals from these websites: **Bankrate.com**, **CardRatings.com**, **CreditCards.com** or **LowerMyBills.com**.

To properly analyze each credit card offer, determine the following information *before* completing an application:

- Is there an annual fee? How much is it?
- Is there an "application" or "processing" fee associated with completing the credit card application?
- What is the APR (annual percentage rate)? The lower the APR, the better. Some credit card offers have an "introductory APR," which only lasts for the first three, six or 12 months. If this is the case, understand what the APR will revert to after this initial period.
- What is the default APR? If you're late on just one monthly payment, skip a payment for whatever reason, pay your monthly bill with a check that ultimately bounces, or fail to adhere to the terms of the cardholder agreement, your APR could automatically jump to the default rate, which is often well over 32 percent.
- What fees and charges are associated with the card? Most cards have late fees, over-limit fees, balance transfer fees, online payment fees, telephone payment fees and other "hidden" fees associated with them. These fees can

add up quickly if you choose the wrong credit card or don't adhere to the terms of the cardholder's agreement.

• What perks or benefits are associated with the card?

RESOURCES
  – American Express Small Business, ♂ **https://home.americanexpress.com/home/open.shtml**
  – MasterCard Business, ♂ **mastercardbusiness.com**
  – Visa Small Business, ♂ **usa.visa.com/business**
  – Discover Business Card, ♂ **discovercard.com**

Social Lending

This is a relatively new concept when it comes to borrowing money. Instead of turning to a traditional bank, credit union or financial institution, using a "social lending service," you can borrow money from everyday people looking for an interest-earning investment opportunity.

While having a better-than-average credit score is definitely beneficial, using this method for borrowing money allows you to tell your unique story to potential lenders and take advantage of a more personalized approval process. The interest rates associated with this type of loan vary, based on your credit score.

Keep in mind, just because you're not borrowing through a traditional bank, this does not mean you can default on the loan without negative repercussions. If you're late on payments or default on a loan, the credit bureaus will be notified and a collections agency will be hired to recover the funds.

For additional information about social lending, visit **Prosper.com** or **LendingClub.com**.

Seek Out an Investor

Depending on how much money you need, it might make sense to seek out venture capital from one or more private investors (sometimes referred to as "angel investors") or from an investment capital firm.

A private investor can be found almost anywhere. It could be a friend, a relative, or an entrepreneur looking for a viable investment opportunity. Typically, investors will receive interest on their loan, as well as a stake (equity) in the company.

According to the Small Business Notes website (**smallbusinessnotes.com/financing/angelinvestors.html**), "Angel investors are individuals who invest in businesses looking for a higher return than they would see from more traditional investments. Many are successful entrepreneurs who want to help other entrepreneurs get their business off the ground. Usually they are the bridge from the self-funded stage of the business to the point that the business needs the level of funding that a venture capitalist would offer. Funding estimates vary, but usually range from $150,000 to $1.5 million."

An investment capital firm is more appropriate for companies capable of generating more than $25 million in revenue within five years. For a list of *Entrepreneur* magazine's Top 100 investment capital firms, visit **entrepreneur.com/vc100/index.html**.

Leasing and Renting

Leasing or renting equipment is another financing strategy that might not fund your entire buy-and-sell enterprise startup, but can greatly reduce the amount of hard cash you need to get things rolling.

Renting equipment or tools means you do not take ownership in any form. You simply pay the rental rate for the time you need the equipment and return it when it's no longer needed. Leasing also means you do not own the equipment, but you are legally bound to pay for a portion of the entire value of the equipment, plus interest by way of scheduled monthly lease payments.

The benefit of renting or leasing equipment, such as computers, is that you need little if any money upfront, which leaves your cash free to buy merchandise that can be resold for a profit right away. Also, rental and lease payments are deductions, unlike the sliding scale of tax depreciation used on owned equipment.

Supplier Terms

Another way to kick off your own buy-and-sell business with minimal upfront costs is to ask your new suppliers for a revolving credit account, which gives you up to 90 days to pay for goods and services you need to operate your business or for resale to customers for a profit.

People with strong credit will have few problems opening revolving credit accounts with suppliers. If your credit is not so strong, you will need to establish a payment history with most suppliers prior to their granting you credit privileges.

The advantage of revolving credit is that you can often sell your goods long before you have to pay your supplier. In effect, your suppliers are bankrolling your business and you get to skim off the profits, all without having to use your own cash.

Banking and Bookkeeping

Money management can be tricky business because—in addition to customers—cash flow is what keeps your buy-and-sell business operational. Consequently, understanding money management should become a priority, even if you elect to hire an accountant or bookkeeper to manage your business's books.

You will still need to familiarize yourself with basic bookkeeping and money management principles. In addition, you'll need to understand how credit actually works, as well as how to read bank statements and tax forms. It's also important that you understand the basic principles of accounts receivable and accounts payable.

Once your business is registered and ready to roll, you will need to open a commercial bank account, separate from your personal savings or checking account. To do this, select the bank you want to work with, and then schedule an appointment to open an account. Be sure to shop around for a bank that offers the best and most convenient services, as well as the lowest fees.

When you sit down with a banker, make sure you bring personal identification, as well as your business name registration papers (incorporation papers) and business license, since these documents are required to open a commercial bank account.

The next step will be to deposit funds into your new account. If your credit is sound, also ask the bank to attach a line of credit to your account, which can prove very useful when buying large quantities of products and during slow sales periods. Also, inquire about a credit card merchant account and other small business services that the bank offers.

Setting Up the Books

When it comes time to set up your financial books, you have two options—do it yourself or hire an accountant or bookkeeper to do it. You might want to do both by keeping your own books and hiring an accountant to prepare year-end financial statements and tax forms.

If you opt to keep your own books, make sure you invest in accounting software, such as Intuit's popular QuickBooks software (877-683-3280/**quickbooks.com**), because it is easy to use and makes bookkeeping much easier than doing it manually.

Most accounting software also allows you to create client accounts with invoicing and mail merge options, and to track account bank balances, merchant account information and accounts payable and receivable. QuickBooks Pro, which is probably the most popular accounting software on the market for small businesses, is priced near $200, and is available wherever software is sold or directly from Intuit's website.

Keep in mind that even with the proliferation of accounting software, hiring an accountant to take care of more complicated money matters is often wise. Like many professionals, accountants pride themselves on the fact that they do not cost you money, but rather make you money by discovering items overlooked on tax returns, by identifying business deductions you never knew existed, and by creating financial plans that will enable you to enjoy the fruits of your labor later in life without having to worry about where the money will come from.

If you are unsure about your bookkeeping abilities, even with the aid of accounting software, hire a bookkeeper to do your books on a monthly basis, and an accountant to audit the books quarterly and prepare year-end business statements and tax returns.

If you are only holding the occasional garage sales to raise a few extra bucks, there is little sense or need for accounting software and accountant services. Simply invest a few dollars in a basic ledger, and enter prices paid versus prices sold for all goods, along with expenses, such as advertising. The ledger book will run you about $5, and keeping on top of it should take all of about fifteen minutes a week.

Remember to keep all business and tax records in a dry and secure place for up to seven years. This is the maximum amount of time for which the IRS and Revenue Canada can request past business revenue and expense information.

Likewise, be sure to track and record every cent coming in and going out of your business. Obtain receipts for everything you buy or spend money on for the business. Keep a logbook in your glove box for times when no receipts are issued, such as when feeding the parking meter. You can record these expenses in the logbook and enter them later into your accounting program or ledger.

Purchase Payment Options

In today's super-competitive business environment, consumers have come to expect many payment options for purchases. A steadfast cash-only payment policy is no longer acceptable even for the small buy-and-sell enterprise, especially if you plan on doing business online.

You must provide customers with multiple ways to pay, including cash, debit card, credit card and electronic cash. There are costs to provide these payment options: account fees, transaction fees, equipment rental and merchant fees based on a percentage of the total sales value. But these expenses must be viewed as a cost of doing business in the 21st century.

Be sure to shop around for the best service with the best prices. Not all banks, merchant accounts and payment processing services are the same, and fees vary widely. Remember, consumers expect choices when it comes time to pay for their purchases, and if you elect not to provide these choices, you can expect fewer sales.

Accepting Cash and Checks

The first way to get paid is by accepting good old cash, which is great because it is instant, with no processing time or fees required. As fast as the cash comes in, you can use it to buy more goods to sell and increase revenues and profits.

The major downside is that cash is risky because you could get robbed or lose it. In that instance, collecting from your insurance company could prove difficult if there is no paper transaction as proof. Even if you prefer not to receive cash, there are people who will pay in cash. For this reason, invest in a good-quality safe for your home and for use on the road. Also get in the habit of making daily bank deposits during daylight hours.

For a small business operator, accepting paper checks from people you don't know is not a sound business strategy. It's too easy for people to write bad checks, which will result in a loss of revenue, as well as additional fees imposed by your bank. If you decide to accept a personal or business check from a customer, ask to see picture ID and write the customer's driver's license number on the back. If the amount of the check exceeds a few hundred dollars, ask the buyer to get the check certified, or pay you using a bank draft or money order instead. The last thing you want to be left holding is a rubber check.

Accepting Debit Cards

Buying or renting a wireless or wired debit card terminal allows you to accept debit card payments, which is much better than accepting checks, and in some cases better than cash, because you do not have the theft concerns.

Having the ability to accept debit cards will often give you a competitive advantage and make it easier for people to buy and impulse shop. Offer debit card payment options if you will be selling at flea markets, from a homebased show-room, mall kiosks, community events, at farmers' or public markets or online.

When you acquire a merchant account to accept major credit cards, you will also be able to accept debit card payments from your customers. To obtain a credit card merchant account, see the next section of this chapter.

Obtaining A Merchant Account

The ability to accept credit card payments requires you, as the business operator, to acquire a *merchant account* through a bank or financial institution. This typically means paying an application fee, filling out a bunch of paperwork, and then paying a per-transaction fee plus a small percentage of each credit card sale to the merchant account provider. If you'll be operating an online business, your merchant account provider must also provide resources that are compatible with your website hosting company, so credit card orders can be processed securely and in real time online.

It's important to shop around for the best deal when trying to acquire a merchant account, because fees vary dramatically. In addition to contacting local banks, do a search using Google or Yahoo! using the search phrase "Merchant Account." You should also contact your website hosting company, as most already have partnerships with merchant account providers, which makes it easier for you to get started accepting credit card payments.

Whatever fees you wind up paying to accept credit card payments must be calculated into your cost of doing business. It may be necessary to forward some of these costs onto your customers by raising your retail prices slightly for the products you'll be selling.

One reason to accept credit cards is to provide convenience to your customers. Studies have shown that consumers are apt to spend more on purchases when using a major credit card (as opposed to writing a check or paying cash, for example).

Most merchant account providers can set you up with the ability to accept Visa, MasterCard, Discover and American Express payments, as well as debit card payments and electronic check payments.

The fees, however, may be different for each credit card or payment type. For example, depending on the merchant account provider, you may wind up paying a higher per-transaction fee and/or discount rate for an order paid for using an American Express card versus a debit card.

The following are five strategies for obtaining a merchant account:

Compare prices carefully and watch out for hidden and recurring fees. Most merchant account providers charge a percentage of each sale (called the *discount rate*), in addition to a fixed per-transaction fee. Additional fees you'll want to compare are the application fees for setting up the account and any recurring monthly fees that you'll be required to pay in order to maintain the account and be able to accept credit card payments. You may be offered a lower discount rate by one provider, but that same provider will have a higher per-transaction fee, or a higher than average recurring monthly fee. Other potential fees to watch out for are associated with having to purchase or lease credit card processing equipment and/or software.

For a startup company with no sales track record, negotiating for lower rates from a merchant account provider will be a challenge. However, once you develop a relationship with your merchant account provider and demonstrate a track record of growing monthly sales, you could go back and try to negotiate for a lower per-transaction fee and/or discount rate. Even a small reduction to your discount rate will save you a fortune over time, plus instantly increase your profit margin on whatever you're selling.

The contract you'll be required to sign with your merchant account provider will probably be a complex and confusing legal document. Before signing it, understand exactly what you're agreeing to in terms of the fees and the duration of the contract. If you sign a two-year agreement, for example, but your business only remains open for six months, you'll still be required to pay the minimum monthly fees for the duration of the contracted agreement (or pay a hefty cancellation fee).

Make sure the merchant account provider you choose offers the tools and resources necessary to seamlessly integrate credit card processing into your website (through your website hosting service). A lack of compatibility will cause tremendous headaches, plus cost you extra when it comes to getting everything to work properly. Ease of implementation and security are important factors to consider.

Not all merchant account providers are alike. In addition to charging different fees, each offers its own level of customer service and technical support. You also need to know how quickly transactions will be processed, in order to determine when the money from incoming credit card sales will get automatically deposited into your company's bank account. How long this takes (between a few hours and several days) varies between merchant account providers. Many merchant account providers also offer lower rates and fees to low-risk businesses. Operating an escort business, online poker site or credit restoration business, for example, will be regarded as a high-risk business.

CREDIT CARD MERCHANT ACCOUNT ADVANTAGES

As a small business operator, the following are reasons why you'll want to acquire a merchant account and be able to accept major credit cards, including Visa, MasterCard, Discover and American Express (as well as debit cards) as payment from your customers:

- Accepting credit cards increases impulse buying. Studies have proven that merchants who accept credit cards can increase sales by up to 50 percent.
- If you have your own merchant account, you can typically accept credit card payments online, over the telephone, by mail or in person.
- You can sell products on an installment basis by obtaining permission to charge your customers' credit cards monthly, or as per agreement.
- Processing time is relatively quick, and money is often deposited in your bank account within 48 hours.
- You can ship products knowing you have been paid in full and do not have to worry about CODs, bum checks or slow payers.

CREDIT CARD MERCHANT ACCOUNT DISADVANTAGES

The following are some potential disadvantages of utilizing a merchant account as a small business operator:

- It can be costly to set up and maintain a credit card merchant account, including:
  - Setup and application fees, $0 to $1,000
  - Equipment and software purchases, $200 to $1,000
  - Equipment and software leases, $25 to $100 per month
  - Administration and statement fees, $10 to $100 per month
  - Processing fees—2 to 8 percent of total sales
  - Transaction fees, from $.15 to $.50 per transaction, in addition to the processing fee.
- Credit card companies can hit you with stiff "chargeback fees" for goods returned and credits returned to customers' credit card accounts.
- If you're not careful to follow your merchant account's policies exactly, you could become responsible for fraudulent credit card transactions perpetrated by your customers.

Online Payment Services: Google Checkout and PayPal Express Checkout

These two services are available to merchants who plan to sell products online via their own e-commerce websites. To make shopping online a more secure and faster experience for all consumers who opt to participate, both Google (**https:// checkout.google.com/sell**) and PayPal (**paypal.com**) have developed services that allows consumers to create a single password-protected account (with either Google or PayPal) and enter all of their personal and financial information just once.

When a participating consumer opts to make an online purchase with any participating online merchant, the customer needs only to click on the Google Checkout or PayPal icon that's incorporated into a site's shopping cart. The consumer is then seamlessly transferred to either the Google or PayPal system, which already has their name, address and credit card data stored. This eliminates the need for the consumer to repeatedly enter this information whenever they place an order with a particular online merchant.

A consumer can feel safer using Google Checkout, for example, because the merchant they're shopping with never actually receives their personal credit card information. Instead, Google processes the payment (and then pays the merchant). The consumer also doesn't need to remember usernames and passwords for every online merchant they shop with. At any time, they can review their purchase history, track orders and deliveries, or contact merchants they've done business with—all from one centralized website operated by Google or PayPal.

For consumers, utilizing Google Checkout or PayPal Express Checkout is totally free. They can set up their own secure account in minutes and there is no extra charge associated with making purchases using Google Checkout or PayPal Express Checkout. It is the merchant that pays fees to use these services as a way to accept online payments.

Theoretically, an online merchant can accept major credit card, debit card and electronic check payments using either of these services and not have a separate merchant account. However, if a customer has not set up a Google Checkout or PayPal account (and does not wish to do so), they would not be able to place an online order from your site.

The number of consumers who have either a Google Checkout or PayPal account is growing quickly, but as of early 2008, we're not yet at the point where an online merchant should only accept one or both of these payment options instead of having their own merchant account. Currently, offering either or both of these online payment options should be considered an optional added convenience merchants can extend to their customers.

As of early 2008, PayPal boasted a network of 150 million active accounts that continues to grow at a rate of 104,500 new accounts opened by online shoppers every day. Google Checkout is a newer service, but is actively marketing to both consumers and merchants in hopes of making it a widely accepted standard for online payments.

PayPal accepts foreign currencies, so you can immediately begin tapping the worldwide market with your online business. In fact, PayPal reports it accepts payments in 16 currencies and allows merchants to sell to shoppers in 190 countries and regions. For the consumer, their Google Checkout or PayPal account can store an unlimited number of shipping addresses and credit cards.

Taxation and the Buy-and-Sell Enterprise

There is no escaping the taxman, regardless of how big or small your business may be. If you earn business profits, the government will want its share. In the United States and Canada, business income/profits are taxed at the federal, state/provincial and municipal levels.

The best and most up-to-date information and advice you can obtain about small business and income tax will come directly from the Internal Revenue Service in the United States and the Canada Customs and Revenue Agency in Canada. These government agencies oversee federal business and income taxation.

Likewise, accountants can help you navigate the murky taxation waters, and there are also many books specifically developed to help the small business owner understand and prepare tax forms. Small-business taxation is complicated and can be very frustrating for the novice entrepreneur to understand. Even seasoned entrepreneurs do not like dealing with tax issues and preparing forms because the rules and regulations change regularly.

RESOURCES

Canada Customs and Revenue Agency, ☎ (800) 959-2221, ♂ **ccra-adrc.gc.ca**

Internal Revenue Service (IRS), ☎ (800) 829-3676, ♂ **irs.gov**

Paying Taxes

How your business is legally structured will determine the taxes you pay, both personal and business, as well as the forms you're required to file. As a sole proprietor or unincorporated partnership, the income your business earns after expenses is your personal income, and you are taxed accordingly.

If your business is incorporated, you are taxed on the income you receive from the corporation in the form of wages and bonuses, and the corporation is taxed on the profits it earns after all expenses are deducted.

Additionally, post-tax corporate profits are taxed once again when distributed to shareholders in the form of dividends. Keep in mind that if you have any employees, you will need to obtain employee identification numbers, prepare and submit employee income tax reporting forms, and withhold and remit the employee and employer portions of Medicare, employment insurance and Social Security.

There are a number of tax advantages for operating a buy-and-sell enterprise. Because of allowable business expenses, it is very possible to claim a portion of your current household expenses, such as rent or mortgage payments and utility bills, against your business and personal income, especially for the sole proprietor. Whenever you are unsure about which expenses are allowable and which are not, it is best to contact an accountant.

The IRS provides small business owners with a number of free publications to explain small-business taxation issues. These publications can be used as a guide for completing small business and self-employment tax forms.

You can pick up IRS small-business information, tax forms, and publications in person at your local IRS office, call to have the publications delivered by mail, (800) 829-3676, or download them online, **irs.gov/business/small**.

Up Next: Establishing Your Business's Infrastructure

Before we start exploring all of the possible products you can buy and sell for a big profit, it's important that you properly set up the infrastructure for your business. This chapter was designed to help get you started with this process. In Chapter 3, many of the other decisions and considerations associated with launching a successful buy-and-sell operation are explored.

THERE'S STILL PLENTY MORE YOU'LL NEED TO KNOW

This chapter focuses on some of the additional considerations and subjects you'll need to become familiar with prior to launching your buy-and-sell business venture. Some of the more important topics covered within this chapter include:

- Effectively selling from home

- Building strong trade accounts

- Developing a marketing plan

- Mastering your personal selling skills

- Creating advertising that works
- Taking your buy-and-sell enterprise online
- The importance of providing top-notch customer service

As you've probably figured out by now, buying and selling as a business is a very broad topic, mainly because there are so many options in terms of how you buy, how you sell, and the types of products you ultimately buy and sell. So there's no single solution for success or one quick and easy answer for generating profits.

The information in this chapter is meant to give you a general understanding of important business fundamentals and marketing. You'll definitely want to build upon specific areas of knowledge, based on the subjects that are directly relevant to the business you'll be operating.

Running any type of business is an ongoing and evolutionary learning process. As your business grows, your goals, policies and methods of doing business will most likely change. Being open and ready to make important decisions and to make necessary changes will afford you the opportunity to fine-tune your business and marketing skills while on the job.

On an ongoing basis, you always want to be learning more—about your products, your industry and your customer base. Keep on top of new trends and shifts in the marketplace. Stay apprised of what your competition is up to. Also, always work toward improving and broadening your own skill set when it comes to what's required of you to successfully operate your business.

Attend industry trade shows, read industry-oriented magazines, do online research, read additional books, interact with your customers, stay in close contact with your suppliers, and pay careful attention to your competitors. These are all ways of making sure you and your business are prepared for the future.

Buying and Selling From Home

Before committing to working from home, you need to determine if you can legally operate a buy-and-sell business from your current residence. Chances are you can, although probably with some restrictions, based on local laws and ordinances where you happen to live. Unfortunately, there is no standard, across-the-board set of rules on allowing businesses to operate from a residential location. Each and every community in the United States and Canada has its own home-business zoning regulations and specific usage guidelines.

The majority of municipalities allow small home businesses to operate from a residence, providing the business activities do not negatively impact neighbors and the neighborhood in general. Some allow only certain types of businesses to operate (such as those that do not involve customers visiting the premises).

From a zoning standpoint, the potential issues include exterior signage, parking, noise, fire, storage of hazardous substances, deliveries and shipping, and customers visiting your home. Long before you decide to launch your buy-and-sell enterprise from home, check out your local zoning rules, regulations and restrictions. Visit your local city or municipal planning department or bylaws office for further information.

Setting Up Your Work Space

The products you sell and how they are sold will determine the type, size and location of the home work space that you need. Homebased work space options range from any corner of a room, to an entire room, or a separate outside structure.

Many people opt to use a converted garage, den, basement or a spare bedroom from which to operate their business. Each of these locations has advantages and disadvantages you'll want to consider before setting up shop.

First, thought must be given to the daily living needs of your family and how space in the home is currently being utilized for day-to-day living, as well as for special occasions, seasonal activities and guests. Because setting up a home work space requires balancing the needs of your business with the needs of your family, compromises will have to be made on both fronts.

Make sure that you have ample space to work, but also that the space offers a suitable work environment from a noise, lighting, temperature and layout standpoint. Is the office space wired for internet access and does it possess enough electrical outlets, for example? When working, will you be able to close the door and block out any family-oriented distractions, such as your kids at play or your dog barking?

Working out of two or three separate areas of the home is far less productive than working from one area. Will you constantly be searching for things rather than working? Try to make your work space a single-use area. Ideally, the room should not double as the dining room at night or the children's playroom.

If you plan to work from home, your work space must be conducive to working efficiently, plus provide ample space for you to conduct your business and potentially store your inventory. (For inventory, many people opt to rent a nearby climate-controlled storage facility, so that their on-hand inventory doesn't clutter their home.)

Considerations Before Welcoming Customers Into Your Home

If you will be selling from home, ask yourself the following questions:

- Are you legally able to welcome customers into your home, based on local laws and ordinances?
- Do you have the interior/exterior space required to showcase products and accept customers?
- Do you have suitable parking, and can you provide customers with access to washroom facilities?
- Do you have ample space to separate your living space from your selling space, to provide privacy for both customers and your family?
- Do you have a separate entrance for customers?
- Is the appearance of your home conducive to welcoming customers? Peeling paint, threadbare carpets and broken porch boards send customers the wrong signals about your business and products. If your home needs a sprucing up, then do it before you get started.

Storage Issues

Whether you have customers coming into your home or not, you will need storage space for equipment, inventory and business records, as well as adequate space for receiving products and shipping orders.

Provided you have enough storage space to meet your needs, the space you use will also need to be easily accessible, dry and free of critters. It must be secure, so there is no risk that valuable business equipment, inventory and records will be stolen. If you do not have suitable storage space for inventory, is there suitable space for rent close by with good access? If so, how much will this increase your cost of doing business?

Equipment and Technology

Every buy-and-sell business has different needs in terms of office furniture, equipment and technology devices. If customers will be visiting your homebased showroom, your furniture, equipment and displays will need to reflect this, both in appearance and function.

If you do not have customers visiting your home office, you will have more leeway because it won't really matter if the colors are mismatched, if you purchased your desk secondhand at your neighbor's garage sale, or if you choose to build a few of the items yourself.

When it comes to your office furniture and equipment, all that really matters is that it's fully functional, reliable, and allows you to handle the day-to-day responsibilities of business operation. Some of your office needs might include:

- *Desk and comfortable chair.* You will need a desk large enough for a computer monitor with tower storage underneath, a printer, and a telephone/fax machine. However, you can save space by using a laptop computer, if necessary. Full-size Apple iMac desktop computers also tend to require less desk space. If you only splurge for one piece of office furniture, a comfortable and ergonomically correct office chair should be that luxury item, especially if your business keeps you in your seat for long periods of time. (Your back, neck and shoulders will thank you!)

- *Paper file storage.* Even in this electronic age, businesses still generate lots of paperwork and paper-based files. You'll definitely need file cabinets to properly organize and store these files.

- *Work table.* Purchase or build a work table that is separate from your desk. Work tables are indispensable and can be used for opening and sorting mail, bookkeeping and record keeping duties, packing and unpacking inventory, and much more. Just make sure you keep this work space clear and clutter-free when it's not in use.

- *Computer system and software.* You will need a complete computer system, including monitor, printer, modem, keyboard and mouse. The main considerations will be processing speed and data storage capabilities. You will also need software. Depending on the products you buy and sell and how they are sold, you might need software in one or more of the following areas: word processing, accounting, database management, website building and maintenance, payment processing, inventory tracking and desktop publishing. In general, Windows-based desktop computers cost less than laptop computers. Apple Mac-based computers tend to cost a bit more, but many people find them much easier to use, more ergonomic and more space efficient.

- *Digital camera.* Digital cameras are indispensable to buy-and-sell entrepreneurs. You can take pictures of products, and because the images (photographs) use digital technology, they are easily transferred to your website, e-mails, classified ads or desktop publishing programs to create fliers, brochures, presentations, catalogs, posters and signs. When it comes to choosing a digital camera, the higher the resolution the better. What's absolutely essential is that your product photographs look professional. This will probably mean you'll need to invest in backgrounds and specialized lighting equipment to create a mini photo studio. If you can't achieve the professional results you need by taking your own photos, either use stock photography provided by the manufacturers of the products you'll be selling, or hire a professional photographer to take the necessary photos on your behalf.

- *Telephone/fax machine.* You will need a desktop telephone with business functions, such as on-hold, conferencing, redial, speakerphone and message storage capabilities. You'll also need some type of answering machine or remote voice mail system. If your budget allows, you might consider purchasing an all-in-one office document center with a telephone, fax, printer, scanner and copier. However, you'll still want a separate, full-featured telephone (perhaps equipped with a good-quality telephone headset) situated on your desk.

- *Cellular telephone.* A cellular telephone is a must, enabling you to keep in constant contact with customers and prospects, no matter where you are. Consider purchasing a smartphone or wireless PDA (such as an Apple iPhone, BlackBerry or Palm Treo) that also has internet features, so you can receive, check and send e-mails, not to mention track eBay auctions, if desired.

- *Internet connection.* Within your office, you will need a high-speed broadband, FIOS or DSL internet connection so you can access web. Depending on the layout of your office, the number of computers you'll be using, and where you'll need to connect to the internet, setting up wireless (Wi-Fi) internet access in your home or office may be beneficial. Depending on your service provider, a high-speed internet connection should cost between $40 and $60 per month.

- *Lighting.* Especially if your office doesn't have windows, you'll definitely want to install ample lighting. Avoid fluorescent lighting or any lighting that will cause eyestrain or fatigue. No matter when you're working (day or night), you want your office and work space to be well lit.

Keeping Track of Inventory and Delivering the Goods

One of your main considerations when setting up your office is inventory management. In addition to storage, you'll need to create a system for tracking your inventory and efficiently shipping it to customers (unless you'll be selling in person).

Starting with the physical aspect, you will need a place to put your inventory. The location where you store your inventory must be easily accessed, dry and secure. If you do not have space at home, you will need to rent space. Should this become necessary, be sure to consider the remote storage location's on-site security, cost, size and proximity to your home.

Public (climate-controlled) mini-storage services are the best, because you are not tied to long-term warehouse leases. At home or off-site, you will probably need to build or purchase new or used shelving to house your inventory. Ideally, the shelving should be adjustable to accommodate various product sizes. Your needs will be based on the size and weight of what you're actually selling, plus the amount of inventory you plan to keep on hand.

In terms of inventory management, once again you have options. If you are an occasional or small buyer and seller, simply invest in a spiral notebook, create a few columns for product description and units, and you are pretty much set. Likewise, you can create your own inventory management system using your computer and a spreadsheet or database management program such as Excel or FileMaker.

Large-volume sellers should definitely invest in inventory or retail management software. Most inventory management software offers valuable, time saving features, such as the ability to manage a customer database, create and manage invoices, make labels, track inventory, scan bar codes, manage tax codes, and automatically reorder inventory.

Prices for this type of software vary, depending on features. You can find this type of inventory management software by performing an online search. Many e-commerce turnkey solutions provide inventory management tools as part of their overall offerings.

Product Delivery

There are many options available for how to get products from your business to your customer's location. You can deliver the items yourself, use a courier service to pick up and deliver your orders, utilize the U.S. Postal Service (**usps.com**), or hire a courier service.

Your decision will be based on several factors, such as cost, schedule, and the size and weight of what is being shipped. You'll also need to consider how quickly you need the products to arrive at their destination (overnight, within three business days, within two business days or within a week).

Prompt and efficient product delivery will play a major role in your business's success. When a customer places an order, chances are they expect that order to be processed and shipped quickly (within 24 hours). If they're willing to pay for overnight shipping, they also want it to arrive the following morning.

How quickly you process and ship orders reflects to customers the kind of service you provide and can have a positive or negative impact on repeat business and word-of-mouth advertising, depending on how customers perceive their overall experience. Of course, shipping costs vary, depending on product weight, overall dimensions, schedule, geography and value. However, some or all of this cost can be passed along to your customers in the form of a "shipping and handling" charge that gets added on to their order subtotal.

You will also need to consider how you will pack items for transport, and your costs for packing and shipping materials, such as boxes, bubble wrap, envelopes, tape, foam packing, shipping labels and plastic bags.

All of the big couriers offer some free shipping supplies, but also sell additional materials, depending on the services you utilize. Office supply superstores—Staples, OfficeMax and Office Depot—generally have the lowest costs on packing and shipping supplies purchased in relatively small quantities.

All the big courier companies—the USPS, Canada Post, FedEx, UPS and DHL—have software (or a website) available to frequent shippers that calculates shipping charges based on the information you enter. You can also print customer labels, track packages, and arrange for pickups and deliveries online.

If most of your shipping needs will utilize the USPS, consider buying or renting a postage machine or using your computer to purchase and print postage, based on your needs. This will save you time making constant trips to your local post office. Pitney Bowes (**pitneybowespostagemeters.com**) and Endicia (**endicia.com**) are two companies that offer various low-cost postage machine and computer-generated postage systems.

Listed below are a few of the major courier companies and postal services. Visit the websites of these companies to establish an account (which usually requires a major credit card) and to order shipping supplies.

RESOURCES
- Canada Post, ✂ **canadapost.ca**
- DHL, ✂ **dhl.com**
- FedEx, ✂ **fedex.com**
- USPS, ✂ **usps.com**
- UPS, ✂ **ups.com**

Product Pricing

Pricing new, used and collectible products for resale can be more difficult than most people think, yet pricing is a very important element of the marketing mix and your ability to turn a profit. If your prices (what you're selling your products for) are too high, you will meet with great resistance to buying. If your prices are too low, you may also meet with resistance, because of perceived quality issues, plus you probably won't make any money on the sales you have.

There are a number of factors influencing how you should price products for resale. Considerations include:

- Product costs
- Overhead (ongoing business expenses)
- Competition
- Method of distribution
- Wages
- Your desired return on investment (ROI)

If your pricing is correct, consumers won't think twice about buying from you, because they will feel what you are charging is fair and commensurate with the perceived value and benefits.

However, as soon as your price goes below or above the threshold of what consumers feel is in the fair range, you will meet with sales resistance. Whether you are selling new, used, customized, modified or collectible products and items, you still have to cover the basics: your fixed costs, direct costs, income and profit.

It is a combination of the aforementioned and common sense that will help you determine what prices you have to, and can, charge for your products. The first factor is overhead, which takes into account all of your costs associated with doing business (equipment, utility charges, rent, salaries, marketing expenses, banking fees, business permit fees, lawyer fees, accounting fees, etc.). Even though fixed costs cannot directly generate a profit, they nonetheless must be present in order to operate the business.

For example, your monthly telephone bill must be paid, regardless of how many sales you make or how much revenue is generated. Some overhead costs tend to increase as sales volume increases, necessitating good record keeping and bookkeeping habits to keep on top of changes.

The next factor affecting product pricing is direct costs associated with the sale and delivery of a product. An example of a direct cost is the wholesale cost of what you're selling, including the product's packaging or customization costs.

The third basic factor influencing product pricing is your wages and profit. People often confuse the two, but they are separate issues. Income is what you trade your time for— say, $25.00 per hour, for example. Profit is the return on your investment and the reward for the risks entrepreneurs take by starting and operating a business.

Pricing New Products for Resale

There are a number of ways to price new products for resale. The simplest is generally a cost-plus approach, which means that you multiply your product cost by a markup factor, such as 100 percent. If you paid $25 wholesale for an item and applied a 100 percent markup, the retail (selling) price would be $50. But at the end of the day, competition will be seen as the greatest influence.

If the majority of resellers charge $35 for that same item, you would be hard pressed to sell it for more, unless you did something to add value to the product, through customization, modification or bundling it with an additional product. Of course, if you were the only vendor selling the item online or elsewhere, you might be able to sell it for $75, if there was a demand from consumers and an absence of competition.

Sales value also has to be factored into pricing. If you pay $1 for an item and resell it for $3, you might earn a whopping 300 percent markup. But, at the same time, you have to sell a whole bunch of that item to cover your fixed costs and also generate an income (salary) plus a profit.

On the other side of the coin, you might only earn 5 percent on the resale of a piece of real estate, but on a $300,000 sale, this adds up to $15,000. Once again, a commonsense approach must be taken when choosing products and prices.

For the small buy-and-sell operator, the best product pricing approach is to conduct research in the marketplace to find out what the same or similar products are selling for, how they are being sold, and who is buying them.

Potential research techniques include:

- Going online to eBay and other marketplaces to study prices; this includes using price comparison websites, such as **nextag.com** or **shopzilla.com**
- Searching through newspapers, fliers and magazine advertisements for prices on identical and similar items
- Doing some "mystery shopping" at retail stores and conducting price comparisons
- Scanning product catalogs for pricing information
- Calling retailers and asking how much they charge for the type of products you are going to be selling
- Asking your suppliers, wholesalers or distributors, as they are one of the best sources of up-to-date product pricing

Obviously, it is in your best interest to find innovative ways to distinguish what you sell from the competition's products and seek out unique methods of distribution, so you can sell your products for more and in greater volume. The methods you ultimately adopt, however, will vary greatly based on what you're selling and to whom, as well as what resources you have available (financial or otherwise).

Pricing Used Products for Resale

Pricing previously owned merchandise for resale shares similarities with pricing new products, especially in terms of pricing research. Use many of the same price research techniques—online searches, classified advertising and mystery shopping comparisons—to help determine the current market value of the used goods you are selling.

There are also online and published pricing guides available for more expensive products, including cars, boats, many type of collectibles, antiques, jewelry and recreational vehicles.

Price guides typically describe the product, including model and features, and assign a value based on these criteria, taking into account the condition of the used item. For example, used car dealers have used price guides (such as *Kelley Blue Book*, **kbb.com**) for decades to help establish a buying and selling price for trade-ins.

You can also have professional appraisals performed on higher-priced items to help substantiate and support your asking price. This is especially true for items like real estate, cars, fine jewelry, art, antiques and boats. Keep in mind that professional appraisals and surveys can be quite expensive, and you will need to factor in this cost when buying and pass the cost along when selling.

Many resellers create a sliding-condition scale when pricing items. For example, when in perfect condition, items are priced at 70 percent of their new cost, while items that are still saleable, but past their glory days, are priced at 30 percent of new cost.

Some products, however, retain value better than others. For instance, used computers are notorious for having poor resale value due to rapidly changing technology, while used jewelry tends to hold its value (or even increase in value).

Ultimately, effectively pricing used products for resale must take into account what the current market will bear. You can greatly increase the odds of securing top dollar by selling products that are in good condition, work properly, and are in demand, and by selling through the right venues to the right audience.

Pricing Antiques and Collectibles for Resale

Pricing antiques and collectibles for resale is another game entirely, mainly because antiques, collectibles and memorabilia items are seldom actually needed by the consumer. Antiques and collectibles are things people *want*, not *need*, and the target audience can be very narrow, especially for uncommon collectibles and highly valued antiques.

Let's face it, few consumers have an extra $25,000 lying around to buy an original Tiffany lamp. Therefore, pricing is largely reflective of what the marketplace will bear. There are price, value and condition guides available for every imaginable type of antique and collectible.

Value or pricing guides are unquestionably a good starting point for pricing certain types of items. The perceived value of antiques and collectible items goes up and down daily, and is influenced by many factors. For instance, the value of nautical collectibles—especially cruise line memorabilia—skyrocketed after the release of the movie *Titanic*, as does the value of first-edition Hemingway novels for a few weeks every year around the anniversary of his birthday.

Pricing antiques and collectibles is as much about choosing the right sales venues and target audience as it is about the actual item—probably more so. Therefore, success comes to antique and collectibles traders who pay close attention to what's going on in the marketplace at all times.

Professional appraisals and authentications also help to substantiate and support asking prices. Indeed, in many situations, having antiques, collectibles and memorabilia items appraised and authenticated will greatly increase their value. Authentication is especially valuable and often necessary.

Building Strong Trade Accounts

If you sell new products purchased from manufacturers, wholesalers, distributors, liquidators, importers or craftspeople, you have to choose your suppliers wisely. In order to sustain long-term stability and profitability, relationships with your product suppliers must be mutually beneficial and equitable.

Buying decisions should not be based solely on low price. You also have to factor in reliability, sustainability and support from the people you do business with. Let's take a quick closer look at these issues:

- *A good match.* The first rule of choosing suppliers is to only do business with people you like, trust and respect. You might love your supplier's products, but if you do not like or cannot get along with the people running the company, there is little hope for establishing a long-term, stable and equitable business relationship.

- *Reliability.* If your suppliers cannot deliver what you need when you need it, this will have a very negative impact on your business. Supplier reliability is perhaps the most important piece of information you should consider when establishing trade accounts. Your supplier's promise to you relates directly to the promises you'll ultimately make to your customers. If your supplier lets you down, you in turn will let your customers down, and lose sales and profits every time this happens.
- *Support.* Consider the support that suppliers offer in terms of warranties, customer service, selling aids (such as product samples, brochures, fliers, catalogs, promotional signage, event displays and website or e-commerce support). The higher the level of support and service supplied to you, the higher level of support and service you can provide to your customers.

Buying on Terms

The payment terms you can negotiate with your suppliers are often more important than the lowest unit-product cost. With the right terms, you have the opportunity to sell products to your customers, get paid, and collect your profits before paying your suppliers.

Ideally, you want to secure 90-day payment terms on a revolving-account basis, but you will generally find most suppliers prefer 30 days and offer discounts for cash orders or early settlement.

People with strong credit will have few problems opening revolving-credit accounts with suppliers. If your credit is not so strong, you will need to establish a payment history with most suppliers prior to their granting you credit privileges.

The advantage of revolving credit is that you can often sell your goods long before you have to pay your supplier. In effect, your suppliers are bankrolling your business, and you get access to your profits without having to use your own cash.

Once you set up accounts with suppliers, always pay on time and in full when required to do so. Credit is a privilege for those who deserve it: it's not a right. If you have your credit privileges revoked by a supplier and you don't have ample cash on hand to pay for your inventory, you could go out of business or sustain tremendous losses.

Drop-Shipping Option

One option available to buy-and-sell entrepreneurs who resell new products is not to purchase inventory for resale at all, but instead to open accounts with wholesalers and manufacturers who offer drop-shipping services.

Drop-shipping is simple. You sell a product to a customer and collect payment via credit card, debit card, cash or check. You then send the order to your supplier via e-mail, fax, or courier. Your supplier fulfills the product order and ships it to your customer under your business name. Your supplier then bills your account for the product shipped and you pay your supplier when the account becomes due.

The big benefits of drop-shipping for the small buy-and-sell entrepreneur are that you do not have to worry about buying inventory upfront, you do not have to rent warehouse space to store inventory, and you do not have to worry about transportation and delivery issues.

One huge potential drawback to using a drop-shipper is that you have no control whatsoever over how quickly items get shipped to your customers. You also have to rely on the drop-shipper to properly label your packages, provide accurate tracking information, and insure all orders are processed accurately. If any mistakes are made, this reflects extremely poorly on your company in the eyes of your customers.

In short, when you rely on a drop-shipper, all you have to do is concentrate on finding customers to buy your products. Many online retailers work with drop-ship wholesalers. You can also work with drop-ship wholesalers and manufacturers if you sell via mail order, at in-home parties, via an e-commerce website, or through consumer shows.

When using drop-shippers, you'll need to have actual product samples on hand, as well as product literature and order forms. To find manufacturers and wholesalers who provide drop-ship solutions for a wide range of products, conduct an online search using the search phrase "Drop Ship Wholesalers."

RESOURCES
- American Drop Shippers Directory, ♂ **bookservices.com**
- World Wide Brands, ♂ **worldwidebrands.com**
- No Minimum, ♂ **nominimum.com**

Developing a Marketing Plan

Developing a marketing plan for your buy-and-sell venture is well worth the effort. Based on your research and the information revealed in the plan, you will be able to prove that there is sufficient demand for your product, that you can compete in the marketplace, and that the market is large enough to support your venture and marketing goals.

Your marketing plan does not have to be highly sophisticated, however. Even a few well-researched and documented pages covering the basics are often sufficient to reveal the information needed to identify your customers, product advantages, sales goals, marketing strategies and action plan.

By answering the questions in the following subsections, you will compile enough information to create your own marketing plan. This information can then be used to help market your products and guide your marketing decisions. All of this information should become an integral part of your overall business plan.

1. Your Buy-and-Sell Enterprise

Describe your buy-and-sell venture in general terms. Include your business's name, legal structure, owners' and partners' special skills and experiences, and who your key product suppliers will be.

If your buy-and-sell venture is currently in operation, use this space to recount successes and failures, as well as growth or decline in sales to date. Describe where your business is now versus where it will be in the future should your goals and objectives be achieved.

A. What is your business name and legal structure? _____

_____

_____

B. Where is your business located? _____

_____

_____

C. Describe your own and any business partner's relevant experience, skills, and training. _____

_____

_____

D. List key product suppliers and the products each supplies.

_____

_____

2. Marketplace

Describe the marketplace in which your business will operate or into which it might expand in the near future. The biggest benefit of conducting and recording marketplace information is that it enables you to greatly reduce your exposure to financial risk. It also allows you to increase your chances of capitalizing on marketplace opportunities, and can help you prove (to yourself and your investors) that there is a big enough marketplace to support your business and forecasted sales.

A. Describe the trading area that your buy-and-sell venture will serve. (City, county, state)

_____

_____

B. How big is the current market?

_____

_____

C. How big is the potential market?

_____

_____

D. In what life-cycle stage is the market—growth, decline or static?

_____

_____

3. Target Customer

For each category, check all that apply specifically to your primary target audience. Once you've carefully narrowed down your target audience, complete this worksheet a second time to define the secondary potential audience for your product.

Gender:	❏ Male	❏ Female	❏ Not Applicable

Marital Status: ❏ Single ❏ Married ❏ Divorced
❏ Widowed ❏ Not Applicable

Age: ❏ Child ❏ Teenager
❏ Age 18 to 24 ❏ Age 25 to 49
❏ Age 50 to 65 ❏ Age 66+ ❏ Not Applicable

Race: ❏ White ❏ African American
❏ Hispanic ❏ Asian
❏ Other:_____ ❏ Not Applicable

Sexual Orientation:

- ❏ Straight
- ❏ Gay
- ❏ Bisexual
- ❏ Not Applicable

Income Level:

- ❏ Under $15,000 per year
- ❏ $15,001 to $25,000 per year
- ❏ $25,001 to $45,000 per year
- ❏ $45,001 to $55,000 per year
- ❏ $55,001 to $99,999 per year
- ❏ $100,000 to $500,000 per year
- ❏ $500,001 to $999,999 per year
- ❏ $1,000,000+ per year
- ❏ Not Applicable

Education Level:

- ❏ Some High School
- ❏ High School Graduate
- ❏ College Graduate
- ❏ Advanced Degree
- ❏ Not Applicable

Occupation:_____ ❏ Not Applicable

Religion: _____ ❏ Not Applicable

Geographic Region:

- ❏ Specific City/State—Specify: _____
- ❏ United States
- ❏ Canada
- ❏ Europe
- ❏ Asia
- ❏ South America
- ❏ North America
- ❏ Africa
- ❏ Australia
- ❏ Not Applicable

Physical Attributes:

- ❏ Tall
- ❏ Short
- ❏ Average Height
- ❏ Thin
- ❏ Overweight
- ❏ Average Weight
- ❏ Not Applicable

Housing: ❏ Owns Home
           ❏ Rents Home
           ❏ Rents Apartment
           ❏ Owns Condo
           ❏ Rents Condo
           ❏ Lives with Parents
           ❏ Lives with Roommate(s)
           ❏ Lives with Spouse
           ❏ Lives with Spouse and Children
           ❏ Other: _____
           ❏ Not Applicable

Primary Computer & Internet Usage:
           ❏ At Home
           ❏ At Work
           ❏ Internet Café/Wi-Fi Location
           ❏ Wireless PDA or Smartphone
           ❏ Not Online

Hobbies / Special Interests: _____ ❏ Not Applicable

Club/Association Membership:_____ ❏ Not Applicable

Spending/Shopping Habits:
           ❏ Typically Shops at Retail Stores
           ❏ Shops Often Via Mail Order
           ❏ Comfortable Shopping Online
           ❏ Readily Uses Credit Cards
           ❏ Readily Uses a Debit Card
           ❏ Writes Checks for Purchases
           ❏ Possesses a PayPal Account
           ❏ Has Below Average or No Credit

Driving Habits:
           ❏ Drives a Compact Vehicle / Hatchback
           ❏ Drives an SUV or Van
           ❏ Drives a Pickup Truck
           ❏ Drives a Sports Car

❏ Drives a Luxury Sedan
❏ Drives a Hybrid Vehicle
❏ Owns Their Vehicle
❏ Leases Their Vehicle
❏ Drives Less Than 15,000 Miles Per Year
❏ Drives More Than 15,000 Miles Per Year
❏ Commutes Daily To Work
❏ Carpools
❏ Other:_____

Media Habits:
❏ Primarily Watches TV
❏ Primarily Reads Newspapers
❏ Primarily Reads Magazines
❏ Primarily Uses the Internet
❏ Not Applicable

Other Relevant Attribute: _____ ❏ Not Applicable

Other Relevant Attribute: _____ ❏ Not Applicable

Other Relevant Attribute: _____ ❏ Not Applicable

4. Product-Related Questions

After defining your primary and secondary audience for your product, answer the following questions as they apply to what you'll be selling and to whom you'll be selling. As you answer these questions on a separate sheet of paper, be as specific as possible. Also, don't forget to put yourself in your target customer's shoes and think the way they would think (taking into account their needs, wants and concerns).

A. What about your product will appeal to your target audience? (Be sure to list specific features, functions, selling points, etc.) _____

_____

_____

B. How, when and why will your target customer use the product?

_____

_____

C. What needs does your product address? _____

_____

_____

D. How does your product satisfy your target customer's wants?

_____

_____

E. Why would someone want to buy your product? _____

_____

_____

F. What problems, challenges or obstacles can your product help the customer overcome? How will it make their lives happier, better, easier, less stressful, more entertaining, etc.? _____

_____

_____

G. What are the biggest and best benefits or features that your product offers?

_____

_____

H. Describe why your product is worth the money people will spend for it.

_____

_____

J. Why should someone use your product as opposed to a competing product?

_____

_____

K. What do you anticipate will be the biggest objections your target audience will have regarding your product? How can these objections be overcome?

_____

_____

L. What misconceptions might your target audience have about your product? What information will you need to convey to help them overcome these misconceptions quickly? _____

_____

_____

M. Why should someone purchase the product from your business?

_____

_____

Based on the information you've compiled, you should now have a relatively detailed profile of your primary customer base, as well as your potential secondary markets. Now you can proceed by learning as much as possible about the people who make up your target market and begin formulating all of the ways your product will address their wants and needs.

5. Competition

Researching and documenting competitor information is important because it tells you who your direct competition is, that is, the other businesses that sell the same or similar products to the same target audience within the same geographical area. You can use information you gather to develop strategies to turn competitors' weaknesses into your strengths.

A. List your competitors

_____

_____

_____

B. What are your competitors' strengths?

_____

_____

_____

C. What are your competitors' weaknesses?

_____

_____

_____

D. What do your competitors do well that you should also be doing?

_____

_____

_____

6. Sales Goals

Your sales goals should be given in easily measured, quantifiable financial terms and the corresponding number of units. Be realistic, and list a firm date when each sales goal should be reached. If you are planning on utilizing more than one sales venue, create a separate list of sales goals for each.

A. What are your first-month sales goals? _____

_____

_____

B. What are your six-month sales goals? _____

_____

_____

C. What are your first-year sales goals? _____

_____

_____

D. What are your three-year sales goals? _____

_____

_____

E. What are your five-year sales goals? _____

_____

_____

7. Product, Price, Place and Promotion

Developing your marketing strategy revolves around the four marketing Ps: **p**roduct, **p**rice, **p**lace (distribution), and **p**romotion. It is the combination of the four Ps that creates your unique marketing mix, which is, in effect, the entire marketing process.

Essentially, the four Ps are about finding the right portions of each, enabling you to create the perfect marketing mix, comprised of the marketing strategies that will allow you to meet and exceed your marketing and sales objectives.

PRODUCT

A. Describe your products in detail, including packaging. _____

_____

_____

B. What special features do your products have, and how do customers benefit by purchasing and using your products? _____

_____

_____

C. What advantages do your products have over competitors' products?

_____

_____

D. Describe your product warranties, return/refund policies and customer-service guarantees. _____

_____

_____

PRICE

A. How much will you charge for your products? _____

_____

B. How did you arrive at your selling price? _____

_____

_____

C. What is your pricing strategy? _____

_____

_____

D. How sensitive are your target customers to pricing issues, and why?

_____

_____

E. How much do competitors charge for their products? _____

_____

_____

F. List the purchase payment options that you will provide to your customers, e.g., credit cards, debit cards, electronic transfers, and the setup and ongoing fees associated with each. _____

_____

_____

PLACE

A. Describe the methods you will utilize to sell your products. If you'll be selling online, describe your methods in detail. For example, will you be using eBay to conduct auctions? Will you create and manage your own e-commerce website? If you'll be selling directly to customers in the real world, will you have a showroom, a mall kiosk or a booth at trade shows, or will you attend flea markets? _____

_____

_____

B. Describe the inventory management system you intend on using.

_____

_____

C. Describe how customers receive your products and describe your logistics system, including order fulfillment, warehousing and transportation needs. _____

_____

_____

PROMOTION

A. Describe what advertising media you will utilize in the promotion of your products, as well as marketing materials (such as fliers, signs, catalogs and business cards) that will be used. _____

_____

_____

B. Describe any direct sales tactics you will employ, including personal, mail, telephone and online selling. _____

_____

_____

C. Describe how you will utilize public relations in the promotion of your products. _____

_____

_____

D. Describe how you will use the internet to promote your goods, including your website, search engine optimization, keyword advertising, online display advertising and other online marketing strategies. _____

_____

_____

8. Marketing Budget

Use a from-the-ground-up approach to calculate the cost of each marketing strategy and activity you plan to use to sell, advertise and market your goods. Break down each marketing activity by individual cost, and add them together to estimate your overall marketing budget.

You also may want to consider the use of a break-even analysis. Once you know how much the marketing activity will cost, you can then calculate how many product units will have to be sold in order to cover, or break even with, the cost of the planned activity.

A. List your main marketing activities and the cost to implement each.

_____

_____

B. Describe how these marketing activities will be paid for. _____

_____

_____

9. Action Plan

An action plan is nothing more than a big do-to list that gets broken into marketing categories and timetables that outline when each promotional activity will be implemented and managed, and how results will be measured.

You may also want to purchase a large wall-mounted calendar that can be written on in erasable marker, and outline promotional activities and relevant dates. An alternative is to use computer software to help with this process.

Your action plan must include details about how and when you will measure progress and the success or failure of each individual promotional activity. By measuring results incrementally, you can make sure that each promotional activity is working and that you are on track to meet your marketing and sales objectives.

A. List each of your marketing strategies. _____

_____

_____

B. Describe how each marketing strategy will be implemented. _____

_____

_____

C. Outline the timetable for when each marketing strategy will be implemented.

_____

_____

D. Describe how you will track and measure the effectiveness of each marketing strategy. _____

_____

_____

Mastering Personal Selling

Preparation is the starting point for mastering the art of selling. What are you selling? Whom are you selling to? Who else is selling it? And what tools will help you sell and ultimately close each sale? Sales preparation can be divided into the following four main categories:

- *Product.* You have to know what you are selling inside out and upside down. Knowledge about your product can be acquired from research, specialized training, suppliers, information in books and other published formats, feedback from customers and hands-on experience. The better you know your product, the more you will be able to identify potential customers and sell them what they need and want.
- *Customers.* You must know who needs what you are selling, where these people are located, how much they buy and how often they buy. Additional customer information, such as what clubs they belong to and what newspapers they read, for example, can also prove valuable. Perhaps more importantly, sales preparation means you know the answers to the questions your prospects and customers have, in advance of their asking.

- *Competition.* Sales preparation also means you know your competition thoroughly—what people like and dislike about competing businesses, prices and guarantees; how those businesses are promoted; and how your competitors secure their customers. Basically, you need to know how your business stacks up against the competition.
- *Sales tools.* The final aspect of sales preparation is to have a toolbox packed with great sales tools, which are the instruments you will use to grab your prospects' attention, create interest and desire, and motivate them to buy. Sales tools can include product literature, product samples, signage, customer testimonials, training and purchase payment options.

Qualifying the Buyer

Qualifying the buyer is the process of asking questions and using their responses to determine if they need, want and can afford what you are selling. The importance of qualifying cannot be overstated.

The better qualified a prospect is, the greater the chance of closing a sale. You might feel uncomfortable asking qualifying questions because you think it's being pushy, nosy or aggressive. Keep in mind, however, that every person must ask questions in order to help others or to determine what the others need.

For example, doctors ask questions about their patients' symptoms so they can make informed diagnoses. A fitness trainer will ask about specific goals of a client so they can develop an exercise program that will help achieve those goals. Focus on five issues when qualifying buyers:

- Do they need it?
- Do they want it?
- Who makes the buying decision?
- Can they afford it?
- When do they want it?

DO THEY NEED IT?

Determine right away if the person you are trying to sell to needs or wants what you have to sell. If not, you are wasting your time (as well as theirs) by continuing the conversation.

If you have in-depth knowledge of what you sell and how people benefit by owning or using it, qualifying a prospect with a few simple questions should be easy. For example, you will want to know:

- What problems need solving?
- What are their requirements?
- What needs to be improved?
- What is wrong with what they currently have?
- What would make their job or life easier?

WHO MAKES THE BUYING DECISIONS?

Always make sure you are dealing with the person who makes the buying decision. Nothing is more frustrating than having a hot prospect on the line, only to discover after spending your valuable time and energy with him that he cannot make the final decision to buy, or that there are more people involved in the decision-making process.

The best way to find out right upfront is to simply ask. Consider posing these questions:

- Who will be making the purchasing decision?
- Will you be making the decision on your own or will there be other people involved in the purchasing decision?
- If you find my [insert product name] suitable, are you authorized to make the purchase?

CAN THEY AFFORD IT?

You do not want to waste time trying to sell your products to people who simply cannot afford them, especially in fast-paced selling venues such as trade shows and flea markets.

Quickly determine if the person you are talking to has the money or access to the money needed to make the purchase. For example, ask your prospects if they have the money to pay for the purchase or if they can utilize a credit card. Regardless of how you phrase the question, determine if they can afford to buy as early on in your sales efforts as possible.

WHEN DO THEY WANT IT?

Some people begin shopping for products they know they will want or need sometime in the future—sometimes weeks, months or even years in advance. While you definitely want this business, at the same time you also need to make the best use of your time at this precise moment.

Determine if you're talking with someone who wants to buy right away or if they're planning two years ahead, for example. Focus the vast majority of your energies and efforts on consumers who are ready to buy right now. To determine someone's needs, you can ask pre-qualifying questions, such as:

- How soon do you need the [insert product name]?
- When will you be ready to have the product installed?
- When would you like to take delivery?

Getting Past Objections

Most new entrepreneurs confuse rejection and objections. Rejection is a flat-out refusal to buy what you are selling. Objections, however, are nothing more than prospects telling you they need more information to help them make the right buying decision.

When prospects start stating reasons why they shouldn't buy, don't turn tail and run for the hills. Instead, welcome and overcome these objections by addressing their needs and concerns, while also answering their questions.

Some of the most common objections you should be prepared to address time and time again include:

- The price is too high.
- I don't have the money right now.
- Let me think about it.
- I need to consult with my wife or partner.
- I need to conduct more research about the product and do some comparisons.

With practice and research, plus paying careful attention to your customers' wants and needs, you will learn how to quickly and effectively overcome these objections and close more sales faster.

GETTING PAST PRICE OBJECTIONS

It should come as no surprise that most people automatically respond, "The price is too high" or "The price is too much," whether or not they have given it much thought.

For most of us, this is a natural response (and often a negotiating tactic) when asked to buy something. Your first reply should be, "The price is too much in comparison to what?" This throws the majority of people off balance, especially if they have not actually considered why the price is too high.

Another strategy for overcoming price objections is to simply agree that your price is more than competitors' prices, but explain why: better quality, longer warranty, more features, or some other competitive advantage that justifies a higher price.

Be sure to ask, "Is price the only objection you have to proceeding with the sale?" The answer will let you know if price is their only objection, or if there are other obstacles currently keeping you from closing the sale. If price is the only objection, look for suitable solutions—such as offering a cheaper model or creative financing options.

GETTING PAST THE "NO MONEY" OBJECTIONS

When prospects tell you that they cannot afford to buy, ask them why. You cannot overcome the "no money" objection unless you know all the details. Based on their response, you might be able to develop one or more workable solutions.

Clearly demonstrate to prospects that the benefits of buying are so important to their particular situation that a "no money" objection would not be wise. In other words, the cost of not buying far outweighs the cost of buying.

When you receive a "no money" objection, one of the first things that you should do is turn over every last stone to find suitable financing—credit cards, consumer loan or potential leasing, if applicable. When you can show people they *can* purchase by using financing means that they had not thought of, often the "no money" objection fades and they warm up to the idea of buying because now they can.

GETTING PAST THE "LET ME THINK ABOUT IT" OBJECTIONS

When people say they want to think about it, consider going over things again while the details are fresh in everyone's mind. Try to ascertain what's not being understood and explain things better or differently.

This tactic opens the door once more and enables you to flush out real obstacles to overcome. You can also try the Benjamin Franklin technique by listing the advantages of a buy decision in one column while listing the disadvantages of not buying in a second column.

When most people see in black and white that the advantages of buying far outweigh the disadvantages, often it is all the persuasion they need to go ahead. Also, try offering an incentive to overcome the objection: a discount, upgraded model, free delivery, or whatever you think will clinch the sale.

Negotiate Like a Pro

By its very nature, a buy-and-sell enterprise means that you will need to master the art of negotiation. This is a skill you will most likely use daily. You will negotiate with suppliers for lower prices and better terms. You will negotiate with buyers to buy more and at higher prices, and you may need to negotiate with flea market managers for lower booth rent and more space.

In short, buying and selling is a constant round of negotiation. Information is the cornerstone of mastering any negotiation. The more information and actual facts and figures you have, the stronger your position becomes for getting what you want.

Obtaining information means you have to find out as much as you can about what the person you are negotiating with wants and needs, and how these are prioritized—by benefits, budget or schedule. Obtaining this information typically requires listening. Having this information lets you know what the other person wants to achieve through negotiations, thus strengthening your position and weakening theirs.

Keep in mind that if someone really needs what you are selling, price often becomes a secondary issue. In other words, what the product will do for them, such as solve a problem or make them healthier, becomes more paramount.

So before negotiations start, position the value of your product in relation to the benefits the person will receive by taking ownership. This is a critical step in the negotiation process. If what you have to sell is properly positioned in terms of value, it gives you increased leverage and power to get what you want out of the negotiation process without having to accept less money or unfavorable conditions.

During a negotiation, never accept first offers. If you do, you will be leaving money on the table or, alternately, paying too much yourself. Few people walk away from negotiations when a first offer is declined. Always make a counteroffer. Depending on whether you are buying or selling, this means telling the other party you want to pay less or sell for more.

Finally, don't be afraid to walk away from negotiations if you are positive you have nothing to gain by continuing. When the result of the negotiations is no longer beneficial to you, walk away. Otherwise, be prepared to sacrifice profits or waste time.

Closing Every Sale

In reality, no salesperson—no matter how skilled he or she is—will be able to close every single sale. However, all buy-and-sell entrepreneurs have to get in the habit of asking for the sale every time they talk to a potential customer.

If you don't ask for the sale, all you will have accomplished is to educate the buyer, making them an easy closing target for the next vendor they talk to. Few people will take it upon themselves to offer you the sale, unless they are asked to do so.

Closing is an essential selling skill, but bear in mind that no matter how much closing intimidates you, in reality, it is nothing more than the natural progression in the sales cycle. You prospect, qualify, present and close. Therefore, asking for the sale should be nothing more than a formality.

The "assumption close" is a good closing technique because it requires doing nothing more than assuming every person you talk to about your products will buy. Do this by making a statement like, "I will have this shipped to you by the end of the week," "I just need your signature on this agreement so we can start processing your order," or "How would you like to pay for this?"

The "alternate choice" close is also an easy one to master. As the name suggests, this closing technique means giving your prospect more than one product option by asking a question such as, "So, which choice would you prefer, the green [insert product name], or the red one?"

The alternate choice close pulls your prospect into making a buying decision and selecting one of the options. Not buying is no longer an available option, based on the alternate choice closing question. The alternate choice questions can also be used effectively to increase the quantity of a particular product you want your customer to buy.

For instance, "Would you like to buy one [insert product name], or two?" Once again, this pulls your customer into a buying decision. The question is no longer will you buy, but rather how many you are going to buy.

Once you have closed the sale, always ask for a referral. Almost all small businesses survive on referral business and positive word-of-mouth advertising.

Advertising That Works

You do not need to spend a bundle to advertise and promote your products. Just make sure the money you do spend is on advertising and promotions aimed directly at your target audience.

So how much do you spend on advertising? The answer will depend on the type of products you sell, how they are sold and how much you can afford to spend. If you do spend considerable money on advertising, you will need to create a system for tracking your advertising activities so you can determine effectiveness.

Results information is important to know, because it allows you to allocate your advertising dollars where they have the greatest impact in terms of reaching your target audience and generating the most revenue.

This section covers advertising basics, such as creating high-impact ads that sell, finding cheap and free classified advertising opportunities and publicity sources, and using two of the buy-and-sell entrepreneur's most powerful promotional tools—fliers and signs.

Creating Ads That Sell

Creating clever and convincing copy that sells is needed for advertising, fliers, presentations, signs, catalogs, newsletters and website content. At the core of creating great copy is the time-tested and proven "AIDA" advertising formula: Attention, Interest, Desire and Action. Your ad copy must grab the attention of your target audience, create interest in what you have to say, build desire for what you have to sell, and compel people to take action and buy.

Creating effective advertising is a skill and an art form that many advertising professionals (and professional writers) spend years fine-tuning. If you don't have existing experience creating advertisements, consider hiring a freelance professional who does. This will ensure that your advertising message makes the most impact possible.

The starting point of any good ad is a powerful headline. You only have a brief moment to grab the readers' attention and pull them into your message. For instance, "Nobody beats our low prices, guaranteed!" is certainly a powerful headline that will grab the readers' attention and pull them into your story.

Also, when it comes to advertising effectiveness, the old adage that a photograph is worth a thousand words holds true. Professional-quality photographs have the unique ability to showcase the best qualities of your product without you saying a word. Whenever possible, be sure to include high-quality detailed photographs of the products you sell in your advertisements and marketing materials.

Clever advertising copy appeals to people on an emotional level. It uses emotional triggers of basic human feelings, such as the need for friendship, the need for security or the desire to achieve. Your ad copy should single out and talk directly to your target audience in the same way that they would think and speak.

The final—and arguably most important—aspect of creating great copy is to always ask for the sale. You can have the best attention-grabbing headline, visually stunning photographs, a high-impact sales pitch plus an unbeatable offer, but all of this will result in nothing unless you ask your audience to buy. Provide compelling reasons to do so, and offer the tools or resources your target audience needs to take action. Never assume that your ad's audience will know what to do next. Tell them what you want them to do, and give them the tools and motivation they need to take action. Create urgency and demand.

Cheap and Free Classified Advertising Sources

In the real world (as opposed to online), classified advertising is unquestionably the buy-and-sell entrepreneur's best friend because it is easy to create, cheap to run, and almost always has a higher response rate than display advertisements.

People generally read the classifieds looking for a specific product to buy, not for the entertainment value they seek in other sections of the newspaper. This enables you to sell your goods aggressively, because readers expect these types of ads.

When creating a classified ad, write short powerful copy that sells. At the same time, create urgency by stating a deadline or limited availability. Most importantly, include the main benefit(s) that a person receives for buying your products.

Start with an attention-grabbing headline that jumps off the page. If necessary, pay a few extra dollars to have the headline displayed in bold type, flagged with an icon, or surrounded by a border. (This strategy also works for online ads and eBay auction listings.)

Also, give thought to the type of publication and the heading or section under which your advertisement will appear. Pick publications that are read by your target audience, and choose a section they are most likely to read. Because classified advertisements are cheap and quick to post, continually look for ways to improve your results by testing new ads in various publications read by your target audience.

Test your headline, your main sales message and your special offers on a regular basis. Classified advertising costs vary by publication, number of words, number of insertions and other factors (such as the use of icons and photographs). There are many print and online classified advertising sources, some of which offer totally free classified ads, while others you have to pay for. For example, Craigslist is a free online service for placing classified-like ads and a great forum for buying or selling almost anything on a local or regional level.

In addition to utilizing your own local newspaper's classified ad section, check out the following list for some of the more popular classified advertising services.

RESOURCES
- BuySell.com, ♂ **buysell.com**
- Craigslist, ♂ **craigslist.org**
- My Town Ads, ♂ **mytownads.com**
- Penny Saver USA, ♂ **pennysaverusa.com**
- The Recycler, ♂ **recycler.com**
- Thrifty Nickel, ♂ **thriftynickelads.com**

Getting Free Publicity Through Public Relations Efforts

Public relations efforts involve working with the same media outlets you'd potentially advertise with, but in a very different way. Using public relations strategies, your goal is to work with reporters, writers, editors and journalists to try to convince them to include information about you, your company and your products within their editorial content.

This might mean getting interviewed as an expert in your field as part of a relevant news story, having your product featured in a review, or having your products somehow included in news, features or human interest stories which comprise the editorial content of newspapers, magazines, radio shows and television talk shows and news programs.

When you use public relations, you provide reporters, writers, editors and journalists with the information they need to incorporate into their articles or stories. However, you have absolutely no control over what's written or said about your products or your company. You run the risk that details about your product will be misrepresented or that important details will be left out.

The benefit to public relations, however, is that when you, your company and/or your products are featured within the editorial content of various media outlets, this doesn't cost you a penny. Plus, when readers, listeners or viewers hear about your product from an unbiased reporter or journalist they trust, they're more apt to buy the product or at least visit your website to learn more about it, as compared to the percentage of people who would respond to a paid ad that the consumer knows is biased.

The trick to generating positive and free publicity for yourself, your company and your products is to develop relationships with reporters, writers, editors and journalists who currently reach your target audience. This relationship can be established initially by sending a detailed press kit or press releases about your company and its products, and—if applicable—also sending a sample of the product for the reporters, writers, editors and journalists to test or review firsthand.

Every day, reporters are literally bombarded with dozens—sometimes hundreds—of press releases and press kits. Thus, the information you provide must adhere to a specific format, be comprehensive, be of interest to the journalist and be timely. You must also take into account the lead time that the reporter is working under, and be conscious of their often tight deadlines.

The easier you make it for reporters to include information about you, your company and your products within their work, the better your chances are of receiving the free media coverage you're seeking.

As with advertising, planning and executing an effective public relations campaign takes skill, creativity, experience and the ability to capture reporters' attention in a positive way. If done correctly, being featured in a single newspaper or magazine article, or on a radio or television program, can easily generate a better response than spending tens of thousands of dollars in paid advertising. Plus, once the publicity starts to appear in the media, you'll begin seeing immediate results in the form of additional sales or product inquiries.

The best way to begin trying to generate free publicity is to write a well-written press release about your company and/or products. This press release must adhere to a standard press release format, contain some type of newsworthy message, be well-written, and contain all of the information reporters need to know. Answer the questions: who, what, where, when, why and how? A typical press release is double-spaced and fits on one or two pages.

A press kit is a folder that contains several specific press releases, details about your product, a one- or two-page company background, short biographies of company executives, product photos and copies of press clippings already generated about the company.

If you've never written a press release or press kit, consider hiring a freelance public relations specialist or a PR firm to assist you with this process. It is essential to determine exactly what information a member of the media will want or need, and to present that information to them properly.

To learn how to write and format a press release, visit one of these websites:

- **publicityinsider.com/release.asp**
- **press-release-writing.com/10_essential_tips.htm**
- **internetbasedmoms.com/press-releases**
- **wikihow.com/Write-a-Press-Release**

Figure 3.1 is an actual sample of a press release created for a buy-and-sell entrepreneur who is handcrafting his own fashion accessories and selling them online as well as through other retail ventures. This sample release will provide you with a general idea about formatting and what can be included within this type of document.

Kiel James Patrick Custom Wristbands

Something Old Has Launched An Exciting New, Trendy and Premium Brand

www.kieljamespatrick.com
For Immediate Release
Contact: [Insert Name]
[Insert Phone Number]
[Insert E-mail Address]

Cranston, Rhode Island – Kiel James Patrick, a 25-year-old entrepreneur and veteran fashion model, has launched a premium fashion accessory brand that specializes in creating custom-designed, irregularly stitched wristbands made from fabrics recycled from vintage neckties.

Available exclusively from the company's own website (www.kieljamespatrick.com), as well as select upscale boutiques in Los Angeles, Rhode Island and Boston, the Kiel James Patrick® Wristbands represent the newest all-American collegiate accessory that has fashion-focused males and females alike clamoring to wrap their wrists in one or more of these truly unique accessory items.

"Since launching the KJP website in February 2008, we've literally been bombarded with orders from high school and college students, young professionals, and even a handful of Hollywood celebrities, including well-known actors, recording artists and models. This has quickly become *the* fashion accessory item people want to be seen wearing in all of the hottest nightclubs, in the classroom, and in the workplace. The wristbands are stylish and custom-designed to reflect the wearer's unique personality," said Patrick.

From the company's website, customers select their favorite vintage material (which comes from recycled neckties acquired from secondhand shops and other sources), and then choose an intricately designed button which serves as the wristband's fastener. There are dozens of fashionable fabrics to choose from, with new styles slated to be released each season. After the customer selects a size and places the order, each wristband is handmade in Cranston, Rhode Island, and shipped to the customer within 48 hours.

FIGURE 3.1: *Sample Press Release*

"We also have in-store displays at a growing number of select, upscale fashion boutiques that display about 45 of our most popular styles and colors, allowing customers to purchase and wear their favorite KJP wristband immediately," added Patrick, who is proud that his creations are able to showcase the timeless style of all American youth.

Prices for the one-of-a-kind KJP wristbands range from $30.00 to $90.00 each, depending on the vintage fabric style and the unique, oversized, customized button (bearing the company's logo) that's selected. The interior of each band is lined with Kiel James Patrick's signature plaid fabric.

"Vintage men's neckties come in all sorts of fabrics, colors and styles. By reworking these old ties and combining them with classic, custom-designed, oversize buttons—currently available in silver, bronze and a handful of other finishes—we've created extremely stylish, modern and comfortable fashion accessories that can be worn alone or in groups of two or three on a single wrist," explained Patrick.

Within weeks of the website's launch, Patrick has been contacted by several Hollywood stylists looking to accessorize their celebrity clients and even incorporate the wristbands into on-screen wardrobe to be seen on popular TV shows. "It's truly become a fashion phenomenon," he added.

Additional information about the KJP wristbands can be obtained at the company's website (www.kieljamespatrick.com), or by calling (###) ###-####. Kiel James Patrick is currently available for interviews and photo shoots. High-resolution product photographs, along with product samples, are available to the media upon request.

# # #

FIGURE 3.1: Sample Press Release, continued

ADD PR MATERIALS TO YOUR WEBSITE

In addition to creating printed copies of your press materials that can be mailed to targeted media, you'll also want to create a "Press," "Press Room" or "Media" area on your website that contains these materials and makes them available for downloading.

POSITION YOURSELF AS AN EXPERT

When you position yourself as an expert in your field, you could be invited to be interviewed by the news media as part of a timely news story that relates to your area of expertise. Or you could be invited to be a guest on a radio or TV talk show. As a guest being interviewed, you can plug your products and direct people to your website while building credibility with the audience at the same time.

COMPILE YOUR PRESS LIST

After your press materials are created, the next step is to compile a list of specific reporters, based on their "beats," or the topics they typically cover. This is your customized media list. If your business involves selling handcrafted sweaters for infants, it's important to target only journalists that cover parenting topics or crafts, for example. In other words, don't approach sports reporters or entertainment reporters.

There are several ways to track down the right people to send your press materials to at various media outlets, but first you need to create a list of media outlets you want to target in hopes of generating publicity. Next, contact each media outlet and obtain the name, title, address, phone number and e-mail address for the appropriate reporter, writer, editor or journalist at that media outlet. An alternative is to purchase a comprehensive media directory that lists this information.

Bacon's Media Directories ([866] 639-5087, **http://us.cision.com/products_services/bacons_media_directories_2008.asp**) provide a comprehensive listing of all newspapers, magazines, radio stations and television stations, along with contacts at each media outlet. The printed directories are updated annually; however, a complete media database is also available online for a fee.

Several other companies offer similar directories and databases. The reference section of a public library may be a good resource for this information. These directories include:

- *The Gebbie Press All-In-One Media Directory*, (845) 255-7560, **gebbie.com**
- *Media Contacts Pro*, (845) 351-1383, **mediacontactspro.com/products.php**
- *Burrelles/Luce*, (800) 368-8070, **burrellsluce.com/MediaContacts**

To save money compiling your media list, consider visiting a large newsstand, looking through all of the newspapers and magazines, and then checking the masthead of each appropriate publication for the proper contact details. You can also review the ending credits of television talk shows and news programs, plus contact news and talk radio stations.

Mastering the art of working with the media to generate free publicity for yourself, your company and your products can be an extremely cost-effective way to promote your business and build its positive reputation on a local, regional, national or even international level, but on a shoestring budget.

Public relations can be an extremely powerful tool if used correctly, and should definitely be a prominent part of your overall marketing/advertising campaign. You'll find that once you start generating positive publicity, other media outlets will eventually start coming to you in order to feature you, your company or your products within their editorial coverage.

To save time and potentially money, once your press release is written you can pay a press release distribution service, such as PR Newswire (**prnewswire.com**), to distribute it electronically, via fax or by U.S. Mail to the media outlets or media contacts you desire. Within hours, thousands of reporters, writers, editors and journalists could have information about you, your company and your products waiting in their inboxes.

Speeches

Another great way to secure publicity is by giving speeches at seminars, trade shows, special events and organized workshops. There are numerous associations, organizations and clubs of every type in every community, and these organizations often have experts speak to members on topics related to the purpose of the club.

Talk Radio

Talk radio is a potential publicity windfall for buy-and-sell entrepreneurs. Get started by developing a story idea. For instance, if you sell antiques, develop a story idea around teaching listeners what to look for when buying antiques.

If you sell personal security devices, for example, develop a story that educates listeners about how to buy and use personal security devices. Once your idea is fully developed, contact radio show producers around the country to pitch your ideas.

Radio Locator, **radio-locator.com**, has links to more than 10,000 radio stations, including talk radio format stations. In addition to talk radio, consider pitching yourself as an expert in your field to news radio stations. These stations might want to interview you in conjunction with a timely news story they're covering.

Talkers magazine ([413] 739-8255, **talkers.com**) is a printed publication that radio show producers, guest bookers and hosts read on a regular basis. Advertising your availability for interviews in this publication is a great way to generate radio publicity for yourself and your products.

Community Publicity

Getting out and meeting people in your own community is another way to inform the public about the products you sell, especially if you are selling from home. It's proven that people like to buy from people they know and like, as well as refer other people to these businesses.

So it makes sense to become active in your community. Clubs and churches—as well as charity, business, and social functions—are all great places to meet new people, hand out business cards and talk about the products you sell. Consider becoming active with your city's chamber of commerce as well. This will help you create valuable connections, plus give your business local credibility.

Phenomenal Promotional Fliers

Many buy-and-sell entrepreneurs find that printed fliers represent one of the best advertising vehicles and values available to promote their products. Fliers are a fast and frugal, yet highly effective, way to promote a wide range of products and services, especially if you take the time to learn basic design skills so you can create high-impact promotional fliers in-house on your own computer.

Having the equipment and skills to produce your own promotional materials in-house gives you the ability to experiment, at little cost, with various print marketing tools, messages and special promotions until you find the right mix. Once your fliers have been created and printed, they can be copied in bulk or professionally printed—which is a much better option to create top-notch results.

The great benefit of printed promotional fliers is that they can be used everywhere and for everything. Hand them out at flea markets, garage sales, auction sales, seminars, trade shows and networking meetings. You can canvas busy parking lots tucking fliers under windshield wipers and leave them in public-transit areas, such as buses, subway cars and train stations, for riders to read and take home.

You can stock a supply of promotional fliers and thumbtacks in your car so you can make a weekly run posting the fliers on every community notice board in your area, in places like supermarkets, libraries, schools, community centers, laundries, churches and gas stations.

Full-color fliers and brochures (as well as matching business cards) can be created on your computer using graphics software. Once created, you can e-mail the file to a printer to have it professionally printed very inexpensively.

VistaPrint (**vistaprint.com**), Overnight Prints (**overnightprints.com**), and Brochure Printing Online (**brochuresprintingonline.com**) are just a few companies that will print full-color brochures in various quantities, for very low fees. If you don't have the graphic arts or creative skills to design your own brochures, consider hiring a freelance graphic artist to help you. Use a service, like **eLance.com**, to help you find an inexpensive freelancer.

Sizzling Signage

Signs are one of the lowest-cost yet highest-impact forms of advertising, especially for buy-and-sell entrepreneurs operating from a home-based location or a flea market, for example. Signs work to promote your products 24 hours a day, 365 days a year, virtually for free once paid for.

Signs are not something you should cut corners on. They must be professionally designed and constructed. Most signs today are designed on a computer and printed on large sheets of vinyl. These signs are easily installed, long-lasting, and very inexpensive to produce.

You always want to make a positive first impression, so keep all of your signage in tip-top condition. Faded signs, peeling paint, torn banners or signs that require maintenance send out negative messages about your business and the products you sell.

Consider using attention-grabbing design elements, colors, graphics and pictures of the products you sell to lend visual appeal to your signs. Installing signs at home is a tricky business because of local bylaws, which stipulate the size of signs, as well as placement and style. Often commercial signage is not permitted in residential neighborhoods.

There is no one set of regulations for home business signage. Each municipality has its own regulations and restrictions. Generally, a call to the planning department or bylaws office is all that is required to get the answers you need. If you are not going to have customers visiting your home to view and buy products, a sign probably isn't needed in front of your home.

Many buy-and-sell entrepreneurs need to obtain professional event signage and banners to use at flea markets, consumer shows, trade shows and other events. Once again, these signs should be professionally designed and made, should grab people's attention, and should perfectly describe the products you sell.

To have signs created, find a local print shop or sign company in your area. The local phone numbers for sign companies can be found in your local telephone directory.

The Importance of Customer Service

No matter what you're selling or to whom you're selling, every single potential customer or actual customer you interact with online, over the telephone, through the mail or in person must always feel as if they're your most important customer. Their satisfaction and happiness is ultimately the key to your success, and every aspect of how you do business should somehow take into account what will make your customers happy.

Satisfied customers often become repeat customers. From an expense standpoint as a business operator, it's always less costly to generate repeat business from an existing customer than it is to find a new customer and make a sale. In addition, satisfied customers provide positive feedback and testimonials you can utilize, plus they're more apt to provide positive word-of-mouth advertising on your behalf (another very inexpensive way to generate new business).

On the flipside, a dissatisfied customer will require more of your valuable time to "fix" or "remedy" the situation, plus he/she could easily generate negative word-of-mouth publicity for your company. This could quickly become detrimental and result in lost business. People who are dissatisfied with an experience they have dealing with a merchant are apt to complain to their credit card company, their friends, coworkers and anyone else who will listen.

You already know that your products should address your customers' needs and wants, potentially help them save time or money, and somehow make their life more enjoyable, more pleasurable, less stressful or easier. These same requirements should hold true for every interaction you have with each of your customers: from their experience exploring your website, to placing their order, to dealing with their questions, concerns, or any problems they may encounter with the products you're selling.

In addition to conveying a professional and friendly attitude, some of the things you can automatically do to improve each customer's experience dealing with your company include:

- Sending a "Thank you for your order" e-mail or letter as soon as a new order is received
- Sending a follow-up e-mail when an order ships, including tracking information and anticipated date of arrival
- Offering a special discount or money-saving offer for repeat customers
- Offering an incentive for current customers to provide you with referrals
- Encouraging customers to interact with you online, via e-mail or by telephone
- Shipping all orders promptly

- Responding to all inquiries, problems, return requests, etc., within 24 hours of receiving them—sooner if possible

Offering the best customer service experience possible to your customers does not have to cost a fortune. It's all about maintaining the right attitude and conveying that attitude in every aspect of your business. In fact, if done correctly, offering top-notch customer service should cost next to nothing. The long-term benefits to your business, however, are incalculable.

Taking Your Buy-and-Sell Enterprise Online

Although there is a lot you need to know to start an online buy-and-sell business, the following information covers the basics: building a website using an e-commerce turnkey solution, choosing a domain name, registering with search engines, keyword optimization, permission-based marketing and online advertising. Additional information about online sales venues, such as eBay and electronic storefronts, can be found in Chapter 5.

To learn more about how to launch a successful e-commerce website, pick up a copy of *Click Starts: Design and Launch Your E-Commerce Website in One Week* (Entrepreneur Press) and *The Unofficial Guide to Starting a Business Online, 2nd Edition* (Wiley Publishing) from any bookstore. These two books provide a lot of valuable information and insight for someone interested in launching an online business.

Creating Your Own Website

Online sales are expected to hit $144 billion per year by 2010. Using an e-commerce turnkey solution, getting in on this potential moneymaking opportunity has never been easier. Plus, as you're about to discover, your initial investment can be as low as a few hundred dollars.

Instead of having to hire a team of programmers to design and launch a website from scratch (which would take weeks or months to create and cost you thousands, if not tens of thousands of dollars in development costs), an e-commerce turnkey solution provides you with a selection of pre-designed, professional-looking website templates that you can fully customize.

Each template includes all of the components needed to create a highly functional e-commerce website capable of handling secure transactions. In addition, website hosting services and the ability to accept major credit cards and other online payment options are available for an additional fee, so you may not need to acquire a separate merchant account.

While the pre-created website templates available to you may not offer all of the flashy bells and whistles you'd ultimately like to incorporate into your site, they do offer the core functionality necessary to launch your e-commerce business and test its viability. Once your business is successful, you should definitely plan on expanding and fine-tuning your website on an ongoing basis.

Many of the companies that offer these turnkey solutions have created an entire suite of easy-to-use online tools to assist you in designing, creating, launching and then managing your online business.

Some of the biggest benefits of using a turnkey solution to design, launch and manage your e-commerce website include:

- *Low startup cost.* One company provides the development tools for the website itself, plus secure website hosting services. For an additional fee, the same company will facilitate the ability to accept multiple forms of online payments, including major credit cards, electronic checks, Google Checkout or PayPal's Express Checkout.
- *Absolutely no programming is required.*
- *You can typically design and launch a basic site in less than 24 hours.*
- *The ability to choose* from dozens or even hundreds of pre-created, professional-looking website templates, and then customize your favorite to give your site a unique look.

Using the same suite of online-based tools, you can design, publish, maintain and promote your site, plus track traffic to the site and synchronize sales data to financial software applications to better handle your record keeping and accounting. Many of the turnkey solutions also offer modules for maintaining a customer database, managing inventory, and keeping detailed order shipment records (including the ability to print shipping labels and track packages shipped via the USPS, FedEx, UPS or DHL).

Before you start creating your website—whether it's from scratch or by customizing a template—spend time on the internet looking for top-quality, well-designed e-commerce websites that you'd like yours to emulate. Determine in advance what features and functionality you might want, as well as what design elements you'd like to incorporate into your site. Knowing your immediate needs, plus what your needs might be in the future, will help you better choose a turnkey solution that's best suited for your business venture.

Every online business will have different needs based on what's being sold, to whom the products are being sold, and what features and functionality the online merchant wishes to incorporate into their e-commerce site. Once you pinpoint what you want and need, finding a complete turnkey solution that meets your requirements, at a price you can afford, will be a relatively straightforward process.

As you look at what each e-commerce turnkey solution offers, don't just look at a list of features and make your decision, visit several actual e-commerce websites that currently utilize the services of the company you're thinking about working with, and invest time exploring those websites. Considering that your own site will be customized, do the sites you're looking at offer the professional look, functionality and user interface that could work well for your business? Will you be able to easily customize the templates to create a site you're proud of and that meets your needs?

Ultimately, choosing the best turnkey solution to meet the needs of your unique online business could mean the difference between success and failure. In addition to comparing startup costs and ongoing monthly fees associated with each of these services, some of the things you'll also want to evaluate before choosing a turnkey solution include:

- The tools and resources offered by the service provider
- The professional quality and selection of the site templates being offered
- The ease of use of the website design tools and other resources offered to help operate your business
- The technical support services provided by the solution provider
- What e-commerce-related functions can be easily incorporated into your website using the development tools provided
- The ability to accept and process online payments from customers
- The online security measures your site will be able to incorporate
- Resources offered to help you market and promote your online business
- Whether or not your site's order and customer data can easily be integrated with your accounting, spreadsheet and order management software
- The ease of use, functionality and professional appearance of the shopping cart module that will be incorporated into your site using the turnkey solution you select
- What extra fees or hidden charges you'll be responsible for in order to get your website designed, launched and operational
- The expandability of your site in the future, using compatible third-party tools and resources

In addition to the e-commerce turnkey solutions offered by Yahoo! (Yahoo! Stores), eBay (eBay Stores and eBay ProStores) and GoDaddy (Quick Shopping Cart), you can find many additional options using any internet search engine and entering the search phrase "e-commerce website," "e-commerce website creation," or "online business creation."

You can also find ads for these services in popular computer magazines and publications, such as *Entrepreneur* magazine, that target small business operators and entrepreneurs.

Selecting a Domain Name

After selecting the name of your business, you'll need to register your website's URL (website address). This process takes just a few minutes and will cost under $10 per URL if you use an internet registrar such as GoDaddy.com (**godaddy.com**).

The first step in this process is to brainstorm the perfect website address for your company. Ideally, the address you select should be easy to remember, easy to spell, and obvious to potential web surfers. For example, if the name of your company is "ABC International," you might want your website address to be "ABCInternational.com."

Obviously, with so many websites already in existence, many website domain names (URLs) are already taken. However, with more than 31.7 trillion domain names ending with the ".com" extension possible, there are still plenty of appealing domain names available.

A typical URL has three main components. The first part typically begins with "www." or "http://www." The second part of an URL is what you actually must select. The third part of an URL is its extension, which is typically ".com"; however, a variety of other extensions are available, such as .edu, .org, .net., gov, .info, .TV, .biz, .name and .us. Some of these extensions have specific uses. For example, a website that ends with the extension ".gov" is a government-operated website.

Most web users are accustomed to URLs ending with the popular ".com" extension, so ideally, you want your URL to use it. Otherwise, potential customers might get confused trying to find your website if it utilizes a less popular extension.

Of course, the same website can have many different URLs that lead to the same place. So, you could potentially register "www.abcinternational.com," "www.abcinternational.biz" and "www.abcinternational.info," to ensure that web users will be able to find you.

As you brainstorm the perfect URL, the part of the website address that you create can only use letters, numbers and the hyphen symbol. No other special characters or punctuation marks (such as "!", "#", "$" or ",") can be used. Also, no spaces can be used within a URL. You *can* use an underscore ("_") to represent a space, but this can be confusing, so it's not advisable.

The customizable part of a domain name and the extension (".com", for example) can be up to 63 characters long. As a general rule, the shorter the domain name, the easier it is to remember and type into a web browser accurately. Virtually all of the one-, two-, three- and four-character-long domain names have long since been taken, however. Most importantly, the customizable part of the domain name you select must be totally unique and not have already been registered by another person or company. It also may not violate someone else's copyrighted name, company name or product name.

Domain names are not case sensitive, so you can mix and match uppercase and lowercase letters to make a domain name easier to read and promote. For example, you could promote your domain name as "www.abccompany.com" or "www.ABCCompany.com" or "www.AbcCompany.com."

As you're in the process of brainstorming the perfect domain name for your business, come up with at least five to 10 options you like. When you're ready to register your domain name, you'll first need to determine if the domain name you've selected has already been registered by someone else. This process takes under one minute.

To check if a domain name is registered to someone else, simply go to the website of any domain name registrar, such as **GoDaddy.com**, **Register.com**, **NetworkSolutions.com** or **MyDomain.com**, and enter your desired domain name in the field marked "Start a domain search" or "Find a domain name." If the domain name you've entered is available, for an annual fee you will have the opportunity to register it on the spot.

After you've determined that the domain name you want is available, you'll need to register it with an internet domain name registrar. There is an annual fee to register a domain name. Depending on the registrar, registering a single domain name will cost between $5.95 and $39.95 per year. Obviously, choose a company with the lowest rates.

GoDaddy.com (**godaddy.com**) tends to offer very competitive rates for domain name registrations, plus this company makes the process extremely fast and easy. Registering your domain name will require you to provide details about yourself and your company, including your name, address, phone number and credit card information (for paying the annual fee). The process will vary based on which domain registrar you use, but it should take no more than five to 10 minutes to complete. After you've set up an account, registering additional domain names can be done much faster.

Part of the domain name registration process will most likely involve the need to provide the registrar with your ISP's IP address. You may also need to provide what are called DNS numbers to the registrar. This is information that will be provided by your ISP, if applicable. The ISP is the company that will be hosting your website. In this case, it'll probably be the company you select to provide you with an e-commerce turnkey solution.

Ideally, you want your website to have a single domain name that you can promote and that will be easy to remember. However, since some people have trouble spelling or get easily confused, you might want to register multiple domain names with slightly different spellings. This way, if someone accidentally types the wrong domain name into their web browser, they'll still wind up at your website. Think about some of the common typos or ways someone might misspell your domain name, and register those domain names as well.

Registering with Search Engines

When more than 80 percent of all web users want to find something online—whether it's a tidbit of information, a particular website or some type of specialized content—the place they typically begin (unless they already know the URL) is with a search engine. There are hundreds of search engines and web directories available. The most popular are Google, Yahoo!, MSN.com, Ask.com, AOLSearch.com and AltaVista.com.

Your goal as an online business operator is first to get your website's URL listed with each of the major search engines, and then work toward optimizing your listing so it receives the best ranking and placement possible. After all, if you're in the balloon delivery business and someone enters the search phrase, "Balloon Delivery, New York City" into Google, several dozen or perhaps hundreds of relevant listings will probably show up. A typical customer will visit the first listing, and maybe the second or third, for price comparison purposes. But all subsequent listings will be ignored. This is why earning a top placement or ranking with each search engine is essential for driving traffic to your site.

The first step is to register your website with each of the major search engines. This can be done, one at a time, by manually visiting each search engine and completing a new website recommendation form. This process is time consuming and often confusing. An alternative is to pay a third-party submission service, such as GoDaddy.com's Traffic Blazer, to register your site with hundreds of the popular search engines simultaneously.

When it comes to hiring a company to help with your business's search engine optimization, there are hundreds of choices. You'll want to compare prices as well as services offered. For example, will the submission service simply get your website listed with the search engines, or will it take added steps to earn you excellent placement or a top ranking? Will the service evaluate your site to make sure its HTML programming will generate the best results with search engines? Also, you'll need to determine if the service will keep your listing up-to-date on an ongoing basis, and whether or not this will cost extra.

The search engines and web directories are like telephone books where people can look up listings based on keywords or phrases. There are literally thousands of search engines and web directories on the internet, but the majority of web surfers mainly utilize the most popular search engines, so it's essential that your site is represented on these same sites.

The cheapest way to get your site listed with the search engines is to visit each search engine yourself and to complete the new listing submission form. This process is free and it involves completing a brief questionnaire that will help the search engine find and then catalog and categorize your proposed listing. It's important to understand that the listing submission process is different for each search engine and web directory, and then once you've completed the process, it will be necessary to update your listing periodically in order to maintain or improve your ranking or position.

When listing your site with some of the search engines and web directories, the process will be as simple as entering the URL address of your site as well as its title. The listing and submission process for other search engines, however, is much more in-depth and must be done correctly. In some cases, your site will need to get approved by a human before it gets listed.

The following links can be used to submit a listing for your new website on some of the most popular search engines and web directories:

- Google, **google.com/addurl**
- Yahoo!, **https://siteexplorer.search.yahoo.com/submit**
- MSN Live Search, **http://search.msn.com/docs/submit.aspx**
- Ask, **countrystarsonline.com/jimweaver/submit/askjeeves.htm**
- AltaVista, **altavista.com/addurl/default**

A comprehensive introduction to search engine marketing and search engine submissions can be found at the Search Engine Watch website (**http://search enginewatch.com/showPage.html?page=webmasters**).

Although more expensive, a quicker way to get your site listed with the popular search engines is to pay a third-party submission service to handle the process on your behalf. If you opt to use one of these services, be sure you understand exactly what you're paying for and what results you can realistically expect.

For example, if you pay a service $39.95 to list your site on hundreds of the major search engines, chances are this will include a listing, but not guarantee prominent placement.

To earn a high ranking or prominent placement on a search engine takes human intervention when submitting a listing with the search engines and when actually programming your website in order to provide exactly the information the search engines look for in the site's HTML programming and meta tags, for example. An inexpensive automated submission process does not typically guarantee that top-ranked listings will result.

To find a third-party company that specializes in submitting URL listings to search engines, as well as search engine optimization, enter the search phrase "search engine submissions" or "search engine optimization" into any search engine. You'll discover hundreds and potentially thousands of paid services you can use, including:

- **buildtraffic.com/indexnew.shtml**
- **engineseeker.com**
- **godaddy.com/gdshop/traffic_blazer/landing.asp**
- **iclimber.com**
- **networksolutions.com/online-marketing/index.jsp**
- **seop.com**
- **submitasite.com**
- **toprankresults.com**
- **trafficxs.com/platinum.htm**
- **worldsubmit.com**
- **wpromote.com/quicklist/landing**

Keyword Optimizing

Because 90 percent of internet users conduct searches using keywords and keyword phrases, you need to optimize your website for keyword searches. Most online marketing specialists suggest that you aim for a keyword density of about 5 percent, meaning that keywords will comprise five out of every 100 words of site content.

Also, include keywords in your page titles, headers, meta tags and hyperlinks. And because each web page is unique in terms of the information featured and its marketing objective, be sure to select different keywords for each.

Be descriptive when selecting keywords and phrases, keeping in mind that few people type in single search words, so combining keywords into short descriptive phrases is wise.

A good starting point is to make lists of words describing the products you sell and conduct search engine and directory searches using these words. The top ten results will help you pinpoint the best and most descriptive keywords to use when optimizing your site.

There are also keyword generators and even keyword creation services that will optimize your keyword selection for a fee. Finally, always include the maximum number of keywords the search engines allow, but keep in mind that directories base ranking more on the quality of the content than just on keywords. So also concentrate on quality content to improve search results.

Permission-Based Marketing

Permission-based (opt-in) marketing is a term used to describe asking for and securing permission from your website customers and visitors to send them information via e-mail. Providing they agree, information you send can range from simple e-special offers to elaborate e-newsletters and e-catalogs, depending on your marketing objectives.

Regardless of the information you send, gaining permission brings three benefits. First, if people ask to be included in your electronic mailings, in all likelihood they have an interest in the products you sell. Second, by securing permission you won't be spamming—that is, sending e-mail messages without the recipient's permission. Third, you will be building a very valuable in-house mailing list, which can be used for any number of research and marketing purposes. On that note, you will need to purchase customer database software so you can compile, store and manage your subscriber base.

Online Advertising

Online display advertising allows you to purchase ad space on other websites that potentially appeal to your target audience. Your ads can utilize text, graphics, animation, sound and even video to convey your marketing message. Unlike traditional print ads, however, someone who sees your online display ad can simply click on the ad and be transferred to your website in seconds in order to gather more information or make a purchase.

Running online display ads on popular websites costs significantly more than utilizing short, text-based search engine marketing ads. What your ad says and the visual elements used to convey the message (the overall look of the ad) are equally important. Thus, in addition to spending more to display your ads, you'll probably want to hire a professional advertising agency or graphic artist to design the ads to ensure that they look professional and are visually appealing.

Depending on where you want your online display ads to appear, the size requirements, ad content specifications, and how much you pay will vary dramatically. In addition to choosing appropriate websites to advertise on, you'll need to select the exact placement of your ad on each website's page. Online real estate has value, based on the potential number of people who will be seeing your ad, and the physical size of your display ad (which is measured in pixels).

In general, the more people who will potentially be seeing your ad, the higher the ad rates will be. Depending on the website, however, you may have to pay based on overall impressions (the number of people who simply see your ad), or you may be responsible for paying a predetermined fee only when people click on your ad. Another alternative is to pay a commission when a website offers a referral that results in a sale. The payment terms will typically be created by the website on which you'll be advertising.

As the advertiser, your main objective—after creating a display ad that expertly conveys your message in a visually appealing way—is to find the perfect websites to advertise on. These should be sites that directly appeal to your target audience. Ideally, you want your ads to be seen at precisely the moment someone is looking to purchase the products you're offering.

The best way to find website advertising opportunities is to put yourself in your target customer's shoes and begin searching sites that offer appealing content. Next, determine if those sites accept display advertising, and then request advertising information. Sites that accept display ads will typically have a link on the homepage that says, "Advertise Here" or "Advertising Information."

Creating, launching and managing a successful online display ad campaign requires specific skills. Instead of throwing away money on misguided advertising experiments, if online display advertising is going to be part of your overall advertising, marketing, public relations and promotional efforts, consider hiring an experienced advertising agency to help you. You'll pay a bit more initially, but being able to utilize the experience and expertise of a trained advertising professional will ultimately generate much better results and higher sales.

Search Engine Marketing (Keyword Advertising)

The first step to launching a search engine marketing campaign in to choose the service or services you'll use, such as Yahoo! Small Business' Search Engine Marketing, Google AdWords or Microsoft AdCenter. If you opt to use Google

AdWords, for example, your ads will appear on Google whenever someone enters a search phrase that matches the keywords you select in your ad (providing you're willing to pay the going rate for that ad to be displayed—a concept that will be explained shortly).

In addition to Google AdWords ads being displayed through Google's own search engine site, the company has partnered with thousands of other websites and blog operators that also display context-sensitive ads through the AdWords service. This is referred to as Google AdWords' content network, and it includes About.com, Lycos.com, FoodNetwork.com, The New York Times on the Web, InfoSpace, Business.com, HowStuffWorks.com, and literally thousands of other sites from around the world.

In fact, according to Google, "The Google content network reaches 75 percent of unique internet users in more than 20 languages and over 100 counties. As a result, if you advertise on both the Google search network and the Google content network, you have the potential to reach three of every four unique internet users on earth."

Yahoo!, Microsoft and Google have similar content networks, which allow targeted, text-based ads to be displayed on a wide range of websites well beyond each company's primary search engine or web directory.

As you compare the search engine marketing programs offered by companies like Google, Yahoo! and Microsoft, not only will you want to compare rates, you'll also want to determine if each respective company's content network will help you reach your company's own target audience.

Search engine marketing has a number of benefits to the advertiser, including:

- It's extremely inexpensive to launch a search engine marketing ad campaign. The initial investment is typically under $50, plus you have 100 percent control over your daily ad spending. Once you set your budget, you pay only for the actual clicks to your site, not the impressions (people who see your ad).

- You can create and launch a fully customizedsearch engine marketing campaign in just minutes and start seeing results within hours.

- The success of your campaign will depend on your ability to select appropriate and relevant keywords that are being used to find specific web content.

- You can track the success of your campaign in real time, using online-based tools provided by the respective service.

- Your ad campaign can be expanded as you begin to achieve success and generate a profit, or it can be modified or cancelled in minutes (not weeks or months), to address changes in your overall marketing campaign or your company's objectives.

Once you choose which company or companies you'd like to advertise with, the process of launching your campaign involves a few simple steps, including:

- Set up an account with the search engine marketing company you'd like to work with. This will require the use of a credit card, debit card or PayPal account, plus a deposit of about $50 to get started. The deposit amount varies depending on the service.
- Create a detailed list of keywords that relate directly to the products your business sells. These keywords can include industry jargon, product names, your company's name and any other keywords you deem relevant.
- Create a text-based ad. Each ad includes a headline, a short body and a URL that links directly to your website.

Decide on how much you'd like to spend on your campaign each day. Part of this decision includes deciding how much you're willing to pay each time someone sees your ad and clicks on it in order to reach your website. With this type of advertising, you do not pay for the number of impressions the ad receives. You only pay each time someone actually clicks on the link to visit your website. Based on the keywords you select, you'll be competing with other companies running ads with similar keywords. Using a complex formula that takes into account how much you're willing to pay per click, your ad's placement and display frequency will be determined. The more you are willing to pay per click, especially for popular keywords, the better your ad placement will be and the more frequently the ad will be viewed by potential customers actively using those same keywords to find what they're currently looking for online. Thus, when you launch your campaign, you must set a maximum cost per click, as well as your total daily spending limit, which can be as little as $10 per day.

As you create your search engine marketing campaign, in addition to setting your own list of keywords, you can also determine who will see your ads based on geographic location.

To help you create a comprehensive and effective list of keywords, the search engine marketing services offer a set of online tools to assist you in creating your ad's keyword list and forecasting how many impressions your ad will ultimately receive, based on your ad budget.

Once your ad campaign is running, you can utilize online tools to keep tabs on the number of overall impressions, click-ons, ad placement, ad positioning and related costs. This tracking is done in real time, so you'll know instantly if your campaign is working.

Some of the reasons why text-based search engine marketing ads work so well are because the ads that appear for each web user are always directly relevant to the topic they're actively seeking. The ads are also very short and to the point, plus they serve as links directly to websites that have the content the user is looking for at that very moment.

From the advertiser's standpoint, this type of advertising can be extremely targeted by region and by keywords. Thus these ads can quickly and efficiently prequalify a potential customer and attract them to your site at the precise moment they're looking for what your site offers.

In addition to ensuring that your ads get the best possible placement on the search engine websites, as well as throughout the appropriate websites within the search engine marketing company's content network, it's your responsibility as the advertiser to create a short, text-based ad that quickly captures the reader's attention and generates enough excitement for them to click on your link.

Creating an effective search engine marketing ad takes creativity, as well as a strong knowledge of your product and your target audience. What you say in your ad must be relevant, appealing and attention getting. However, you have relatively little space to accomplish this rather significant task.

Regardless of whether you use Yahoo Search Engine Marketing, Google AdWords, Microsoft AdCenter or another service, the anatomy of the ad that viewers actually see will be basically the same. Every ad will be comprised of the following components:

- *Title:* This can be up to 40 characters long. It should be brief but attention-getting.
- *Description:* This portion of your ad can only be 70 characters long, so again brevity is essential, but what you say must make an impact and appeal directly to your target audience. When possible, incorporate one or more of your keywords into the ad itself (in both the title and the description). Two goals of your ad should be to announce that your online business offers the product the person is looking for, and then to somehow differentiate your online business from the competition (which may also be advertising using ads that surround yours on the surfer's screen). One way to do this is to announce that you offer free shipping or some other incentive for the potential customer.
- *Display URL:* This is the website address that will be displayed within the

ad. The actual link, however, can lead to a different website, or a sub-page within your domain. Ideally, the link should take the surfer directly to the product description page for what they're looking for—not to your website's home page. Don't make visitors to your site who are responding to an ad have to search for the product they're shopping for. Clicking the link in your ad should take them to that exact information.

From your perspective as the advertiser, it's easy to create and utilize a handful of different ads that run simultaneously, incorporate different headlines and messages, and will appeal to slightly different target audiences, but that ultimately lead to the same place—your website. It's common for online business operators to run several different campaigns simultaneously, using different content and keywords.

As you create your ads and each overall campaign, you'll need to create a list of relevant keywords that perfectly describe your product and/or your company. Who ultimately sees your ad will depend heavily on the keywords associated with each ad. Ideally, the keywords you utilize should also correspond very closely to the content on your actual site. Each keyword can be a single word or a phrase that's up to 100 characters long. The web users who see your ad, however, don't actually see your keyword list.

The service you use will help you select appropriate keywords if you're having trouble compiling your list. Most of the services allow advertisers to associate up to 50 unique keywords or phrases with each of their ads. As you create your keyword list, you do not have to use multiple variations of a single word (such as "widget" and "widgets"). Just make sure each word is spelled correctly.

Price Comparison Websites: Drive Price-Conscious Consumers to Your Site

Savvy internet shoppers know they never have to pay full price for anything. If they want to find the absolute lowest price possible on virtually any item, they visit a price comparison website, enter in the exact name of the product they're looking for, and within seconds a listing of online merchants offering that product will be displayed, along with their lowest advertised price for that product.

As an online business operator, advertising using a price comparison website (so you can be included in a list of referrals requested by a web surfer) can generate traffic to your site. The drawback, however, is that the potential customer will be looking for the lowest price possible and if you're not offering it, they'll simply shop elsewhere.

If the products you're selling have a high profit margin, or you're willing to compete with countless other online merchants based mainly on price, price comparison websites can be an extremely viable sales tool.

This type of service also benefits merchants that focus on providing top-notch customer service, since the majority of these price comparison websites display customer ratings or rankings. A savvy web shopper will know to visit an online merchant that has the lowest price and the best customer feedback, all of which is displayed when they use a price comparison website.

Some of the popular price comparison websites include:

- AOL Shopping, **http://shopping.aol.com**
- BizRate, **bizrate.com**
- Nextag, **nextag.com** and for merchants, **http://merchants.nextag.com/serv/main/advertise/Advertise.do**
- Price Grabber, **www.pricegrabber.com/sell_here.php**
- Shopping.com, **shopping.com**
- Shopzilla, **shopzilla.com**

Up Next: Choosing What to Sell and Where to Get It

Thus far, this book has offered a lot of information about setting up a successful buy-and-sell enterprise, but little has been said about what you can actually sell in order to start generating profits. Well, the next chapter focuses on choosing products to sell, and will help you find suppliers for those products.

If you're still having trouble coming up with ideas about what you could sell after reading the next chapter, don't panic just yet. In Chapter 6, you'll discover details about 202 potentially profitable products and product categories that buy-and-sell entrepreneurs have found to be lucrative.

CHAPTER

WHERE YOU CAN BUY THINGS CHEAPLY

here are two major steps involved with a buy-and-sell business venture. The first step is to acquire (buy) your inventory as inexpensively as possible. Step two involves reselling that inventory for the most money possible in order to generate a profit. This chapter focuses on step one, and highlights just some of the popular sources for acquiring products to sell.

Your ability to buy your inventory cheaply is of paramount importance. Once you have decided what type of products you

straightforward. First, find a wholesaler that carries the type of merchandise you want to sell. Second, contact that wholesaler and open an account. Step three involves actually making your purchases, typically in large quantities in order to obtain the lowest possible pricing.

Your choice of which wholesaler you buy from will be determined by your own specific needs and additional factors, such as:

- Wholesale Pricing
- Reliability
- Product Availability
- Purchasing / Financing Terms
- Product Quality
- Customer Service Offered
- Promptness and Accuracy with Order Fulfillment
- Merchandising, Marketing and Advertising Support Offered
- Extended Services Offered (such as drop-shipping and warranties)

Given that there are many factors to consider, you will want to talk with several potential wholesalers before deciding to buy from one. It's also an excellent business strategy to have at least one or two suppliers as backup, just in case an unexpected problem arises with your primary supplier and you can't get your hands on enough inventory quickly enough to meet customer demand.

It is also a good idea to open accounts with more than one wholesaler early on, so you can shop for the lowest prices and take advantage of the specials each offers. In addition to the wholesale sources, directories and associations listed below, you will find many more featured in Chapter 6. You can also use an internet search engine to find additional wholesale suppliers for the products you ultimately decide to sell.

Resources

- Buck Wholesale, ☎ (770) 904-2052, ✄ **buckwholesale.com**
- Buy N Save, ☎ (888) 868-0900, ✄ **buynsavedirect.com**
- Crazy Discounts, ✄ **crazydiscounts.com**
- Dollar Days, ☎ (877) 837-9569, **dollardays.com**
- Go Wholesale, ☎ (877) 566-4849, ✄ **gowholesale.com**
- Hot Dandy Wholesale Superstore, (800) 875-8211, ✄ **hotdandy.com**
- National Association of Wholesaler-Distributors, ☎ (202) 872-0885, ✄ **naw.org**
- Wholesale Hub, ☎ (336) 830-2679, ✄ **wholesalehub.com**

Liquidators

Buying merchandise from liquidators will generally be your cheapest wholesale source of new products. However, the products you're able to acquire might be outdated models or surplus.

Liquidators differ from wholesalers, distributors and importers in that they do not carry a steady supply of the same items all the time. Instead, they purchase many types of merchandise from various sources, including retailers trying to unload out-of-season goods, returns and slow-moving inventory; manufacturers selling seconds and end-of-run; insurance companies disposing of damaged and recovered merchandise; and inventory of all sorts from bankrupt retailers, wholesalers, distributors and manufacturers.

The variety of products that can be purchased from liquidators knows no limits. All merchandise is new, though it may be slightly damaged, seconds, store returns, out-of-season or discontinued. In some instances it is possible to purchase products with warranties, which add value to the goods when you're reselling. Never assume, however, that any merchandise purchased from liquidators is covered by any type of warranty or guarantee unless it is in writing.

If you buy frequently and in large quantities, it is possible to arrange incremental discounts, so be sure to arrange this from the outset. Also, there are auctions for liquidated merchandise, which is one way to buy for less. Liquidators are a great buying source for good, easily saleable merchandise at very low prices, provided you do not need a regular supply of exactly the same products. If you do, buy from wholesalers, distributors or manufacturers that can provide the same products on a regular basis.

Before acquiring a large quantity of any product from a liquidator, get your hands on a few samples to ensure that what you're purchasing is of decent quality, easily resalable and not total junk.

RESOURCES
- 1AAA Wholesale Liquidators, ☎ (800) 661-9430,
  ✆ **1aaawholesaleliquidators.com**
- Liquidation Online, ☎ (800) 498-1909, ✆ **liquidation.com**
- Merchandise USA, ☎ (773) 579-0600, ✆ **merchandiseusa.com**
- Overstock.com, ✆ **overstock.com**
- Quitting Business, ☎ (866) 222-7992, ✆ **quittingbusiness.com**

Importers

Importers are another source of new merchandise at wholesale prices. As a rule of thumb, however, importers are usually product- or industry-specific. General merchandise importers do exist, but they are not common. Most importers deal in specific products or product categories, and sometimes in very highly specialized products.

All importers deal in new merchandise. Some import items such as antiques, but they are generally referred to as import dealers. Likewise, importers only bring products into the country. Those that ship products out are referred to as exporters, or importers/exporters if they do both.

Buying from importers is the same as buying from wholesalers, distributors or manufacturers. Source one or more and open a buying account. However, don't be surprised if more than one importer refuses to sell to you. This is because some importers only work with large-volume clients.

A few potential drawbacks to working with an importer directly are that you'll typically need to deal with people from other countries (via telephone, fax or e-mail) who are in different time zones. You'll also need to consider currency conversion rates, wire transfer charges and international shipping charges in your financial model.

Another consideration to take into account is long shipping times, sometimes up to a month or longer, for products to arrive from the originating country into the United States. There's also the issue of U.S. Customs, and having to fill out additional paperwork and potentially having to pay special import taxes.

As you consider doing business with an importer, you'll want to consider the following:

- Wholesaler Pricing
- Reliability
- Product Availability
- Purchasing / Financing Terms
- Product Quality
- Customer Service Offered
- Shipping Charges
- Currency Conversion Rates
- Language Barriers
- Promptness and Accuracy with Order Fulfillment
- Merchandising, Marketing and Advertising Support Offered
- Extended Services Offered (such as drop-shipping and warranties)

RESOURCES
- American Importers Association, ☎ (727) 724-0900, ✄ **americanimporters.org**
- Canadian Association of Importers and Exporters, ☎ (416) 595-5333, ✄ **importers.ca**
- Global Importers Directory, ✄ **export-import-companies.com**
- Import-Export Internet Advertising, ✄ **importers-exporters.com**
- World Trade AA, ✄ **worldtradeaa.com**

Buying from Manufacturers

Another buying source for new products is manufacturers, which also include farmers, producers, growers, and sales or manufacturers' agents. When buying from manufacturers, the inevitable question arises: Should you buy from local or domestic manufacturing sources and support your own economy, or should you shop overseas manufacturers in hopes of lower prices?

The answer is that each person will have to make that decision individually, but there is a strong argument for supporting your own economy, especially in light of labor laws and practices in some foreign countries.

It is no mystery that products generally cost less from foreign manufacturing sources. On the other hand, domestically manufactured and produced goods are generally of much higher quality. Ultimately, what you're selling, to whom you're selling and wholesale pricing will play a huge role in where you acquire your inventory.

Buying Factory Direct

When you buy directly from the manufacturer of a product, there are no middlemen, agents, distributors, importers or wholesalers of any kind to deal with. This fact alone can save you money. Buying factory direct for the small operator was not an easy or very accessible option as recently as 10 years ago, but it's definitely a viable option today in many situations. With the aid of the internet, you can easily source product manufacturers from around the globe and buy direct.

Even with the assistance of the internet, however, the fact remains that you often have to buy in extremely large quantities (in the hundreds or thousands of units), especially from overseas manufacturers that need to sell by the container load to justify expenses and their competitive pricing.

Nevertheless, there are plenty of domestic and international manufacturers that welcome new wholesale customers, regardless of their current buying power. It might just require a little more homework on your part to flush them out. For some of the products featured in Chapter 6, purchasing directly from the factory is the best and least expensive option.

Some of the things to consider when doing business directly with a manufacturer include:

- *Fair pricing.* You need the ability to buy from manufacturers at a price level that enables you to resell competitively while still retaining the ability to profit. Virtually all manufacturers will negotiate to a certain degree.
- *Quality products.* You need quality products to sell. What you sell must be able to stand up to consumer scrutiny. A super-low price is of no benefit if the product quality is so poor that your potential customers won't buy.
- *Reliability.* You need a reliable buying source. The manufacturers you choose to work with must be able to supply the products you need when you need them. Buying and selling is very much a now, or impulse, business. You cannot ask customers to wait days or weeks for products.
- *Terms.* Seek out manufacturers that will offer you payment terms on purchases. Initially, you will probably have to apply for and be approved for credit, or establish a payment record by paying in full for your first few orders. However, beyond this, you should expect manufacturers to extend 30-, 60- and even 90-day payment terms. From your standpoint, the longer the payment terms offered, the better.
- *Consider exclusivity.* If you're buying a large quantity of a specific product, try to negotiate exclusivity within a geographic region. This will help limit your competition.

RESOURCES
- Alibaba, ✄ **alibaba.com**
- Asian Products, ✄ **asianproducts.com**
- Canadian Manufacturers & Exporters Association, ☎ (613) 238-8888, ✄ **cme-mec.ca**
- Global Sources, ☎ (480) 951-4400, ✄ **globalsources.com**
- India Mart, catalogs, ✄ **indiamart.com**
- National Association of Manufacturers, ☎ (202) 637-3000, ✄ **nam.org**
- Online International Business, ✄ **b2b-bestof.com**
- Taiwan Products Online, ✄ **manufacture.com.tw**
- Thomas Register, ☎ (800) 699-9822, ✄ **thomasnet.com**
- Webster's Online, ☎ (800) 316-2363, ✄ **webstersonline.com**

Manufacturers' Agents

Many manufacturers, especially small ones, enlist the services of sales agents, otherwise known as manufacturers' agents, to find new customers for their products in new geographic markets, both nationally and internationally. This is especially true of manufacturers that do not have the financial resources or people in-house to undertake establishing distributorships in far-flung locations, or that currently have a limited product line, too small to grab the interest or attention of major wholesalers and distributors.

The job of the agent is to prospect for new business for the manufacturer, often establishing accounts with retailers to buy products on a frequent basis. Buying through a manufacturer's agent generally means you will be paying slightly more for the product on a per-unit basis, but over time, as your buying volumes increase, incremental discounts can reduce unit costs. The best way to source manufacturers' agents is to harness the power of the internet and search manufacturers' agents directories, or to contact manufacturers' agents associations.

If you contact a manufacturer directly and they're unwilling to work with you because you don't represent a large enough account, ask if that manufacturer uses a manufacturer's agent who might be more apt to do business with you.

RESOURCES
- Find a Sales Agent, ✂ **findasalesagent.com**
- Manufacturers' Agents National Association (MANA), ☎ (949) 859-4040, ✂ **manaonline.org**

Craftspeople and Artisans

Talented craftspeople across North America make everything from custom furniture to woodcraft decorations, garden ornaments, stained-glass items, and everything imaginable in between. According to the Craft Organization Directors Association (CODA), the crafts industry generates in excess of $14 billion in sales annually.

Crafts (and one-of-a-kind handmade items) are very big business in America. But how do craftspeople distribute their goods? Once again according to CODA, approximately 60 percent of them retail their goods directly to consumers through craft shows, mail order and online marketplaces. An additional 10 percent place their products on consignment with retailers such as gift shops, furniture stores and fashion retailers. The remaining 30 percent wholesale their crafts to retailers and resellers of all sizes. This 30 percent wholesale market adds up to a whopping

$4 billion worth of wholesale crafts that are up for grabs every year for resale.

Most craftspeople who do retail direct to consumers are the first to admit they are not the best marketers of their own goods. These people often miss out on a lot of profit because of their lack of sales and marketing skills. Therefore, persuading them to sell to you on a wholesale basis should not prove too difficult.

Start by talking with craftspeople right in your own area to inquire about the goods they make and their wholesaling policies. You can also contact craft guilds and associations to track down people who make specific products you would like to buy and sell.

Rather than buy crafts wholesale for cash, consider working out a revenue split or consignment arrangement for all goods sold. This way, you'll be able to minimize the amount of investment required to get started. The crafters supply you with inventory, you do the selling and both parties profit.

RESOURCES
- Canadian Crafts & Hobby Association, ☎ (403) 291-0559, ✄ **cdncraft.org**
- Crafts Shows USA, ✄ **craftshowsusa.com**
- Indian Arts & Crafts Association, ☎ (505) 265-9149, ✄ **iaca.com**
- National Association of Artists' Organizations, ✄ **naao.net**
- National Association of Independent Artists, ✄ **naia-artists.org**

Inventors (Patent Holders)

If you're looking for a product to sell exclusively—meaning you'll have no competition whatsoever—consider working directly with a product inventor and purchasing or licensing all worldwide rights and patents to a specific product.

When you do this, you will need to have the product manufactured at your expense. Depending on the product, the potential market for it, the target audience and your available financial resources, this could become a lucrative opportunity.

There are many clubs and associations for inventors, such as the National Congress for Inventor Organizations (**inventionconvention.com**) and The Inventor's Network (**inventnet.com/invorg.html**) that you can tap for referrals or to find product ideas worth pursuing.

Drop-Shippers

See Chapter 3 for more information about manufacturers and distributors that also serve as drop-shippers for their wholesale customers.

Buying at Auction Sales

Live or offline auction sales provide a host of excellent buying opportunities for entrepreneurs who are willing to spend time researching and attending them. These efforts are usually rewarded with incredible buys, which can be resold for two, three or even four times what you spent.

In this section, you will learn auction terminology and buying tips, as well as information about four popular types of offline auction sales:

- Public Auction Sales
- Police Auction Sales
- Government Surplus and Seized-Items Auction Sales
- Estate Sales

There are other types of offline auctions, such as charity auctions and retailer inventory-reduction auctions, but these seldom provide buying opportunities with resale potential.

Likewise, seldom will you find new merchandise being offered at auction sales, unless it is a retailer's or manufacturer's bankruptcy sale. For the most part, live auctions exist for selling secondhand goods such as cars, homes, furniture, antiques, art, tools and equipment. Therefore, buy-and-sell entrepreneurs dealing in the sale of new products should focus their buying efforts on sources that are better suited, such as wholesalers and manufacturers.

AUCTION TERMINOLOGY

Before bidding at an auction, you first have to know auction terminology. Much of this terminology also applies when participating in online auctions (on eBay, for example).

The following are a few of the more common auction terms:

- *Conditions of sale.* These are the terms under which the auction will operate, including buyer's premium in effect, reserves in place, payment options and terms, and date by which items must be removed from the sale site. These sale conditions are generally printed on the registration agreement, announced by the auctioneer at the beginning of the sale, and printed in the auction lot catalog.
- *Bidder's number.* Before being able to bid on items, you must obtain a bidder's number, which is issued at the registration desk. The bidder's number is boldly printed on a paddle or piece of cardboard. It is large enough to be seen by the auctioneer or bid spotter during the sale. When you have suc-

cessfully purchased an item, the auctioneer will ask for your bidding number and assign this number to the item purchased, so you can claim it at the end of the sale.

- *Bid.* A bid is the amount of money you offer on a particular item you wish to purchase. Low-value items will generally increase by dollar increments, while higher-value items can increase in hundred- or thousand-dollar increments.

- *Opening bid.* The auctioneer usually opens bidding, at which point bidders can wait as the opening bid drops, or begin to bid, driving the price higher.

- *Absentee bid.* People who are not physically at the auction sale can bid on items by telephone, by e-mail, by pre-delivered letter stating the lot and bid price, or through the auctioneer's website.

- *Reserve.* A reserve is the minimum price a seller is willing to accept for an item. For instance, if bids top out at $200 for an antique desk, but the reserve is $250, the desk will not sell because the reserve price was not met. The auctioneer informs bidders that the reserve was not met, though he will not disclose the reserve amount, and moves on to the next lot for sale.

- *Buyer's premium.* To increase revenues, many auctioneers now add a buyer's premium to the total value an item has sold for, which can be represented as a flat fee or a percentage of the total value. For instance, if an antique desk sells for $200 and the buyer's premium is 10 percent, then the buyer must pay $220 for the desk, plus applicable taxes. As a rule of thumb, buyer's premiums are generally 5 to 10 percent of the total sales value of items purchased.

- *Preview.* A preview is the opportunity for bidders to inspect items before the sale. Larger sales generally have a preview day or half-day preview time anywhere from one week before the sale to the day of the sale; smaller sales generally have the preview an hour or two prior to the sale. Some auctioneers also list sale items on their websites for preview prior to sales. The purpose of the preview is to give bidders the opportunity to closely examine the items for condition and details prior to bidding.

- *As-is.* As the term suggests, when you purchase items at auctions on an as-is basis, these items are sold without any warranties whatsoever. You get what you see, with no guarantee it will work or as to its overall condition.

- *Lots.* The term lot(s) has two meanings. First, every item being auctioned receives a number, which is referred to as a lot. Second, often a number of small items, such as hand tools, are grouped together in one lot and sold to the highest bidder. So a lot can be one item, or a number of items grouped together.

- *Pick.* When more than one identical item is being auctioned, such as six computer monitors of the same size and age, the first successful bidder will get to choose which one they want and how many they want at the same price. The buyer may choose to buy one, some, or all. He or she gets "the pick of the lot." The items not purchased by the first successful bidder are auctioned once more until all have sold, or the auctioneer has moved on to the next lot.

Auction-Buying Tips

"Let the buyer beware" is the most powerful and truthful auction tip that can be offered! Seldom are auction items covered by a warranty or guarantee of any kind. There are the occasional exceptions to the rule, but for the most part, you get what you buy. Therefore, the onus is on you, and no one else, to ensure that you know what you are buying, its condition and its value, *before* you make a bid.

The following are a few tips for buying at auction sales:

- Go to the preview to inspect items of interest, and be sure to take your auction toolbox, which should include a flashlight, magnifying glass, camera and mirror. These items will help you to properly examine an item to determine its condition *before* bidding. Also, recheck items you intend to bid on the day of the sale to ensure no damage occurred during the preview.
- Do your homework and know the value of what you want to purchase *before* bidding. Make sure to factor in all costs, including buyer's premiums, time, transportation, repair or alterations (if required), shipping fees, plus a return on investment. You have to buy cheaply enough that you can add in all related expenses and still be able to resell the item(s) at a profit. It is a good idea to keep a logbook and list expenses for each individual sale, along with items purchased, and what they were later resold for.
- Don't get carried away in all the excitement and bid on items you did not intend on buying. Also, never bid higher than your preset limit on any one item.
- Once the auctioneer has said "Sold!" you cannot retract your bid if you were the successful bidder, but you can at any time up until that point. If you are feeling uneasy about the item or the price, get out of the bidding by telling the auctioneer or bid spotter you are dropping out *before* the gavel drops.

- If you are an absentee bidder, submitting by phone, fax, e-mail or online, make sure you know the currency the sale is dealing in before you bid.
- If possible, try to attend midweek auctions as opposed to weekend auctions. There are generally fewer people in attendance, which usually means less pressure to drive bids into the stratosphere.
- Look for auctions listing "fish out of water" items because these items can usually be bought for a song. For instance, if you deal in antique furniture and you notice an auction selling mainly computer and office equipment, but that also lists a few pieces of antique furniture, then at least go to the preview to examine the antiques. Dealers generally shy away from these sales because of the limited number of items of interest. The other bidders in attendance are more likely to be interested in the computers than the antiques, which could provide you with a good buying opportunity.
- Get to know auctioneers in your area so they can keep you informed about items of interest to you prior to sales. Also, ask to be included on their auction notification and schedule lists, which are generally sent by fax or e-mail, and list forthcoming auction sales and the items available.
- On items that interest you and are within your preset price range, enter the bidding late, as this often discourages other bidders from continuing because they feel the item will go out of their range. Last-minute bidders coming into the game can even force the most determined bidders to give up.
- Come to the sale with suitable transportation and equipment, such as a loading dolly and rope, so you can leave with your purchases. Trips back to pick up purchased items cost time and money, driving up the prices of items that must be resold to make a profit.
- Look for deals in need of a little elbow grease or minor repairs. Some of the most profitable auction finds are ones that require a little TLC to bring them back to their former glory.
- If you are interested in items that did not sell because the reserve was not met, be sure to give the auctioneer your business card with the lot number of the item and the maximum price you would spend for the item printed on the back of the card. The auctioneer can easily present your card to the seller, who may accept the offer after the sale and contact you.

PUBLIC AUCTIONS

The most common type of auction is a public auction. As the name suggests, these events are open to the general public. Items available for sale vary greatly: cars, real estate, furniture, business equipment, restaurant equipment, antiques, jewelry, art, collectibles, tools, machinery and anything else imaginable. Items being auctioned can be supplied by private sellers, estates, businesses, trustees or any combination of these supply sources.

Auction sales featuring household items are generally conducted on weekends and evenings, when most of the target audience is available to attend. Business and bankruptcy sales are typically held Monday through Friday, during normal business hours.

Regardless of the type of auction you attend, make the experience worth your while in order to justify your time and expense. Buying an item for $20 and reselling it later for $40 might be doubling your money, but if it was the only item bought at the sale, a $20 gross profit hardly justifies the time and expense. In fact, you would be losing money.

Only attend sales that have the potential to make you money. Buy items that are $100, $1,000 and more, and look to double or triple these amounts when reselling. Calculate your total fixed costs for the day, including an hourly rate for your time, and factor in your costs to market and resell items.

Chances are you will come up with a figure in the range of $250, which means if you cannot earn $250 in gross profit from the items you intend to purchase at the sale and then resell, in all probability it would be best for you to skip the sale. Depending on your overhead and other factors, the $250 minimum gross-profit base may be less or more than you need. The trick is to know, in advance, how much profit you have to generate from each sale before attending.

RESOURCES
- Auction Guide, ✄ **auctionguide.com**
- Auctioneers Association of Canada, ☎ (866) 640-9915,
  ✄ **auctioneerscanada.com**
- National Auctioneers Association, ☎ (800) 662-9438, ✄ **auctioneer.org**
- Net Auctions, ✄ **net-auctions.com**

POLICE AUCTIONS
Police auctions represent an excellent opportunity to purchase a wide variety of secondhand products at very low prices. Many police forces in the United States and Canada host quarterly, semiannual or annual auctions to sell off stolen items that were recovered but never claimed by the owners.

At police auctions you will find a vast array of products for sale, including bicycles, tools, car parts, home electronics, computers, jewelry and shoplifted merchandise, much of it for a mere fraction of the original retail value and current resale market value.

There are several levels of police forces: city, county, state and federal. So the best way to find out about police auctions in and beyond your area is to log on to police websites, or call and ask who conducts sales and how the organizer can be contacted.

Most police forces hire auctioneers. Whether they're hosted online or offline, police auctions are conducted in the same manner as any auction: You bid on the items you wish to purchase, and—providing your bid is the highest—you will get it. As always, preview items of interest first, stick to your preset bid amounts, don't buy on impulse, and have the right transportation to cart away your acquisitions. The Property Room Police Auctions website (**propertyroom.com**) is a great resource for learning more about police auctions, and it offers an opportunity to participate in online-based auctions.

GOVERNMENT AUCTIONS

Government surplus and seized-item auctions and tender sales are excellent buying sources, especially for large-ticket items that can often be purchased for 10 percent of their original value, making them extremely profitable for resale purposes.

Many government agencies routinely hold auction sales or sealed-bid tenders to dispose of government surplus assets and equipment, foreclosed property, seized property and unclaimed property.

A few of these agencies include:

- Internal Revenue Service (IRS)
- U.S. Department of Housing and Urban Development (HUD)
- U.S. Justice Department
- U.S. Marshals Service
- U.S. Postal Service
- U.S. Small Business Administration (SBA)
- U.S. Treasury Department

There are many more government agencies at the federal, state, county and city levels that also routinely hold auction sales to dispose of surplus, foreclosed and seized property. Most of these sales are conducted like traditional auction sales.

To find government auctions in your area, contact city, county and state offices. Items routinely auctioned at these events include used computers, real estate, automobiles, machinery and tools, jewelry, furniture, electronics and boats.

Depending on the agency and type of items auctioned, sales can be conducted live, online or both.

RESOURCES
- Public Works and Government Services Canada–Crown Assets Distribution, ☎ (905) 615-2025, ♪ **http://crownassets.pwgsc.gc.ca/text/index-e.cfm**
- U.S. Department of Housing and Urban Development–HUD Home Sales, (202) 708-1112, ♪ **hud.gov/homes/index.cfm**
- U.S. Department of the Treasury, ☎ (202) 622-2000, ♪ **ustreas.gov/auctions/treasury/rp**
- U.S. General Services Administration, ☎ (800) 473-7836, ♪ **gsa.gov**
- U.S. Marshals Service, ☎ (888) 878-3256, ♪ **usdoj.gov/marshals/assets/assets.html**
- U.S. Postal Service, ♪ **usps.com/auctions**

Estate Sales

Estate sales can be conducted in a similar fashion to an auction, as buyers bid on items live or by sealed bid to purchase one or more items from the sale. The organizer of the estate sale may elect to price items individually and hold the sale over a number of days or weeks, until all or most items have been sold.

Estate sales can be organized and conducted by auctioneers, estate sales specialists, family members, lawyers or executors. Regardless of who organizes the sale and how it is conducted, one thing remains constant: Due to the need to settle accounts and inheritances and to dispose of property, it is very possible to purchase items at well below their true market value.

Your ability to buy cheaply will be enhanced further if you are prepared to purchase more than one item, or even all of the items for sale. Estate sales are typically advertised in the newspaper classifieds and on websites, as well as in newsletters of companies that organize such sales.

To find these companies, search under "Estate Sales" in your local Yellow Pages directory, or conduct a search online using Yahoo! or Google. Regardless of who organizes the sale or how the sale is conducted, your ability to resell for a profit rests on your ability to out-negotiate the seller, buy at well below market value, and buy items that are in demand.

Buying Through Online Marketplaces

Almost all wholesale buying sources of new products—such as wholesalers, distributors, importers and manufacturers—now have a website or some sort of online presence. The advantages of buying online are obvious. For example, you can save time because shopping for inventory can be accomplished from home, and you save money because there is no need to travel in most cases.

Of course, there are also a few disadvantages, such as sifting through junk to find what you are looking for, and there are plenty of scammers who conduct online fraud using popular auctions sites.

When buying through an online auction, know who you are dealing with and try to pay with a major credit card. This gives you an added level of protection as a buyer. Sites such as eBay rely heavily on buyer and seller feedback. Pay careful attention to feedback scores, how long a seller has had their account open, and whether or not contact information is provided by the seller.

Online Auctions

Most people think of eBay as a great place to buy products for personal use, or as a forum for selling products. They don't, however, necessarily think of eBay as a viable venue to buy new and used products for resale purposes. In reality, eBay provides opportunities for both buying new products wholesale (for resale purposes) and buying used products cheaply (which can also be resold for a profit).

Opportunities to purchase new products in bulk are listed under the "Wholesale" link in the navigation bar on eBay's home page. The wholesale lots page is segmented into numerous product categories, so finding what you're looking for is a quick and easy process.

Via the wholesale lots page you can purchase new products, liquidated merchandise, seconds, pallet lots, remainders and returns posted by wholesalers, liquidators and manufacturers. Some products are available by way of no-reserve and reserve-bid auctions, while others have volume pricing through individual eBay stores.

If you are going to experiment with no-reserve auctions in hopes of obtaining merchandise at super-cheap prices, use one of the auction-bidding software programs available. Constantly checking auction listings before an auction closes to see if your bid is the highest can be very time-consuming, especially if you are tracking numerous items in multiple auctions.

Automated bidding software is often referred to as sniping software. Sniping means waiting until the last moment to place your bid. The software enables you to do this automatically, and generally allows you to get products at a lower price than if you tried the same tactics yourself without the software.

The sniping software literally swoops in at the last moment to make bids slightly higher than those already placed. Doing this keeps other bidders from increasing their bids before time runs out.

Two of the more popular auction bidding software programs and services are Auction Stealer (**auctionstealer.com**) and Auction Sniper (**auctionsniper.com**). This service may be free, incur a monthly fee, or the cost may be based on a percentage of the purchase price.

If you're looking to buy big-ticket used items cheaply and then resell them for a profit (possibly after cleaning them up or doing some minor repair work), there are companies that operate eBay Stores or other online auctions that specialize in offering this type of merchandise.

For example, there's InterSchola (888-653-7360/**interschola.com**), a certified eBay Power Seller, which acquires surplus goods from public and private schools (and school systems) and then resells these products to the general public, often for a fraction of their actual value.

While the offerings through InterSchola change daily, you can expect to find used vehicles, food service equipment, school supplies, furniture, computers, musical instruments, sports equipment, wood shop and metal shop equipment, plus many other items offered for sale using online-based auctions.

There are many books, online tutorials and other resources available to help you learn how to master the art of bidding when it comes to participating in eBay auctions. Start with the tutorials offered on the website, and then visit your local bookstore or library.

E-Classifieds

E-classifieds can also be a source for tracking down previously owned items to buy for resale. The best e-classifieds are those that also have a print version, such as your local newspaper or buy-and-sell-style publications.

The downside to shopping for deals in online classified ads is there is often a lot of junk to sift through, descriptive ads with photographs are rare, and the geography can be problematic on larger items because of travel needed for inspections, unless you are searching strictly in your area.

The upside is that there are deals to be found, and it is quick, easy and free to scan thousands of ads every day right from home. The rules for buying from e-classified private sellers are the same as the rules for buying from private sellers advertising in print classifieds. These rules are outlined in the next section.

RESOURCES
- AdPost, ♂ **adpost.com**
- Buy and Sell, ♂ **buysell.com**
- My Town Ads, ♂ **mytownads.com**
- The Recycler, ♂ **recycler.com**
- Sell.com Classifieds, ♂ **sell.com**
- Thrifty Nickel, ♂ **thriftynickelads.com**
- Trader Online, ♂ **traderonline.com**

Buying From Private Sellers

People who sell items through auction sales, through flea markets or online, as well as through other methods, can also be private sellers. But for the sake of simplicity, this section deals with five private seller sources for buying previously owned items such as cars, furniture, jewelry, antiques and sporting goods.

These five private seller buying sources include:

- Garage Sales
- Moving Sales
- Print Classified Advertisements
- Bulletin Board Advertisements
- For Sale Signs

Just as you qualify a buyer for your products, you also have to qualify private sellers and the items they are selling, mainly because your first contact with private sellers will usually be on the telephone. You do not want to waste time and money going to see items for sale unless they meet your predetermined buying criteria.

Depending on what types of products you decide to specialize in buying and selling, these criteria could include size, age, overall condition, price, make and model, and any other information that will help you decide if an appointment to inspect the item is warranted.

Once an appointment has been set, you must then be comfortable asking questions—potentially lots of questions. You want to know the history of the item for sale, especially if it is mechanical, such as a car, boat, riding lawn mower or shop tool.

You also want to know if any work or repairs have been done. If so, look at the receipts for a description of the work and warranty information. Remember, sellers have reason to embellish the truth. You, on the other hand, must work like a detective, uncover any telltale signs of a fishy story, and satisfy yourself that the item meets your buying criteria.

Find out as much as you can about the item from the seller: how long they have owned it, what changes have been made, what is the overall condition, and why they are selling. Through careful questioning, you will also be able to determine their level of motivation to sell. By asking questions, you stay in control of the buying process and negotiations.

The following are a few more helpful tips for buying from private sellers:

- Only buy what you know and, more importantly, what you know can make a profit on resale.

- Get a receipt for every purchase, including the date, product description, any guarantees the seller is willing to provide, the seller's complete contact information, the selling price, and the method of payment. Once you pay, request that the seller sign their name beside a statement that says, "Paid in Full." Professional buyers carry their own carbon copy receipt books.

- Always insist that the seller include the extras. For instance, you need a helmet to ride a motorcycle, so get the seller to include the helmet, leather jacket and any other accessories. Or, if you are buying a computer system, make sure you get the printer, scanner, software and monitor. Having the extras is very valuable when it comes time to resell. First, you can charge extra for the accessories and increase your profit. Second, people prefer to buy a package because it is more convenient and represents a better value.

- Always make your first offer half of what you are really prepared to pay. If you want to become a professional buyer, you have to get comfortable with making lowball offers and participating in the negotiation process. Flush out the seller's reason for selling. What is their true motivation? Once you know, you can use this information to support your offer. When you can explain to people why they should accept your offer, based on their own reasons and motivations for selling, it will make logical sense, and most will bite.

Garage Sales

Some people who regularly attend garage sales do so for fun and entertainment, and to find treasures for their homes. However, garage sales can also be a gold mine for buyers looking for profitable reselling opportunities.

Professional buyers always arrive early to garage sales. They are often pushy, drive the hardest bargains, and are the ones snapping up the true treasures, leaving all the junk in their wake. If you do not like this description, look for alternative buying sources.

The world of the professional garage sale hunter can be furiously competitive.

Buying previously owned merchandise for resale at garage sales starts with the advertisement. Carefully examine the ad to differentiate a good sale from a bad one. The best garage sales tend to be estate sales, moving sales, multifamily or block sales and "first sale in 20 years" type sales.

Basically, the aforementioned tend to have lots of great merchandise and sellers who have reason and great motivation to dispose of what they're selling. They'll usually accept any reasonable offer.

The worst garage sales are those at the same addresses week after week (telling you they are professional garage sale sellers), charities (because people will donate junk just to feel good), and those that list the best available items as used tires.

The following are a few additional garage sale buying tips:

- Garage sale hosts generally don't like it, but be sure to show up early to the most promising sales so you get to see the best selection of merchandise. The best items always sell on the first day, in the first hour and to the first shoppers on site.
- If possible, try to buy items more than one at a time. Purchasing a number of items at once can often save you 50 percent or more of the individual selling price. If the seller does not want to budge on price, say you'll pay full price, but that you want whatever other item interests you for free. Buying in volume, regardless of the items or place, always nets lower purchase prices.
- Pay with cash. There is only one currency at garage sales—cash—so bring lots of small bills and stash them in various pockets. When you are negotiating, you do not want to pull out a wad of bills.
- Follow the in-and-out rule. Get in quickly and check the merchandise for what you want. If it's not there, get out quickly and go on to the next sale. Remember, this is your business, so there is no time for idle chitchat or browsing.
- Prioritize the garage sales you intend to visit, starting with the most promising. After the most promising, group the rest together geographically so you can get to more sales in less time. A GPS system will help you navigate the quickest routes between destinations.
- Always avoid impulse buying, and stick to your specialty. If you specialize in antiques, don't buy toys, no matter how good the deal seems. Only buy what you know and what you know you can resell for a profit.
- Always go shopping with suitable transportation: a van, truck or trailer.

Larger items such as machinery, tools and furniture can often be purchased for a song, because many potential buyers do not have the ability to transport them. Most sellers frown on buyers who say they'll come back with suitable transportation. Besides, making trips back to pick up items is a waste of time and fuel, which cuts into your resale profits.

- It is OK to buy items in need of a good cleaning or basic repair, but never buy anything in need of a major overhaul. Always look for reasons to offer less—chipped paint, scratches, no owner's manual and so forth.

- Don't be afraid to make lowball offers. Remember, most people holding garage sales are doing so to rid their homes of clutter, not to pay off their mortgage with the proceeds. Ten bucks for an antique rocker might seem like a ridiculously lowball offer to you, but to the seller it may seem reasonable for something that was collecting dust in the attic just one day earlier.

RESOURCES
- Craigslist, ♂ **craigslist.org**
- Garage Sale Planet, ♂ **garagesaleplanet.com**
- Garage Sales Daily, ♂ **garagesaledaily.com**
- Yard Sale Search, ♂ **yardsalesearch.com**

Moving Sales

Like garage sales, moving sales can be an incredible buying source for previously owned items that can be resold for a profit. There are basically two ways to locate moving sales. You can wait for people to advertise their moving sale in the newspaper classifieds or with bulletin board fliers. Or you can be proactive and create your own ads stating that you buy partial or entire household lots—everything from furniture to books.

Option one requires you to scan your local classified ads and community bulletin boards. Option two requires you to place classified ads and post flier ads on bulletin boards. Most entrepreneurs engaged in buying partial or entire household lots opt to combine both options to maximize buying potential and profit.

The majority of people who hold a moving sale do so over the course of a few days or a week, and as a general rule, most items will be displayed in the seller's home and be individually priced.

The same buying rules apply here as with other types of sales. Know what you want and what it's worth, and negotiate for a bargain every time. Driving a hard bargain and getting products for the price you want to spend is usually not difficult because the seller is moving and, depending on how soon, may be very motivated to liquidate personal belongings at any price.

Classified Ads

Private-seller print classified ads represent a wealth of buying opportunities for previously owned merchandise, especially when dealing with motivated sellers. Their motivation or reason for selling could be based on any one of a number of considerations.

Regardless of the motivation, when under pressure, sellers are more apt to take much less than their asking price or fair market value for what they're selling. These are the types of sellers you want to find.

Look for ads in which the seller provides a reason for the sale, such as "moving." Also, look for strong statements that show desperation, such as "must sell," "best offer by a certain date," or "will accept any reasonable offer."

Scan the classifieds in your newspaper or circular each morning, circle ads of interest, and call right away. When talking with the seller, try to gauge their level of motivation to sell, and make sure the item for sale meets your buying criteria. If so, set an appointment to inspect the item right away.

Remember, what separates the professional buyer and the average person selling is the fact that you do this for a living and they do not. All they want or need to do is dispose of an item. Sellers often accept first-but-low offers because they worry they might not get any other offers, especially if they are motivated to sell and need the money.

Another option is to cut out classified ads of interest and then wait a week to 10 days before calling to see if the item is still for sale. If it is, and it meets your buying criteria, there is a good chance the seller will accept considerably less than the asking price because they have not been able to sell yet.

In addition to your local newspaper classifieds, there are a host of classified-advertising-only newspapers, such as the *Thrifty Nickel*, *Penny Saver* and *Buy and Sell*. All are excellent places to find great items to buy for resale. Also, don't overlook specialty publications relevant to the specific products you deal in, such as boating publications if you buy and sell boats, or antique publications if you buy and sell antiques. Online, Craigslist is an excellent resource for finding used items that are for sale in your geographic region.

The primary steps for purchasing items from private sellers using classified ads include:

Things You Can Buy and Sell for Big Profits

- Scan newspaper and specialty publication classified ads daily for items of interest.
- Qualify sellers and the items for sale over the telephone before setting an appointment to view the products. If items do not meet your buying criteria, don't bother wasting your time with an appointment.
- Carefully inspect all items, and ask sellers for the complete history of the product. Be sure to take along your inspection and buying tools. Depending on the items you specialize in, these tools might include a camera, flashlight, pricing guides, receipt book, magnifying glass and angled mirror.
- Negotiate like a seasoned professional. *Never* pay full asking price. Look for reasons to offer less.
- Factor in all costs, including highest possible purchase price, which will still leave you a reasonable return on investment when resold. If you cannot meet your profit needs and expectations because the purchase price is too high, do not buy.
- Get as much original documentation as possible, including repair receipts and warranties, original purchase receipts, and the owner or operator's manuals. All are valuable marketing tools for reselling.
- Get every available extra you can with the product you are buying. For example, if you buy a bicycle, request that the seller include a helmet, bike rack, tool kit and spare parts. All can be resold separately or as a package to increase sales value and profits.
- Always take your own receipt book, and list a full description of products purchased, including serial and model numbers. Date the receipt and list the purchase price and the payment method. On the receipt, list the seller's full contact information, as well as your own, and have the receipt signed by the seller. If the seller is offering any type of guarantee, warranties, or return options, make sure these are also included on the receipt.

Any *Penny Saver*-type publication (**pennysaverusa.com**) will also have a "freebie" or "recyclers" section, where many very resalable items can be picked up absolutely free. For a few hours' worth of work and a bit of elbow grease, you could probably net $500 to $1,000 (or more) per week, just from these freebie sources alone.

RESOURCES
- Penny Saver USA, ✆ **pennysaverusa.com**
- The Recycler, ✆ **recycler.com**

- Thrifty Nickel, ♂ **thriftynickelads.com**
- Your local or regional newspaper

Bulletin Boards

People often utilize community bulletin boards to post fliers that advertise things they have for sale: furniture, cars, jewelry, electronics, computers and tools. Typically, these bulletin boards are found in grocery stores, public markets, gas stations, convenience stores, libraries, laundries, fitness clubs, universities, colleges and community centers.

There are really two approaches you can use when purchasing items from private sellers who use bulletin boards to advertise the items for sale. The first approach is to call right away on items of interest, get all the information you need, set an appointment to view what's for sale, and then use all of your sales and negotiation skills to get the item for the lowest possible price.

If you choose this route, do not try to pre-negotiate over the telephone before you see the item. Instead, make sure you ask the right questions to ensure the item meets your buying criteria, and save the price negotiations for the face-to-face meeting. When you make a cash offer in person, sellers are far more likely to get excited and take your offer seriously than when you make it over the telephone.

The second approach is to start a bulletin board logbook, which requires nothing more than a spiral notepad. Make a weekly run to all bulletin boards in your area and record items listed for sale that interest you, including product description, price, date posted and seller's contact information.

Wait a week to 10 days, and then begin calling to inquire if the items are still for sale. The reason you wait is because many businesses and organizations that provide bulletin board space require all ads to have a posting date on the flier so ads older than one week can be taken down, making space for new ads to be posted. Otherwise, the bulletin boards would become an overcrowded mess of items, many no longer for sale.

If the item is still for sale after a week to 10 days, there is a better than average chance you will be able to negotiate a substantially lower purchase price. It is also useful to create your own fliers listing the products you are looking to purchase— antiques, cars, furniture, electronic devices or whatever—and post your own fliers when you make your bulletin board runs.

For Sale Signs

No matter where you travel around your own geographic area, you're apt to see "For Sale" signs posted on cars, boats, houses, bicycles and other large items. It is very possible to buy some of these items low and resell them for a profit. You never know a person's reason for selling or their level of motivation to sell at any price until you ask or make an offer.

Additional Buying Sources

There are other buying sources in addition to those already mentioned, such as flea markets, thrift shops, storage companies, hotels replacing furnishings and contractors for reclaimed building materials.

Flea Markets

In spite of the fact that dealers are there to make a profit, flea markets do provide ample buying opportunities for previously owned merchandise, especially for antiques, collectibles and items in need of some spit and polish. You need to practice the same shrewd negotiations you would for any other buying source. Do not buy anything if you are not sure you can resell it for a profit. Also, whenever you make a purchase, always ask for a receipt and the vendor's full contact information. Thieves often use flea markets as a front to fence stolen merchandise, so you want (and perhaps may even need) proof that all items in your possession have been purchased.

The following are a few additional tips for buying low at flea markets:

- To strike the best deals, shop early or late in the day. Flea market vendors have the most power in terms of negotiations at the busiest time of day, which is usually midday. If you find something early and the vendor refuses to budge on price, return later in the day to see if it is still for sale. If so, restate your offer, but no more. Some might bite because it beats having to reload, transport and store their unsold goods.

- Never pay full asking price. Always start low and hesitantly work your way up incrementally, if need be. If the dealer still won't budge, suggest he or she throw in another item for free. If the dealer still won't budge, walk away, unless you are absolutely sure you can resell the item for a generous profit. If not, there is no sense in wasting your time.

- Cash speaks volumes at flea markets, so leave the plastic and checks at home and take only cash—preferably small bills stashed in various pockets so it appears you are short on cash, which supports your need to negotiate and buy low.

- Don't judge a book by its cover. A busy flea market is fantastic for selling, while a slow flea market is great for buying. A lack of customers equals hungry vendors ready to make deals.

- You know the products you are looking for, so don't get sidetracked and buy things on impulse, especially if you are clueless in terms of value, condition, and how and where they can be resold for a profit.
- Have suitable transportation when you go flea market buying. A truck, van or trailer means you may be able to purchase larger items others cannot buy, and be able to negotiate a lower price because of it. Also, having to make multiple trips wastes time and gas and cuts into your profitability.
- Look for dealers with items that seem out of place in their inventory. When any retailer of used goods sells something out of their normal range, there is a good chance the item will be undervalued, especially in the case of antiques and collectibles.
- Take a flea market toolbox stocked with the tools of the buyer's trade, including a magnifying glass, flashlight, retractable search mirror, camera, price guides and tape measure, all of which can be used to closely examine items prior to buying.
- Go shopping in poor weather when other shoppers are likely to stay home. When customers are few, dealers get hungry and are willing to make deals.
- Look for items that are otherwise sound, but in need of a little TLC. These items can generally be bought at bargain prices. Make a few repairs and add a bit of elbow grease, and that product's value could increase dramatically.

RESOURCES
- Collectors, ♂ **collectors.org/FM**
- Craigslist, ♂ **craigslist.org**
- Flea Market Guide, ♂ **fleamarketguide.com**
- Flea USA, ♂ **fleamarkets.com**
- Keys Flea Market, ♂ **keysfleamarket.com**
- Secondhand Stores

Junk shops, secondhand shops, thrift shops, and pawnshops also provide potential buying opportunities, although not as many as the other buying sources listed in this chapter. Because the retailer needs to generate a profit to stay in business, products sold through these sources tend to be priced at true (retail) market value.

With that said, it is still possible to find valuable hidden treasures that can be bought inexpensively and resold for a profit. The keys to success when looking for bargains in these shops are twofold. First, try to stick with shops that are run by or aligned with local or national charities. There is a much higher chance that neither the person donating the items for sale nor the volunteers in the shop will have any idea of the item's true value.

Second, look for fixer-upper items, though not ones in such poor condition that you end up spending too much time fixing and not enough selling. Preferably, items should need no more than basic repairs and a good cleaning to quickly transform them into valuable, resalable merchandise.

RESOURCES
- Consignment Shops Online, ✆ **consignmentshops.com**
- National Association of Resale & Thrift Shops, ☎ (800) 544-0751, ✆ **narts.org**
- National Pawnbrokers Association, ☎ (817) 491-4554,
  ✆ **nationalpawnbrokers.org**
- Pawnshops Online, ✆ **pawnshops.net**

Moving and Storage Companies

Moving and storage companies, as well as towing companies, can represent a wealth of incredible buying opportunities for the innovative entrepreneur. When people do not pay their moving, storage or towing storage bills, companies often sell any goods stored or still in their possession to recover all or some of the monies owed.

Typically, the personal belongings stored at public storage centers will include furniture, clothes, antiques, sporting goods, books and records. Occasionally business owners who fall behind in their rent will have equipment and inventory seized that can often be purchased for less than wholesale value. Larger yard-stored items, such as boats, cars, RVs, motorcycles and trailers, can also be purchased.

Registered items, such as cars, however, require owner transfer. A bailiff or another official is typically brought in to seize and sell the items so they can be legally transferred to new owners. It is best to contact moving, storage and towing companies directly to inquire about how they sell or dispose of goods seized for nonpayment. Each company will have its own disposal methods and policies.

RESOURCES
- American Moving and Storage Association, ☎ (703) 683-7410,
  ✆ **moving.org**
- Self Storage Association, ☎ (703) 921-9123, ✆ **selfstorage.org**
- Towing and Recovery Association of America, ☎ (800) 728-0133,
  ✆ **towserver.net**
- Check your local phone directory for self-storage facilities in your immediate area.

Junkyards

Individuals and companies alike often throw away valuable equipment, products and items that could potentially be resold. The original owner simply doesn't want to deal with the hassle, so the items get discarded. Simply by making regular visits to a local junkyard or garbage dump, you can probably find valuable items and purchase them for little or no money.

One Last Thought ...

Opportunities for finding bargains are everywhere! Use your own creativity, investigative skills and ability to negotiate in order to discover products that you can ultimately resell for huge profits. As the saying goes, think outside the box! Try to find products that have little competition, that are in high demand, and that you know you'll easily be able to find a market for. The internet can be a powerful tool for uncovering potential profit-generating opportunities.

What's Next: Discovering Where To Sell Your Products

Okay, so now that you know all of the different sources for buying products to resell, let's take a look at all of the different places and opportunities you have to sell your products in order to generate a profit. This is the topic that's covered within Chapter 5.

WHERE YOU CAN SELL THINGS FOR BIG PROFITS

If *buying low* represents 50 percent of the buy-and-sell equation required to succeed, *selling high* represents the other 50 percent. The objective of this chapter is to show you where and how you can potentially resell items for top dollar in order to maximize revenues and profits.

In both the real world and in cyberspace, there are a vast number of ways and places to sell, certainly more than are featured here. In fact, many of the same venues and methods for buying products for resale can also be utilized to sell your products to consumers. This chapter provides a sampling of the popular venues that buy-and-sell entrepreneurs just like you are using to achieve success. These include:

"REAL WORLD" COMMUNITY RETAILING
- Arts and Crafts Shows
- Community Events
- Farmers' and Public Markets
- Flea Markets
- Live Auction Sales
- Mall and Shopping Center Kiosks
- Selling Direct to Businesses (also referred to as "B2B")
- Sporting Events, Parades, Carnivals and Festivals
- Street Vending
- Trade Shows, Consumer Exhibitions and Seminars

ONLINE MARKETPLACES
- Craigslist
- eBay
- E-Classifieds
- Other Types of E-Storefronts
- Your Own E-Commerce Website

HOMEBASED SALES
- Garage Sales
- Homebased Showrooms and Exterior Displays
- In-Home Sales Parties
- Selling Direct to Collectors

Most of the ideas and concepts detailed within this chapter work in conjunction with information from previous chapters. For example, the information about personal selling that you read about within Chapter 3 can easily be applied to flea market vending (selling at flea markets). Keep in mind that most tips featured for one type of retailing are portable, and can be used in other retailing venues as well.

Your own creativity will also come into play as you pinpoint innovative and unique ways to reach the target audience that would be most interested in buying your products. As you grow your business, you'll probably find that utilizing several of these selling opportunities simultaneously will help generate even greater profits.

For example, you might opt to sell your products at flea markets every weekend, but also operate an e-commerce website that sells the same products via the internet to a much larger potential audience. An e-commerce website could also potentially generate orders from people who saw your products at the flea market, but—for whatever reason—failed to make a purchase on the spot. The same website could help generate repeat business from flea market customers long after the flea market has ended.

Community Retailing

Beyond traditional retail storefronts, there are numerous retailing opportunities within every community that are available to the innovative entrepreneur. A few examples include selling tools at a weekend flea market, selling flowers from a rented mall kiosk, selling antiques at auction or selling organic vegetables at the local farmers market.

This section focuses on some of the most lucrative community retailing opportunities: flea markets, arts and crafts shows, live auctions, mall (and shopping center) kiosks, farmers' and public markets, street vending, community events, trade shows, seminars and B2B sales.

Unlike operating a traditional retail store located along Main Street in your community or within your local mall or shopping center (which typically requires a financial investment in the hundreds of thousands of dollars), the opportunities described here cost relatively little to get involved with.

Depending on the items you sell and your objectives, you might opt to participate in only one of these selling opportunities. If, however, you have a true entrepreneurial spirit and the right resources at your disposal, consider combining two or three of these opportunities to maximize your potential for success and profits.

Flea Markets

There are an estimated 750,000 flea market vendors peddling their wares in the United States and Canada at more than 1,000 flea markets, bazaars and swap meets, some of which attract crowds in excess of 25,000 a day.

Typical flea market vendors are comprised of professional and amateur sellers working full time, part time, seasonally or only occasionally, and it is not unusual for vendors to earn a significant income working only a few days per week. Keep in mind, on the days you're not actively working at the flea markets, you'll probably need to handle other aspects of your buy-and-sell business, such as bookkeeping, inventory management, marketing and customer relations.

Locating the Best Flea Markets

Flea markets that provide awesome opportunities for selling your products are everywhere. However, it's important that you don't judge a flea market by its size (number of sellers) or average attendance figures alone. Instead, conduct research by visiting a few before deciding which one to set up shop at. Check out other vendors and determine what they sell, how much they are charging, how much they are selling and how many are selling products that are similar to yours.

Also check out the people in attendance. Are they buying or browsing? How many are there and—most importantly—do they meet your target customer profile? You have to get a feel for the venue, vendors and customers *prior* to participating as a seller at a flea market in order to determine which events are right for you.

As you'll discover, there are many types of flea markets. Some are held only on weekends and/or holidays. Some are open every day throughout the year, while others are open seasonally (such as during the summer months). Where these events are held also varies. Some are held indoors (within a large, climate-controlled environment), while others are held outside, within tents or in open fields. Ultimately, you'll need to find one or more flea markets that you believe are the most suitable for what you'll be selling and that are held in an environment where you'd enjoy working.

When choosing between different types of venues where flea markets are held, keep in mind that each has advantages and disadvantages. For instance, outside flea markets are subject to weather, such as wind, rain, intense sun, heat or bitter cold.

You'll also need to factor in the cost of booth rentals and the size of the booth you require to properly sell your products. Some flea markets charge vendors as little as five dollars per day to participate. Others charge hundreds of dollars per day or take a commission on every sale you make.

Often, you can reserve space for a month or longer at a time, and while this method secures your cheapest rent, be sure to test it out for a few days before getting locked into a long-term lease.

Other considerations include:

- Availability of Ample and Convenient Customer and Vendor Parking
- Hours of Operation
- Size and Location of Available Booth Space
- Access to Electricity
- Access to Phone Lines (for credit card processing)
- On-Site ATM Machines
- Availability of Restrooms

- Food Services
- Overall Event Organization
- Reputation of Market Operators

Online flea market directories, such as the ones listed in the Resources section that follow, offer the best way to find flea markets in your target geographic area. Most of the directories are indexed geographically.

Products That Sell Best at Flea Markets

There are always exceptions, but generally the best new products to sell at flea markets include: dollar store items, fad/trendy items, toys, hand and power tools, crafts, costume jewelry, sunglasses, auto parts and novelty products. The best used products to sell include glassware, antiques, collectibles, toys, tools, children's clothing, vintage clothing and books.

Equipment for Vendors

In most cases you will need a vendor's permit and sales tax ID number to get started selling at flea markets. Some flea market organizers also require vendors to have their own liability insurance.

You will also need to supply your own transportation and equipment, such as dollies to load and unload merchandise and displays. Some flea markets provide merchandising tables, canopies and displays as part of your booth rental fees. Others rent these items separately, while some do not supply anything except for the empty booth space.

Therefore, be sure to clarify your equipment and merchandising needs with flea market organizers or managers upfront. You will also want to bring along a few extra items to insure your own comfort, such as comfortable shoes (you'll be doing a lot of standing), lots of water and snacks, a stool (instead of a chair) to sit on (which looks more professional and keeps you up higher), and an umbrella or overhead covering for outside events. A basic first-aid kit, at least one roll of duct tape and a basic tool kit are other items that'll probably come in handy.

The following are 15 additional tips to help you get started earning huge profits at flea markets:

1. Create a flea market vendor's toolbox that's stocked with lots of handy items such as duct tape, string, receipt books, a calculator, pens, fliers, business cards, credit card slips, magic markers, a price gun or label marker, scissors, cleaning products and rags, and supplies such as newspapers, plastic bags and cardboard boxes to pack customer purchases.

2. Buy small, inexpensive items related to your main product line, and boldly advertise and resell these at low cost to draw shoppers to your tables. For instance, if you sell new hand and power tools, fill up a box with assorted screwdrivers priced at just one dollar each. The idea is to grab the attention of people and draw them into your booth; once you have their interest, sell your higher-priced merchandise.

3. Offer numerous ways for customers to pay by getting a merchant account and wireless terminal so you can accept debit cards and credit cards. Most customers will pay cash, but accepting plastic increases impulse buying by as much as 50 percent. Let shoppers know you accept credit cards by posting a large sign. Don't, however, accept checks, even with proper ID! It's not worth the risk and added expense of having people bounce checks on you. Also, make sure you have an ample supply of small bills. You do not want to risk losing sales because you cannot make change.

4. Invest in professional displays, banners and signs to help boost revenues and profits. Have bold and colorful signs and banners made and purchase high-quality and attractive display units. Keep your merchandise and sales area clean and organized.

5. Hand out fliers to everyone passing, even if they did not buy. The fliers should describe your products and list ways for people to buy—including your website address, telephone number and mail order address. To increase the effectiveness of this simple marketing trick, print tips or other valuable how-to information on the back of the flier so people have reason to hang on to it. For example, if you sell fishing tackle, list 20 tips for catching, cleaning or preparing fish on the back of the flier.

6. Develop a system for capturing names and addresses or phone numbers so you can later utilize this information for direct marketing purposes. Hold a contest and use the information on the entry ballot to build a database, or ask people to subscribe to your free electronic or print product catalog, for example.

7. Everyone shopping at flea markets expects to bargain and wants to flex their negotiation muscle, so be ready to haggle. Price items 10 to 25 percent higher than you expect to get, so you have plenty of negotiating room and can still be able to generate a profit off of every sale. Also, there are pros and cons to pricing each item individually. The pro is that if each item is tagged with a price, you will not have to continually repeat the price each time someone asks. The con is that if people think the price is too high, they may move on

to the next vendor and not try to negotiate.

8. Stand out in the sea of vendors by using professionally created and colorful banners, balloons, lights, music (if allowable by the show's organizers) or flags. Any and all types of attention-grabbing devices will help attract people to your booth space. Large flea markets have hundreds—sometimes thousands—of vendors, and all are vying for the attention of shoppers. Be creative and stand out from the crowd.

9. Flea market vendors cannot afford to be wallflowers. There are far too many competitors chasing the same consumers. You have to be creative. Develop ways to engage people and get them into your booth. For example, use live product demonstrations to pull them in. You can't sell to people if they don't stop and check out your goods. Create a hook and provide reasons for people to stop and shop.

10. At flea markets, avoid offering a return or refund policy. You must, however, post your policy using signage, so customers know that all sales are final. If you do offer returns, only offer exchanges for items of equal or greater value. Ideally, there should be no returns or refunds. Post signs that state, "ALL SALES FINAL," and have this printed on every receipt. (If you're operating an online business, you will definitely want to offer returns and a money-back guarantee.)

11. Whenever possible, try to sell items with their original packaging, manuals and accessories. Doing so greatly increases the value and makes the products much easier to sell.

12. In order to prevent theft, always keep more expensive items grouped together so they are easier to watch. Always look inside larger items to make sure smaller ones are not hidden. Likewise, keep your cash with you, in a lockbox, or within a safe.

13. Never hold items for people who say they will be back to pick them up, unless they have left a substantial deposit. Many shoppers say they will return later to pick up items after they have browsed the event or have suitable transportation to carry larger items, but they often never return. All merchandise must remain for sale unless paid for in full or a substantial deposit has been obtained.

14. Price products according to competition and demand, but aim for at least a 50 percent markup on new products. Price used products as a percentage of new cost, but be sure you'll generate a profit based on the prices you set.

15. Only sell items in good working order and free of rips, rust and excessive

wear (unless they're antiques). Also, if power is available on-site, have an electrical cord so people can test electronics and appliances, and have batteries for battery-powered items. Clothing should be cleaned, neatly pressed and displayed on hangers.

RESOURCES
- Collectors, ☞ **collectors.org/FM**
- Flea Market Guide, ☞ **fleamarketguide.com**
- Flea USA, ☞ **fleamarkets.com**
- Keys Flea Market, ☞ **keysfleamarket.com**
- National Flea Market Association, ☎ (424) 247-1152, ☞ **fleamarkets.org**

Arts and Crafts Shows

Providing you have the right products to sell, arts and crafts shows and fairs can deliver excellent selling opportunities. These shows come in different styles and sizes, from church-sponsored crafts shows to international fine arts and crafts shows that last for a week and attract buyers from around the globe.

Most, however, are small events lasting a day or two that take place in community centers, exhibition buildings, hotels, convention centers and school gymnasiums. Often arts and crafts shows are held outdoors, so vending at these shows can be greatly affected by weather.

Rent for booth space also varies widely—from free to $500 or more per day. Some show organizers charge vendors a commission on every sale they make. The key to success is the same as for any vending opportunity: sell unique products that are in demand, and then select shows that allow you to reach your target audience.

Just as with flea markets, other factors to consider include admission fees, parking, competition, rent, operating history and attendance statistics. You should visit larger, more expensive shows before signing on to vend to make sure the show and audience meet your exhibiting criteria. Whenever possible, try to talk to other vendors to get firsthand feedback about the show and audience.

In terms of what you're selling at these shows, try to come up with hand-crafted, collectible or one-of-a-kind items that people will want for themselves and to give as gifts. Often at arts and crafts shows, there are a lot of similar products being displayed among vendors. One key is to differentiate yourself and your products. This will help build demand, plus potentially allow you to charge more for what you're selling.

The following are a few more helpful tips for selling at arts and crafts shows:

- Create a checklist a week before any show, and check off each item or task as completed. Make sure you're 100 percent ready to sell come show time.
- If you are the artist or you make your own crafts, try in-booth demonstrations as a way to draw in a crowd. People love to meet the artist and see them at work! Booths and displays that are alive with activity always grab more attention than static ones. Plus a busy booth equals more selling opportunities.
- Keep your booth, displays and inventory clean and organized. Use mirrors and clamp-on lighting to brighten your booth and displays. Also, bring along a basic toolbox for last-minute changes or emergencies. Stock the toolbox with a hammer, screwdrivers, a flashlight, a wrench, extra light bulbs, duct tape, cleaner, rags, a stapler and garbage bags.
- Have materials for packaging purchases on hand, including newspapers, plastic bags, boxes, packing tape, string and scissors. Consider offering free gift wrapping as a way to distinguish yourself from competitors. (This, however, takes time away from generating new sales, so make sure you have ample help at your booth if you offer gift wrapping or product demonstrations.)
- Consider cash management and purchase payment options. Ideally, you will want to accept credit cards and debit cards. Also, you will need a receipt book, credit card slips, a calculator, pens, a price gun or blank price tags, and a cash lockbox. Avoid accepting checks.
- You should bring 50 percent more inventory than you expect to sell, especially if you are traveling far from your home base. You do not want to chance losing sales and profit because you are out of stock or don't offer an ample selection of your products.
- Because arts and crafts shows can be very busy, make sure you price all items to save the time of repeating prices to everyone who asks. Also, make sure you create a couple of worthwhile show specials to really grab attention and pull shoppers into your booth. A 50-percent-off show special may seem excessive, but what profit you lose on one or two items can be made up in volume sales and through upselling opportunities.

RESOURCES
- Canadian Crafts & Hobby Association, ☎ (403) 291-0559, ♂ **cdncraft.org**
- Crafts Fair Online, ♂ **craftsfaironline.com**

- Crafts Shows USA, ♂ **craftshowsusa.com**
- Festival Network Online, ♂ **http://festivalnet.com/events.html**
- Indian Arts & Crafts Association, ☎ (505) 265-9149, ♂ **iaca.com**
- Open Directory Project, ♂ **http://dmoz.org/Arts/Crafts/Events**

Live Auction Sales

Good news! According to the National Auctioneers Association, the live auction industry exceeded $270 billion in revenues during 2007. "The live auction industry continues to grow at an amazing pace," said NAA president Tommy Williams. "More and more consumers are realizing the benefits of buying and selling at live auctions. Consumers are now buying or selling their homes, purchasing art and antiques, or raising capital for charitable causes through auctions."

Live auction sales are great for selling specialized and high-value products such as boats, antiques and power equipment. The downside is that you have to pay a commission, which is generally 10 percent. Think of this sales commission as a cost of marketing or cost of doing business.

The true downside associated with auction selling is that you have no guarantee of how much the product will sell for, although there are two ways to combat this. First, make sure you are consigning your item for sale at the right type of auction—one that will attract the right types of buyers. About half of all auctioneers specialize in one particular field, such as cars, real estate, heavy equipment, art or antiques.

The main advantage of consigning with specialist auctioneers is their contact lists. Before sales, auctioneers send out a catalog of available items to people who have purchased similar items in the past. This marketing practice assures that qualified buyers will attend the sale, which usually equates to higher bid prices.

 Second, you can place a reserve bid on the products you're selling. This means that if no one bids at least the minimum acceptable price, the item will not be sold during that particular auction. Be aware that most auctioneers charge a fee for items with reserve bids that do not sell. The fee can be a flat rate or a percentage of the reserve bid amount, so be sure to check with the auctioneer.

Participating in live auctions to sell your products is not the ideal selling solution for many types of items—especially inexpensive products—or sellers. Experience a few auctions firsthand before you decide to participate.

Keep in mind that selling through live auctions is very different than participating in online auctions, where virtually anything can be successfully bought or sold.

The following are additional tips for selling through live auction services:

- Not all auctioneers are the same. Some are masters of merchandising and driving up bids, while others are not. Attend sales to get a good feel for the type of auctioneer before consigning your products.
- Before consigning items, get the following information in writing: commission charges, reserve-bid charges, length of time to process and payout for items sold, and any storage and transportation issues and charges.
- If you are selling expensive items, find out how much insurance the auctioneer carries in the event your property is damaged or stolen before, during or after the sale up until the time you get paid.
- Before consigning items, make sure they are clean and in working condition, and include all manuals and documentation.
- It is illegal to bid on your own merchandise in the hope of driving up the price. The best way for you to get top dollar is to make sure you have an excellent item for sale, through the right auction service, with the right bidders in attendance.

RESOURCES
- Auction Guide, ♂ **auctionguide.com**
- Auction Network, ♂ **auctionnetwork.com**
- Auctioneers Assoc. of Canada, ☎ (866) 640-9915, ♂ **auctioneerscanada. com**
- National Auctioneers Association, ☎ (800) 662-9438, ♂ **auctioneer.org**
- Net Auctions, ♂ **net-auctions.com**

Mall and Shopping Center Kiosks
Kiosks and pushcarts located in malls, shopping centers, airports and train stations, for example, represent great selling opportunities for vendors with the right products. These kiosks and pushcarts can be adapted for selling any number of items, such as jewelry, clothing, electronics, leather goods, cosmetics, cell phone accessories, gifts, CDs, DVDs, flowers, pet accessories and souvenirs.

Many people achieve success selling fad or trendy items from mall kiosks. During the 2007 holiday season, some popular products sold successfully through mall and shopping center kiosks included Webkinz, Crocs, tiny remote-controlled helicopters, specific brands of cosmetics and skin care products (including Proactiv Solution), hair care products, iPod skins/cases, gourmet dog biscuits and designer sunglasses.

Many of these carts and kiosks are available to rent on a short- and long-term basis, from one week to a full year. Generally speaking, it is the building or property management company that rents vending space, so these are the people you should contact. If you want to set up a kiosk in a local mall, visit the mall's on-site management office. Before signing up and renting space, however, ask about the following:

- All fees associated with the kiosk rental (including whether or not the venue collects a percentage of every sale)
- How long you must rent the kiosk for
- During what hours you must remain open each day
- The average traffic within the mall or venue
- The demographics of the mall or venue traffic
- What competition may also have a kiosk or retail store within the mall or venue
- Availability and cost of electricity, phone service, plumbing and other services
- The exact size and dimensions of the kiosk
- The rules for displaying signage on or around your kiosk

In addition to a vendor's permit, most locations also require you to have liability insurance. Locations can be lucrative in terms of revenues, but vendors who specialize in selling from mall kiosks tend to fare the best and produce the highest sales, especially during the Christmas shopping season (between Thanksgiving and New Year's).

RESOURCES
- Entrepreneur.com (*How To Start A Mall Kiosk Business*),
   ♂ **entrepreneur.com/startingabusiness/startupbasics/location/ article63012.html**
- General Growth Properties, ♂ **ggp.com**
- Simon Malls, ♂ **simon.com**
- Specialty Retail Report, ♂ **specialtyretail.com**
- The Fixtures Group, ♂ **fixturesgroup.com/content.php?parent=kiosks**
- The Kiosk Expert, ♂ **kioskexpert.com**

Farmers' and Public Markets

Farmers' and public markets come in many shapes and sizes—open-air, under tents, inside buildings, summer only, weekends only, or seven days a week year-round. Public markets tend to be more formal and have more long-term merchants selling from upscale booths and kiosks. Farmers' markets tend to be more laid-back affairs, but also can be strict and limit themselves to vendors who sell food products. Others allow food-related items such as cookware, or even have a more open-door policy and allow vendors to sell just about anything.

Bestselling food products at both include seafood, baked goods, vegetables, fresh fruits, herbs and spices, organic foods and candies. Bestselling nonfood items include cookware, recipe and food books, clothing, flowers, crafts, antiques, gifts, costume jewelry and souvenir items.

RESOURCES
- Farmers' Market Online, ☞ **http://farmersmarket.com**
- The North American Farmers' Direct Marketing Association, ☎ (413) 529-0386, ☞ **nafdma.com**

Street Vending
Many cities offer street-vending opportunities, but obtaining a street vendor's permit/license can be difficult. City or municipal street vendor permits are usually issued and renewable yearly, or they can be issued in a lottery-type drawing and range in price from $25 to $1,000 or more annually. Contact your local city or municipal government to inquire about street-vending opportunities.

In addition to a vendor's permit, you may also have to obtain liability insurance, a health permit and a fire permit, depending on goods sold. It is not uncommon for people to disregard regulations and street-vend without a permit, but this is no way to build a long-term successful business and reliable revenue stream.

Popular products sold by street vendors include hot dogs and ice cream, T-shirts, sunglasses, costume jewelry, wristwatches, souvenirs, umbrellas, hats and flowers. Selling knock-off or counterfeit merchandise—such as fake designer purses or designer label clothing—or illegally pirated DVDs or CDs is against the law. Selling these types of products is not recommended and could lead to hefty fines or even criminal prosecution.

Before you decide what type of products to sell, do the rounds. What are other vendors selling? Who is the busiest? Which days are they busiest? Who are their customers? Duplicating a successful business model is one of the easiest ways to eliminate or substantially reduce financial risk.

Street vendors can work from portable kiosks and pushcarts or right from a suitcase, depending on what they sell. Depending on your budget, you can rent, lease or purchase new and used pushcarts and kiosks, which come in many styles and price points. Some can be towed behind vehicles or placed on a trailer for transport, some are motorized, and others are pedal-powered.

RESOURCES
- Carriage Works, ☎ (541) 882-9661, ♂ **carriageworks.com**
- Cart Owners' Association of America, ☎ (559) 332-2229, ♂ **cartowners.org**
- Kiosks & Carts, ♂ **http://kioskscarts.com**

Community Events

Local community events—such as parades, fairs, holiday celebrations, rodeos, music festivals and swap meets—provide a host of vendor opportunities to sell candy, clothing, gifts, helium-filled balloons, crafts, small flags, souvenirs, costume jewelry and a wide range of other products.

As a general rule, community events are organized by local associations, such as the chamber of commerce, charities, community social or sports clubs or churches, or by a department within local government. Start planning your participation in these events well in advance.

Trade Shows, Consumer Shows and Seminars

Trade and industry shows, consumer shows and seminars are all fantastic venues for buy-and-sell entrepreneurs. Most merchandising and selling techniques that work for flea market and craft show vending, for example, will also work at trade and consumer shows.

TRADE AND CONSUMER SHOWS

The only real difference between trade shows and consumer shows is that trade shows are generally businesses exhibiting for and selling to other businesses, while consumer shows are for the general public to attend, browse, gain information and shop.

For the buy-and-sell entrepreneur, few offline marketing venues can match the effectiveness of trade and consumer shows as a way to showcase and sell your products to a large audience at one time, in one place and in a cost-effective manner.

Over the course of one day to a few weeks, depending on the show, you can make personal contact with hundreds, if not thousands, of qualified prospects, affording you hundreds, if not thousands, of opportunities to sell your products.

These days there is a trade or consumer show for every type of product. There are home and garden shows, food shows, industry-specific shows, sports and recreation shows, car shows, antique and collectible shows, and many other types of specialized shows held throughout the country. In fact, there are in excess of 10,000 trade and consumer shows hosted annually in North America.

When selling at this type of event, your sales plan should revolve around four key elements: engage prospects, qualify prospects, present your products and close the sale. Rarely will your booth, exhibits or displays do the selling.

Resources
  – Trade Show Exhibitors Association, ☎ (312) 842-8732, ✆ **tsea.org**
  – Trade Show Exhibits Sales & Rentals, ✆ **trade-shows.org**
  – Trade Shows Online, ✆ **tradeshows.com**

Seminars

Seminars also provide a potentially lucrative selling opportunity. The best products to sell in the seminar or workshop environment include information in print or electronic format, such as how-to manuals, CDs and videos.

Product sales at seminars are often referred to as back-of-room sales, because tables displaying your merchandise are located at the back of the room near the entrance and exit. Before and after a seminar, guests must pass by your merchandise display.

Seminars and workshops do not have to be formal; they can be held in a banquet room, living room, supplier's warehouse or local restaurant. The specific place will depend on the audience, the objective of the event, and the topic or subject matter.

To learn about seminar opportunities in your area, look into adult education programs, locally held trade shows and The Learning Annex (**learningannex.com**). Of course, you can also coordinate, market and host your own seminars and present yourself as an expert in your field.

Selling Directly to Businesses

Selling your goods directly to businesses is another sales option, provided you have the right products such as office equipment, restaurant equipment, candy for vending, arts and crafts items for decorations, new books, and gift and promotional items.

The downside to B2B sales is that business owners are bombarded daily by people who want to sell them everything imaginable, and because of this, most become hardened to even the most professional sales pitches. This sales method is not suitable for people who are easily put off by rejection, because you will get lots of it. Know your product inside and out, especially user benefits; know what your prospects need, and know the reasons they should buy from you and not competitors.

One of the best ways to mingle with business owners and prospective customers is to join business and non-business clubs and associations, so you can network with members. This is a grassroots approach to building your business through personal contacts and word-of-mouth. Groups such as the Chamber of Commerce provide many valuable networking and business-building opportunities.

RESOURCES

- Canadian Chamber of Commerce, ☎ (416) 868-6415, ✆ **chamber.ca**
- United States Chamber of Commerce, ☎ (202) 659-6000, ✆ **uschamber.com**

Online Marketplaces

The innovative entrepreneur can take advantage of a nearly unlimited number of selling opportunities in a nearly unlimited number of online marketplaces. You can sell products on eBay, through electronic classified ads or by developing your own e-commerce website.

Selling online means you can reach consumers around the globe quickly, easily and at very modest costs. The internet enables you to specialize in selling your own niche products even when your local market cannot support it. In addition to the information featured here, additional information about taking your buy-and-sell enterprise online can be found in Chapter 3.

eBay

There are countless books, magazines, online tutorials and live seminars held throughout the country dedicated to helping people operate a successful online business enterprise using online auctions hosted by eBay. This has become an extremely popular worldwide marketplace where virtually anything and everything can be bought and sold.

In addition to a bit of creativity, all you need to get started is something to sell and a free eBay account, which you can set up in minutes online. To help you generate huge profits by selling online, eBay offers sellers numerous types of auctions to meet individual marketing needs.

These auction types include:

- Traditional Online Auctions
- Reserve Price Auctions
- Dutch Auctions
- Private Auctions
- Restricted Access Auctions

Traditional Auction. Still the most popular and common type of eBay online auction is the traditional or classic auction. In this type of auction there is no reserve price set, and at the end of the one-, three-, five-, seven-, or 10-day auction period, the highest bid wins. The advantage of a short auction is that it may enable you to generate more heat and bidding excitement than a longer auction, in which bidders can take their time to bid, which might eventually lead to diminished interest as time passes.

On the other side of the coin, a longer auction means your item will be exposed to more potential buyers and might fetch a higher price. Ultimately, you will have to play around with auction lengths a bit to find what works best for what you sell.

eBay also offers sellers a "Buy It Now" option, which simply means you can set a price for your item and a buyer can purchase the item for the set price without having to wait for the auction to end.

Every auction begins with the seller creating a listing for their product. A perfect listing includes:

1. Assigning the auction to the proper product category (there are literally thousands to choose from). Select what's most appropriate for what you're selling.
2. The title. Create a title that's attention-getting and catchy, and makes a strong statement. Use keywords and descriptive phrases.
3. Incorporate one or more full-color, professional-quality photographs of what you're selling. For example, show off your product from different angles or perspectives. Use the photos to showcase features, as well as the condition and/or authenticity of the product.
4. Create a detailed and informative description of your product. This should include details about its features and answer all of the potential questions a consumer might have about what you're selling.
5. Choose a price and auction format.
6. Select payment and shipping options.

To generate their own profits, eBay charges sellers a variety of different fees to host auctions. Listing fees vary and change periodically, so it's important to determine what these fees will be and build them into your cost of doing business.

- To learn more about eBay's current fees, visit **http://pages.ebay.com/help/sell/fees.html**.
- To help you learn how to best sell products on eBay, take advantage of the

site's online Learning Center tutorials, found at **http://pages.ebay.com/education/index.html**.

- To participate in live eBay University seminars, visit **http://pages.ebay.com/university/index.html**.
- To learn about the annual eBay Live! Trade show, where sellers from around the globe come to meet with eBay executives and learn about new products, services and selling techniques, visit **http://pages.ebay.com/ebaylive**.

eBay offers the following 10 tips for being an effective seller using its popular online auction service:

1. Maximize your products' appeal with low prices and no-reserve auctions.
2. Include reasonable shipping costs.
3. Accept online payments (such as major credit cards or PayPal).
4. Maximize your item title by including keywords and descriptive phrases.
5. Describe your products in detail.
6. Include one or more professional-quality, detailed photographs of your product.
7. Focus on customer service and generating the highest feedback scores possible from your customers. This includes offering a fair return policy and product warranty or guarantee.
8. Take advantage of inexpensive shipping options offered by the USPS, which offers free boxes and shipping labels for Priority and Overnight shipments (**usps.com**).
9. Establish yourself as an expert in what you're selling. This builds customer confidence.
10. Consider selling for a cause. Think about donating a portion of your profits to a charity.

Reserve-Price eBay Auctions. Sellers have the option to set a reserve price for the item on sale. A reserve price is the lowest possible price a seller is prepared to take for the item, but buyers do not know how much the reserve price is, only that there is a reserve.

Once a bid exceeds the reserve price, the item sells to the highest bidder. If the reserve price is not met before the auction expires, the item does not sell and the seller can choose to relist or not.

Often sellers like to set a reserve price that matches their cost price as a way to protect their investment and not sell for less than cost. Reserve prices can be set for all auctions discussed here, with the exception of Dutch auctions.

Reserve-Price Auction Sellers' Fees. Sellers using a reserve-price bid option pay the same fees as for a traditional auction, with two exceptions: (1) the insertion fee is based on the reserve price and (2) in addition to the insertion fee, you also pay a reserve-price auction fee, which is refundable if your item sells for the reserve bid or higher. If it does not sell, the reserve-auction price fee becomes part of the insertion fee and is nonrefundable.

Dutch Auction. A Dutch auction is a good choice when you have multiple units of the same product for sale, such as 50 pairs of identical sunglasses, or 200 identical wristwatches. There is no upper limit to how many items you can list using a Dutch auction—10 or 10,000, it's up to you.

Bidders also have the option of selecting how many of the items they want to purchase: one, some, or all. Sellers start by listing the number of items for sale, along with the starting bid. Bidders enter the amount they are willing to pay along with the number of units they want to purchase.

The winning price is determined by the lowest successful bid at the time the auction closes, and all winning bidders receive this price even if their bid was higher. The idea is that if you receive bids for more items than you have for sale, then the lowest bids drop off, raising the price. Bidders can rebid a higher amount to stay in the game if they choose. A Dutch auction is a great way to move large quantities of high-demand products quickly and efficiently.

Private Auction. A private auction protects the identity of the buyer by not listing any e-mail address in the bidding history screen. If and when the item is sold, only the seller knows the buyer's identity. You can use the private auction feature on any of the auctions listed here, with the exception of a Dutch auction.

Sellers may choose to use the private auction option when selling very valuable or controversial items, once again to protect potential buyers who may not wish to be identified.

Restricted-Access Auction. If you sell adult-themed products, your only selling option on eBay is through its restricted-access auction service. Be aware, however, that eBay offers restricted-access sellers limited promotional tools, and only visitors with credit cards and visitors who have agreed to the terms and conditions are granted entry into restricted-access auctions.

eBay Stores. For online sellers that do considerable business using eBay, the eBay Stores services are available to allow these sellers to create their own online storefronts and be able to host a large number of separate auctions at once more easily.

At present eBay offers three eBay Stores service tiers, ranging from the Basic to an Anchor Store. There are many benefits to having your own eBay store, including the opportunity to build repeat business with customers, longer-duration listings so you can spend more time selling and less time listing, your own web address, plus you receive a listing in the eBay Store directory (an internal in-store search engine enabling customers to conveniently browse through your products). There is a monthly fee, plus additional per-listing fees associated with operating an eBay Store.

According to eBay, sellers who have upgraded from selling through standard auction services to their own storefronts have realized a 25 percent increase in sales, on average, after a three-month period. To find out more and to get started, go to **http://pages.ebay.com/storefronts/start.html**.

eBay Stores is a totally different service than eBay ProStores, which enables online merchants to create their own e-commerce websites. ProStores does not use the online auction business model, however.

In addition to its regular site, eBay also offers spin-off services, such as eBay Motors (**motors.ebay.com**), where people can buy and sell new and used cars, trucks, boats, airplanes, scooters, motorcycles, recreational vehicles and trailers.

Your Own E-Commerce Website

As you learned in Chapter 3, one way countless buy-and-sell entrepreneurs have made fortunes is by establishing their own e-commerce websites to market and sell their products to a potentially worldwide audience. You can also develop, build and publish your own e-commerce website on the internet, so you can sell your goods 24 hours per day, every day, to anyone capable of using the internet.

If you opt to launch an e-commerce website, one of the fastest and least expensive ways to do this is by taking advantage of the services offered by a complete e-commerce turnkey solution provider, such as Yahoo! Stores, eBay ProStores, OSCommerce or GoDaddy.com. These services are described within Chapter 3. Additional services can be found online, using the search phrase "e-commerce turnkey solution."

Instead of having to create a website from scratch, which requires extensive programming knowledge—not to mention weeks or even months of your time— an e-commerce turnkey solution takes advantage of professionally designed website templates that can be fully customized in hours or days to properly market, showcase and sell your products online. Absolutely no programming knowledge is required, plus you can potentially get your website created and operational within a few days.

Resources

- *Click Starts: Design and Launch Your Own E-Commerce Website In One Week,* written by Jason R. Rich. Published by Entrepreneur Press.
- eBay ProStores, 💾 **prostores.com**
- GoDaddy, 💾 **godaddy.com**
- Network Solutions, 💾 **http://ecommerce.networksolutions.com/ shopping-cart-solutions.asp**
- OS Commerce, 💾 **oscommerce.com**
- Yahoo! Stores, 💾 **http://smallbusiness.yahoo.com/ecommerce**

Other Online Auction Opportunities

In addition to eBay, there are many other online auction sites. They are listed in online auction directories, such as The Internet Auction List. Some of these sites are general auction sites with numerous categories, ranging from collectibles to cars to electronics. Others are product-specific, concentrating on categories such as fine art, boats, antiques and sports memorabilia.

Without a doubt, however, the largest and most popular online auction site in the world is eBay. People selling very specific items, however, should be encouraged to explore alternate auction services because they attract targeted buyers.

Resources

- Auction Fire, 💾 **auctionfire.com**
- Bid 4 Assets, 💾 **bid4assets.com**
- Buy Sell Trades, 💾 **buyselltrades.com**
- Live Deal, 💾 **livedeal.com**
- Net Auctions, 💾 **net-auctions.com**
- On Sale, 💾 **onsale.com**
- The Internet Auction List, 💾 **internetauctionlist.com**

E-Classifieds

Advertising products for sale within online or electronic classifieds is the same as in print classifieds. Your goal should be to make your descriptive ads jump off the page (or computer screen) and grab readers' attention .

Just about every print newspaper now has an electronic edition with classified advertising opportunities. There are also a number of e-classified advertising opportunities that are available exclusively online. One of the biggest benefits of online classified advertising is you can include a link in your ad to direct readers to your website, eBay auction, or any other online location you want to send them to for further information or to buy.

Additional benefits are: e-classifieds are cheap, and sometimes free; your ad can be posted in minutes instead of days; ads can be changed, altered, or deleted in minutes; and you can reach consumers worldwide. Craigslist (**craigslist.org**) is one of the most popular city-specific e-classified websites on the Internet.

Here are a few tips for selling via e-classifieds:

- Pay a few dollars more to flag your ad with a bold border, animation or other attention-grabbing devices. This will help your ad stand out from others.
- Get creative with your headlines so you can catch the attention of skimmers.
- Advertise only in e-publications and classified-only sites frequented by your target audience.
- Use photographs whenever possible. They are invaluable.

RESOURCES
- Adpost,   **adpost.com**
- Buy and Sell,   **buysell.com**
- Classifieds for Free,   **classifiedsforfree.com**
- Craigslist,   **craigslist.org**
- My Town Ads,   **mytownads.com**
- The Recycler,   **recycler.com**
- Sell.com Classifieds,   **sell.com**
- Thrifty Nickel,   **thriftynickleads.com**
- U.S. Free Ads,   **usfreeads.com**

Homebased Sales

All across North America, signs are popping up in front of homes. But they are not house-for-sale or foreclosure signs. In fact, they are signs advertising homebased businesses and the products and/or services these homebased entrepreneurs sell.

Almost all buy-and-sell ventures are operated or managed from a home office. This section, however, focuses on actually selling goods directly from your home by utilizing interior showrooms, exterior displays, garage sales and in-home sales parties. One of the advantages of selling goods from home is that you can combine this method of distribution with many others, such as online sales, flea markets, auctions and vending at community events.

There are a great number of other advantages of selling from home, including the fact that you'll have no commute to work, plus there are significant tax advantages. Of course, one potential downside is that strangers will be invited into parts of your home, so you'll probably want to keep your living areas separate from your work areas.

Not every home is suited for retail sales. Many communities, apartment buildings and housing complexes (including gated communities) do not allow homebased businesses that involve customers visiting the premises. But for entrepreneurs who have suitable homes and products, operating a homebased businesses can have the potential to generate enormous revenues and profits, without the huge cost associated with operating a traditional retail store in a shopping center, within a mall or along Main Street, for example.

Homebased Showrooms and Exterior Displays

There are two basic methods to display and sell merchandise from home: an interior showroom or an exterior display. Depending on what you sell, you might choose to utilize both.

INTERIOR SHOWROOM

You can convert your garage, basement, den or just about any room of your home into a well-stocked showroom. Ideally, the space you choose should have a separate entrance to afford privacy for your family.

Display and merchandise your products just as you would within a traditional retail store by taking advantage of display cases, racks, lighting, mirrors and signage. There are many types of products that can be successfully sold from a homebased retail business. Just a few types of products that could work well include: clothing, arts and crafts, jewelry, antiques, sporting goods, cookware and computers.

The trick to operating a successful homebased retail business is to have pre-set hours of operation that will appeal to your target customer. This might include having extended hours on evenings and weekends.

EXTERIOR DISPLAY

Displaying products for sale outside of your home is the second option. Depending on where you live, you could receive a fair amount of interest from passing motorists and pedestrians.

Perfect products to display outdoors include cars, small boats on trailers, RVs, patio furniture, greenhouses, plants, sheds and weathervanes. Theft could become an issue, so be sure to install motion lights, fencing, a security system and gates as required.

Information about setting up a homebased work space and additional homebased business issues can be found in Chapter 3.

PROMOTING HOMEBASED SALES

If you are going to sell from home, consumers have to know what you sell, where you are located, and how they can contact you. Consequently, you will need to advertise. For budget-minded entrepreneurs, the best and least expensive ways to promote homebased sales are with attention-grabbing signage, classified advertisements, fliers and word-of-mouth. Detailed information about these and other sales and marketing topics can be found in Chapter 3.

In addition to using public relations efforts, for example, consider promoting your business and goods utilizing cheap and free classified advertisements. People seldom search the classifieds for entertainment purposes; they are usually looking to buy, which make these ads the buy-and-sell entrepreneur's best friend. Your ads should include a product description, contact information, a price and an attention-grabbing device such as a border.

Fliers and brochures are the ultimate fast and frugal promotional tool for advertising a homebased business (as well as the products you're selling). Pin fliers to community bulletin boards, tuck them under parked cars' windshield wipers, or have them delivered door-to-door.

Finally, word-of-mouth advertising is the ultimate cheap source of highly effective advertising—it costs nothing. To obtain this type of free advertising, you must provide top-notch customer service and treat all of your customers like they are royalty. Also, get out in your community and network with people so you can tell them about your products.

GARAGE SALES

More than 60 million people go garage sale shopping annually in the United States. If you plan on hosting garage sales from home, the first step is to make sure you can do so legally. Most communities permit garage sales, but some don't. Sometimes there are no regulations governing garage sales. In some communities, you must purchase a permit.

If garage sales are not permitted where you live, or if your home is not suitable for hosting garage or yard sales, you can still participate by renting space at larger community sales. Charities, schools, churches and sports clubs all routinely hold sales to raise revenues for any number of reasons, and most happily accept vendors willing to pay a small rent or a portion of their sales to the cause.

Another option is to partner with a friend or family member who does have a suitable location and share the work and profits. Saturday is the number one day to host a garage sale. Fridays and Sundays are also ideal days to host this type of event.

Before deciding to host a garage sale, it's important that you offer items that you know will sell well and that will be in demand by shoppers. Popular garage sale items include power tools, hand tools, toys, sporting goods, kitchen items, glassware, things for babies, lawn and garden equipment, crafts and decorations, collectibles, books, music CDs, movie DVDs, kids' clothing and adult designer clothes.

Once you're ready to host your own garage sale, event promotion is crucial to success, so have signs professionally made in the shape of an arrow pointing in the direction of your home. The signs should display the phrase "Garage Sale Today" and have your address printed on them in large, easy-to-read lettering.

On the morning of the sale, attach balloons and streamers to your signs to make them stand out. Install the signs in a two-block radius around your home, as well as around major intersections close to your home. Be sure to remove them immediately following the sale, however.

Many newspapers will publish free garage sale ads, so take advantage of these opportunities by contacting your local newspaper advertising office. Also, print fliers promoting the event and post them on community bulletin boards at supermarkets, gas stations, sports arenas and libraries.

The following are additional tips for hosting a successful garage sale:

- Have one central checkout table that's well stocked with tools that will speed purchase transactions and streamline your entire operation. These tools should include a calculator, a receipt book for customers, and packaging materials such as string, rope, scissors, tape, boxes, newspapers and plastic bags.

- Garage sales can attract hundreds of shoppers during the course of a day, so give some thought to traffic flow and congestion. You want enough space so people do not feel crowded and leave without making a purchase. Think wide aisles. Display large items on the ground. Smaller items can be displayed higher up on tables. Use two long lines of tables, or a grid pattern of tables, to keep traffic flowing.

- Garage sales also attract lots of drive-by shoppers who slow down to see what you have. These people will stop only if they see something of interest. Therefore, it is a good idea to display some of your best merchandise nearest to the road.

- Hold back some of the better merchandise to put out as the day goes on. This way you will always have stuff that will appeal to people coming late, so they will stay longer and browse and, with luck, impulse buy.

- Whenever possible, try to sell items with their original packaging, manuals and accessories, such as a remote control with the television. Doing so greatly increases the value and makes the item much easier to sell.

- To prevent theft, always keep more expensive items grouped together so they are easier to watch. Likewise, look inside items to make sure smaller items have not been hidden there. This is a favorite trick of thieves.

- Never hold items for people who say they will be back to pick it up later unless you get a 50 percent deposit upfront. Most don't return, especially if they have not paid a deposit.

- Don't hold your sale on a holiday weekend, because there are generally too many other events going on that will keep shoppers away. But if you live in a resort or vacation area, holiday weekends are the best times to hold your sale.

- To avoid sounding like a parrot and repeating prices all day long, price all items individually, unless you have many of the same. In this case, create one sign—for example, "All video games $10 each" or "All DVDs $5 each."

- Clean and press clothing before displaying and hang it on hangers. (Make up a sign advising that hangers are not included.) Also, check pockets to make sure nothing is inside.

- When pricing, anticipate that people will want to haggle, so initially price your items 10 to 30 percent higher to give yourself room to negotiate.

- Don't accept checks, even with ID. Work on a cash-only basis and keep your money in a fanny pack or your pocket. Put large bills inside your home, within a safe or locked cashbox, for example. Only keep enough money on hand to make change for people.

- Have an "ALL SALES FINAL" sign posted at your checkout table and printed on your receipts. You do not want people showing up at your door a day, week or month later, trying to return something.

RESOURCES

- Craigslist, ♂ **craigslist.org**
- Garage Sale Daily, ♂ **garagesaledaily.com**
- Garage Sale Planet, ♂ **garagesaleplanet.com**
- Yard Sale Search, ♂ **yardsalesearch.com**

Things You Can Buy and Sell for Big Profits

In-Home Sales Parties

Home sales parties are an excellent selling option for the right products, such as cosmetics, lingerie, health care items, Tupperware and jewelry. In a nutshell, you hire contract salespeople to organize and host parties right in their own homes to sell your products. Or you host your own in-home parties to sell your products.

Salespeople can be paid a commission based on total sales, or they can buy products wholesale and resell at retail, allowing them to keep the profits.

The biggest advantage of home party sales is zero competition. Salespeople have the undivided attention of party guests. In a few hours, sales agents can earn hundreds in profits. This can be the perfect opportunity for stay-at-home parents, students, retired folks, and anyone else looking to make extra money working from their home.

Many multi-level marketing opportunities encourage people to host this type of party in order to generate sales while expanding their sales network. Be extremely careful before getting involved with any type of multi-level marketing business opportunity or pyramid scheme. Often, these are scams or illegitimate business opportunities.

Once you pick what products to sell using this method, you will need product samples, sales brochures and other sales tools. The following are some tips for generating higher profits while hosting a sales party:

- Design and print gift certificates and distribute one to each guest attending, but mark them void if not used that night. Many people feel compelled to buy rather than risk losing a freebie. Keep the amount of the certificate to $10.00 or $20.00, depending on what you're selling and your profit margin.
- Offer additional savings at various purchase levels. For example, buy $50 worth of product and receive a $5 credit; $100 receives a $10 credit; and $200 receives a $30 credit toward the purchase of more products.
- Display your entire product line—not just a few items—and offer guests multiple ways to pay: check, cash, credit card or debit card. Accepting credit cards will increase impulse buying.
- Tell each guest that if they bring a friend, both will receive a predetermined percent discount on all purchases.
- Offer free gift-wrapping at the party so people will feel compelled to purchase products as gifts for others not in attendance.
- Hold a contest and give away a prize at each party. Have guests complete an entry form, including full contact information, and draw for the prize. The entry forms may then be used to build a database of potential cus-

tomers, who can be routinely contacted with special offers via e-mail, mail and telephone.

RESOURCES
- Amway, ☎ **amway.com**
- Avon Cosmetics, ☎ **avoncompany.com/about/selling.html**
- Home & Garden Party, ☎ **kimlipe.com**
- Home Party Plan Network, ☎ **homepartyplannetwork.com**
- Mary Kay Cosmetics, ☎ **marykay.com**
- My Mommy Biz, ☎ **mymommybiz.com/party/partyplans.html**
- Party Plan Moms, ☎ **partyplanmoms.com**
- Silver Success, ☎ **silversuccess.com**
- The Ultimate Girl's Night In, ☎ **yourpassionconsultant.com/consultants/ purelypassionate/hostess.html**
- Tupperware, ☎ **http://order.tupperware.com/coe/app/tup_opportunity. opportunity**

Selling Direct to Collectors

If you are going to specialize in antiques or collectibles, you can sell directly to collectors by exhibiting at collectible shows and sales, joining associations and clubs to network at, or consigning items to live and online antique and collectible auctions.

More often than not, however, selling directly to collectors will garner the highest price. Collectors are a fickle bunch. What's hot today is not necessarily hot and valuable tomorrow. Antique furniture seems to be the most stable in terms of value and gradual appreciation, however.

There are many factors involved with determining how much you can sell antiques and collectibles for, including condition, rarity, special history (famous owners, etc.), and what the marketplace will bear.

Selling antiques and collectibles is as much about choosing the right sales venues and target audience as it is about the actual item—perhaps more so. Success comes to antique and collectible traders who pay close attention to what's going on in the marketplace at all times. Professional appraisals and authentications also help to substantiate and support asking prices. In many situations, having antique, collectible and memorabilia items appraised and authenticated in advance will greatly increase the value.

RESOURCES
- About.com Collectibles, ➸ **http://collectibles.about.com/ od/priceguidesonline/ tp/priceguideindex.htm**
- At Oncer, ➸ **atoncer.com**
- AuctionPal, ➸ **auctionpal.com**
- Collector Online, ➸ **collectoronline.com**
- Online Collectibles, ➸ **onlinecollectibles.com**
- Selling Request, ➸ **sellingrequest.com/eBaySellingService.html**
- The Online Auction Company, ➸ **theonlineauctioncompany.com**
- World Collectors, ➸ **worldcollectorsnet.com**

Up Next: 202 Awesome Product Ideas That You Can Sell

Now that you know all about how to buy and sell products, the next biggest piece of your success equation is to come up with the very best products for you to sell. That's the focus of the next chapter. In fact, Chapter 6 offers 202 different product and product category ideas to help you get started.

THE MEGA-LIST: 202 THINGS YOU CAN BUY AND SELL FOR BIG PROFITS

Thus far, you have learned about business structure and registration, the legal and financial issues facing the buy-and-sell entrepreneur, how and where to buy new and used products at low prices, and how and where to resell products for profit.

In this chapter, you will discover more than 202 products that you can start buying and selling almost immediately. Actually, both this book and this chapter title are a bit misleading. There are many more than 202 product ideas featured herein. Some products have been grouped together by category, under a single heading, such as antiques. Within some of the product categories listed, you can choose a specialty and narrow down what you'll buy and sell to one or more very specific niche products.

The criteria used to select the best things to buy and sell were based on a number of factors, including:

- Products that are widely available
- Products that are in demand and that have long-term appeal
- Products currently selling well on eBay, at flea markets and through other sales venues
- Products with excellent profit potential

As you already know from previous chapters, in addition to knowing the best things to buy and sell, you also have to know what *you* personally might be best suited to buy and sell.

What Should You Buy and Sell?

Not every person has the resources or knowledge needed to buy and sell all of the different products listed within this book. Some people are better equipped and better suited than others to buy and sell specific items or categories of products.

For example, if you have no interest or knowledge whatsoever about outdoor power equipment, do not try to start a buy-and-sell enterprise specializing in these products.

As you read this chapter and begin to learn about just a few hundred of the many different types of products you could potentially sell, you'll quickly discover at least several products that are best suited to your interests, skills, experience and available resources.

Ultimately, you will be the best judge of what things you are best suited to buy and sell. To help you make this important decision, there are six key issues to consider: knowledge, investment, location, resources, experience and interest. Let's take a closer look at these issues.

1. *Knowledge.* Knowledge is one of your biggest and most marketable assets in a buy-and-sell venture. The more you know about the product, industry, and people who are most likely to buy, the better off you will be. Capitalize on your knowledge by selling products you know about to a target audience you truly know and understand.

2. *Investment.* You need to have—or have access to—enough investment capi-

tal to get your buy-and-sell enterprise rolling and profitable. Some products described in this book are inexpensive to buy and market. Other products, such as cars, consumer electronics and jewelry, will require you to have access to a substantial amount of startup capital.

3. *Location.* Unless you'll be selling entirely online, where you live will have a bearing on the type of products you sell. Obviously, if you live in Florida, buying and selling snowmobiles would not be a wise choice. Your home or apartment will also be a factor, especially if you plan to sell from a home-based showroom or need considerable storage space.

4. *Experience and Skills.* Your life experiences, professional experiences and education all make up your personal and unique skill set. The skills and experience you already have will benefit you if you take full advantage of them as you launch your buy-and-sell enterprise. Your personal skills and experience may already make you an expert about a specific product or product category. Or your experience may provide you with the know-how to successfully operate, market and promote your business and sell your products without having to invest the time needed to learn any new skills or acquire new expertise.

5. *Interest.* The biggest key to success when choosing a product to sell will be whether or not you have or can quickly develop a true passion for that product or product category. It is tough to stay motivated when you do not like what you are doing, regardless of profit potential. Only buy and sell items that you have an interest in. Start by considering your hobbies. For example, if you're an avid fisherman or golfer, consider buying and selling fishing gear or golf-related products. If you have a passion for fashion, consider buying and selling clothing. If throughout your life you have collected baseball cards, consider starting a business that buys and sells collectible trading cards or sports memorabilia. When it comes to choosing a product to sell, carefully examine the profit potential, but just as importantly, be sure to follow your heart!

How to Use the Information in This Chapter

For each product or product category described within this book (yes, there are 202 of them), there is an explanation of the product. You'll also find a handful of helpful resources, such as wholesaling sources, associations and price guides, to help you get started buying and selling that particular product.

Keep in mind, none of the resources presented in this chapter are meant to promote or endorse any specific company, association, product or service. All resources are included to provide you with helpful tools. Should you decide to pursue any of these products to buy and sell, you may elect to contact and even do business with some of the sources listed, or you may choose to find your own resources and wholesale sources. You will definitely need to invest the time and effort to conduct additional research about the products you ultimately decide to buy and sell.

Ultimately, you must be 100 percent comfortable doing business with reliable and honest sources. The only way this can be accomplished is through conducting your own extensive research. Don't take any shortcuts! Learn everything you can about any company or organization you intend to do business with.

The List: 202 Products You Can Buy and Sell

Okay, it's time to put on your thinking cap and begin learning about the many individual products and product categories you can start buying and selling. This book's listings are provided in alphabetical order, starting with "allergy protection products" and ending with "wine."

Through additional research, you can easily determine what specific items are selling well on eBay. To read eBay's free 40-page Hot Categories Report, visit **http://pages.eBay.com/sellercentral/hotitems.pdf**. To obtain specialized and customized research reports for particular products or product categories offered on eBay, you can pay a small fee to access eBay's Marketplace Research (**http://pages.eBay.com/marketplace_research/index.html**). Whether or not you opt to buy and sell using eBay, this research will give you additional insight into the types of products people are buying and how much money they're spending on them.

The Mega-List of Products

The rest of this is chock full of information about specific products and product categories you could potentially take advantage of in order to launch your buy-and-sell enterprise. The products listed herein are only meant to be a sampling of the millions of products potentially available to you. So use the information in this book as a launching pad for your brainstorming sessions as you develop ideas for what you personally would be interested in buying and selling in order to generate a profit. Remember, the more creative you are, the better your chances of success!

Allergy Reduction Products

According to the Asthma and Allergy Foundation of America, "Allergies are diseases of the immune system that cause an overreaction to substances called allergens. Allergies are grouped by the kind of trigger, time of year, or where symptoms appear on the body: indoor and outdoor allergies (also called "hay fever," "seasonal," "perennial" or "nasal" allergies), food and drug allergies, latex allergies, insect allergies, skin allergies and eye allergies."

When it comes to Americans who suffer from allergies—to allergens such as pollen, ragweed or pet dander, for example—the numbers are truly staggering. For the buy-and-sell entrepreneur who understands the needs of these sufferers, there are profits to be made selling allergy reduction products, such as air filters, specialized bedding, chemical-free cleaning products and a wide range of other products. Sellers should seek out only new and quality products that are proven to somehow help sufferers reduce or control allergy symptoms.

BUY
Wholesalers, Distributors

SELL
E-Commerce, Flea Markets, or any other sales method

RESOURCES
—Allergy Control Products, *✆* allergycontrol.com
—Allergy Guard Direct, *✆* allergyguarddirect.com
— Asthma and Allergy Foundation of America, *✆* aafa.org
— Health Solutions, *✆* pharmacy-solutions.com
— National Allergy Supply, *✆* natlallergy.com
— Wonder Laboratories, *✆* wonderlabs.com

Antiques

The potential to profit from buying and selling antiques is as great as the potential to lose money. Replicas, paying too much and purchasing items in poor condition are just three of the hazards you need to hone your knowledge and skills to guard against if you choose to buy and sell antiques.

However, those who do take the time required to become antique experts can be rewarded with big profits and gratifying work. "Antiques" is a broad category, so pick an area in which to specialize, such as furniture, art, lamps, jewelry, dolls, lamps or architectural antiques.

The best places to dig up antique treasures include garage sales, auctions, estate sales and advertisements placed by private sellers. Secondary buying sources include flea markets, secondhand shops and online marketplaces. The best way to sell for top dollar is directly to collectors via clubs, associations and shows. Next to selling to collectors, selling on eBay is another popular option.

Buy
Auctions, Flea Markets, Garage Sales, Estate Sales, Classified Ads

Sell
Collectors, B2B, Auctions, Homebased Sales, eBay, Flea Markets

Resources
—Antique and Collectibles Dealers Association, *ℰ* antiqueandcollectible.com/acda.shtml
—Antiques Roadshow Online, *ℰ* pbs.org/roadshow
—Go Antiques, *ℰ* goantiques.com
—Kovels Online, *ℰ* kovels.com

Aquariums and Tropical Fish

Selling aquariums, accessories and tropical fish right from home is definitely a viable business opportunity. Sell glass and acrylic tanks, freshwater and saltwater tropical fish, and fish accessories such as stands, canopies, filters, foods, lights, aquatic plants, skimmers, ornaments and cleaning supplies.

All of these items can be purchased at deeply discounted prices from manufacturers, wholesalers and tropical fish farms. Beware that there are laws and regulations that you must comply with for importing and exporting tropical fish, so research will be required if you are planning these activities.

Additional sales venues include an e-commerce website, pet shows and even direct to businesses.

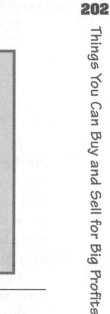

> **BUY**
> Manufacturers, Wholesalers, Breeders
>
> **SELL**
> Online Marketplaces, Homebased Sales, Pet Shows, Flea Markets
>
> **RESOURCES**
> —Acrylic Tank Manufacturing, ☎ (702) 387-2016, ✆ acrylicaquariums.com
> —Florida Tropical Fish Farms Association, ✆ ftffa.com
> —Pet Edge, ☎ (800) 698-9062, ✆ petedge.com
> —Tropical Fish Find, ✆ tropicalfishfind.com/Importers.asp

Arcade Games

If you want to combine fun and profit, consider buying and selling new and used coin-op arcade games. It is not uncommon for vintage pinball machines to fetch a few thousand dollars each, while *Pac-Man*, *Space Invaders* or *Frogger* arcade games can sell for $1,500 or more.

New machines can be purchased through wholesalers and distributors, while used arcade games can be purchased at auctions, through classified ads and through various online marketplaces. Sell directly to business owners, especially coin-operated machines, which can earn them money.

Homeowners also love coin-op arcade games for their recreation rooms, and professionals often add them to their offices as nifty decorations or conversation pieces, or to play the occasional quick game as an escape from work. Invest in arcade game price guides to help value machines for purchase and resale.

> **BUY**
> Online Marketplaces, Auctions, Classified Ads, Wholesalers
>
> **SELL**
> Online Marketplaces, Collectors, Homebased Sales, Collectible Shows, B2B
>
> **RESOURCES**
> —Backyard Entertainment, ✆ backyardent.com/games4sale.html
> —BMI Gaming Wholesale, ☎ (561) 391-7269, ✆ bmigaming.com

—Game Room Antiques, ♂ gameroomantiques.com
—Yahoo! Wholesaler Directory, ♂ http://dir.yahoo.com/Business_and_
Economy/Shopping_and_Services/Games/Arcade

Archery Equipment

Online and from home are the two best ways to sell archery equipment and supplies, especially if you have enough outdoor space to safely and legally establish a test range. A converted garage—stocked with bows, arrows, cases, replacement parts and accessories such as bow stands, targets, chest guards, finger tabs, shooting gloves and instructional videos—will work well as a showroom.

Most retailers of archery equipment do not limit their potential audience and carry many types of bows, such as traditional, cross, compound and recurved. You would be well advised to do the same. Though you should concentrate on selling new equipment, you can also profit on buying and reselling used equipment, especially if you take in inventory on trade or consignment. Factory direct and wholesalers will be your two primary buying sources of new products. In addition to homebased and online sales, you can also exhibit products at sports, recreation and hunting shows.

BUY
Wholesalers, Manufacturers, Classified Ads

SELL
Homebased Sales, Online Marketplaces, Sports and Recreation Shows

RESOURCES
—Archery Direct, ♂ archerywholesalesources.com
—Jake's Archery Wholesale, ☎ (801) 225-0509, ♂ jakesarchery.com
—Lancaster Archery Supply, ☎ (800) 829-7408, ♂ http://lancasterarchery
.com/shop
—Pacific Bow Butts, ♂ pacificbowbutts.com/wholesale_archery_
targets.htm

Arts and Crafts Supplies

In North America alone, there are millions of people engaged in some sort of art or craft as a hobby, such as painting, needlepoint, knitting, drawing, costume jewelry making and folk art, just to name a few. All of these people have one thing in common—they need supplies in order to participate in their hobby.

Where there is demand, the clever entrepreneur will make sure there is also the supply to fill it. As a buy-and-sell entrepreneur, you can purchase arts and crafts supplies from wholesalers and manufacturers at deeply discounted prices, and resell them online, from a homebased showroom or at craft shows or flea markets.

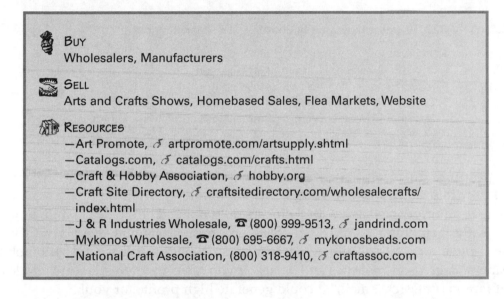

BUY
Wholesalers, Manufacturers

SELL
Arts and Crafts Shows, Homebased Sales, Flea Markets, Website

RESOURCES
—Art Promote, artpromote.com/artsupply.shtml
—Catalogs.com, catalogs.com/crafts.html
—Craft & Hobby Association, hobby.org
—Craft Site Directory, craftsitedirectory.com/wholesalecrafts/
  index.html
—J & R Industries Wholesale, ☎ (800) 999-9513, jandrind.com
—Mykonos Wholesale, ☎ (800) 695-6667, mykonosbeads.com
—National Craft Association, (800) 318-9410, craftassoc.com

Automated Teller Machines (ATMs)

The deregulation of ATMs (automated teller machines) allows any entrepreneur to purchase one or more ATMs, place them at their locations of choice, and operate them as an ongoing revenue-generating business.

Since deregulation, thousands of ATMs have been sold, and a secondary market is now emerging. While a lucrative income can be earned by purchasing secondhand ATMs low and reselling them at a profit, another business model involves purchasing secondhand ATMs and locating them in busy places where they can earn ongoing revenues. Good placement locations include taverns, nightclubs, convenience stores, grocery markets and other buildings with high foot traffic.

Typically, the owner of the building or operator of the business where an ATM is located will split the revenues the machine earns with the ATM owner. The revenue split can range from 50-50 to 90-10 in the favor of the ATM owner, depending on the agreement and how much revenue the machine generates. Be prepared to invest the necessary time, however, in maintaining the machines and keeping them stocked with cash and receipt paper, for example.

Buy
Classified Ads, Auctions, Wholesalers

Sell
B2B, Business Opportunity Shows, Online Marketplaces

Resources
—ATM Marketplace, *⌂* atmmarketplace.com
—ATM Wholesaler, *⌂* atmwholesaler.com
—Cord Financial Services, *⌂* cordfinancial.com
—National ATM Wholesale, *⌂* atmmachines.com/atmmain.htm

Automobile Cleaning Products

The love affair people have with their cars does not end at the dealership. In fact, this is the beginning point. From there, car enthusiasts and everyday drivers spend huge amounts of money on custom auto parts, stereos, and automobile cleaners, degreasers, polishes and waxes. If you have an interest in cars and love that famous "new car smell," it could generate high profits for you!

Automobile cleaning products and equipment are big business, and cashing in on this worldwide demand is easy. Buy your products at rock-bottom prices from wholesalers, distributors and manufacturers, and then resell those products for top dollar at auto shows, on eBay (and eBay Motors), at swap meets and flea markets, online via an e-commerce website, and through mail order. When selling these products live, make sure you demonstrate how well they work. When people can see the benefits of a cleaning product firsthand, resistance to the sale becomes almost nonexistent.

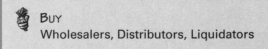

Buy
Wholesalers, Distributors, Liquidators

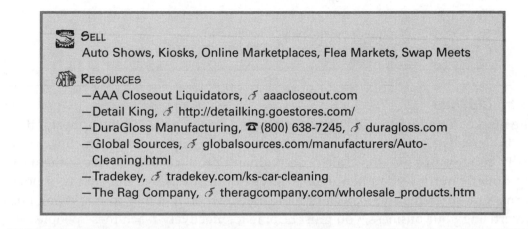

🤝 **SELL**
Auto Shows, Kiosks, Online Marketplaces, Flea Markets, Swap Meets

🏚 **RESOURCES**
—AAA Closeout Liquidators, ♂ aaacloseout.com
—Detail King, ♂ http://detailking.goestores.com/
—DuraGloss Manufacturing, ☎ (800) 638-7245, ♂ duragloss.com
—Global Sources, ♂ globalsources.com/manufacturers/Auto-
Cleaning.html
—Tradekey, ♂ tradekey.com/ks-car-cleaning
—The Rag Company, ♂ theragcompany.com/wholesale_products.htm

Automotive Electronics

North American consumers spend several billion dollars every year on automotive electronics, such as stereo systems, alarms, DVD players and GPS devices. This has become one of the fastest growing segments of the automotive industry.

Start purchasing new, brand-name automotive electronics from reputable wholesalers, distributors and liquidators. Avoid dealing in used merchandise, since there's not too much profit to be made there, plus the chances of coming across stolen goods are very high.

Sell your goods at auto shows and swap meets, on eBay, during community events from a vendor booth, via an e-commerce website and at flea markets. When shopping around for products to sell, focus on profit potential. This is a highly competitive marketplace. In addition to having other buy-and-sell entrepreneurs as competitors, you also have car dealerships, full-service garages and consumer electronics stores such as Radio Shack, Best Buy and Circuit City.

🐚 **BUY**
Wholesalers, Distributors, Liquidators

🤝 **SELL**
Auto Shows, Kiosks, Online Marketplaces, Flea Markets, Swap Meets

🏚 **RESOURCES**
—Car Audio Distributors, ♂ caraudiodistributors.com
—ChinaTronic, ♂ chinatronic.com
—Global Sources, ♂ globalsources.com

> —Online Wholesaler, ♂ online-wholesaler.com
> —Sylvester Electronics Wholesale, ☎ (800) 388-7344, ♂ sylves.com

Baby Clothes

The market for new and used baby clothing is a steady one, and the opportunities for the creative entrepreneur are extremely viable, especially if you develop a really good source for wholesale or secondhand products and can resell them for top dollar. Your target audience for this type of business will be parents of newborns, grandparents and expectant mothers, so when it comes to marketing and advertising your business, you must be able to effectively reach these people.

If you opt to sell used baby clothing, it's your responsibility to have these garments professionally cleaned prior to reselling them. If you're looking to resell new garments, look into buying closeouts and products being sold through liquidators.

BUY
Wholesalers, Distributors, Thrift Shops, Secondhand Stores, Online, Flea Markets

SELL
Online Marketplaces, Flea Markets, Swap Meets

RESOURCES
—Children's Wholesale, ♂ childrenswholesale.com
—Kids Wholesale Wearhouse,   ♂ kidswholesalewearhouse. builderspot.com
—Kids Blanks, ♂ kidsblanks.com
—Sckoon, ♂ sckoon.com
—Wholesale Kid, ♂ wholesalekid.com

Baby Gifts

Soon-to-be parents often have baby showers, which means all of their friends and relatives buy them baby-oriented gifts. This happens again when a new baby is born, and for its first few birthdays. Thus the market for baby gifts and gear—such as toys, blankets, rattles, strollers, car carriers, etc.—is tremendous.

To differentiate your business, consider focusing on one or two types of upscale or customized baby gifts, and learn how to market your business specifically to your target audience. For the creative buy-and-sell entrepreneur, there is a lot of potential when dealing with this vast product category.

BUY
Wholesalers, Distributors, Crafters, Online, Flea Markets

SELL
Online Marketplaces, Flea Markets, Swap Meets, Homebased Showroom, Parties

RESOURCES
—Baby Aspen, ✍ babyaspen.com
—Kids Blanks, ✍ kidsblanks.com
—Princess H Designs, ✍ princesshdesigns.com
—Sckoon, ✍ sckoon.com
—The Cashmere Bunny, ✍ babygiftbasketco.com
—Wholesale Central, ✍ wholesalecentral.com/Baby_Products.html
—Wholesale Kid, ✍ wholesalekid.com

Baby Items

The list of potential new and used baby items you can buy and sell is extremely long. It includes cribs, strollers, car seats, swings and rockers, changing tables, high chairs, audio and video monitoring systems, bumper jumpers, bath and crib mobiles, hampers, bedding and bassinets. New parents and grandparents will be your primary customer base.

New items can be purchased at deeply discounted prices directly from manufacturers and wholesalers, while used equipment can generally be found in good condition at garage sales and via private seller advertisements. New or used, establish a homebased showroom for sales and sell online as well as at flea markets and by spreading the word through local day-care centers, parent-to-be groups and birthing classes.

BUY
Manufacturers, Wholesalers, Garage Sales, Classified Ads, Liquidators

---

SELL
Online, eBay, Mall Kiosks, Flea Markets, Homebased Sales, Parenting Groups and Classes

RESOURCES
—1 AAA Wholesale Liquidators, ☎ (800) 661-9430, ✄ 1aaawholesaleliquidators.com
—Dollar Days Wholesale, ☎ (877) 837-9569, ✄ dollardays.com
—Empire Discount Wholesale, ☎ (914) 684-1455, ✄ empirediscount.net
—Kids Blanks, ✄ kidsblanks.com
—Wholesale Central, ✄ wholesalecentral.com/Baby_Products.html

Balloons

If you are searching for a low-investment business opportunity that has high profit potential, then look no further than balloon vending. There are three ways to buy balloons wholesale. First, you can sell advertising balloons to local businesses and salespeople to promote a sale or special event. These balloons are printed with your customer's business name, logo and sales message. Potential customers include car dealers, restaurateurs, retailers, schoolteachers, politicians and home sellers. Many balloon wholesalers offer printing services.

Another business model involves purchasing latex or foil balloons with preprinted messages, such as "Happy Birthday" or "Get Well Soon," and reselling them at kiosks, community events and flea markets. You could also offer delivery service within your local area or region.

A third business opportunity related to balloons involves purchasing balloons and related products, such as ribbon and confetti, and then providing a balloon decoration service for weddings, parties and special events. If you choose this route, you will need to invest in a helium tank and a few additional pieces of equipment. To market this venture, build alliances with wedding, event and party planners, as well as with banquet-hall owners and restaurateurs.

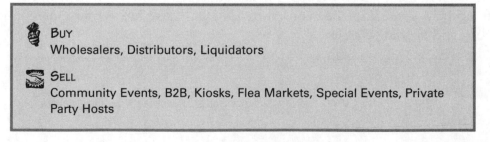

BUY
Wholesalers, Distributors, Liquidators

SELL
Community Events, B2B, Kiosks, Flea Markets, Special Events, Private Party Hosts

RESOURCES
—Balloons Wholesale, ☎ (800) 239-2000, ✄ balloons.com
—B&C Balloons Wholesale, ☎ (888) 629-8545, ✄ bcballoons.net
—Wholesale Balloons, ☎ (919) 676-5998, ✄ wholesaleballoons.com

Baseball and Trading Card Collectibles

Trading card collectibles are a huge business, especially on the secondary market among collectors. To succeed in this business, not only do you need to understand the sport (baseball, etc.) that the trading cards relate to, you also need to understand the intricacies of this collector's market, including how specific cards are priced and their demand. Collector's shows, magazines and websites, as well as flea markets, offer great buy and sell opportunities. Be sure to pick up several different pricing guides and stay on top of current trends.

BUY
Wholesalers, Collectors, Flea Markets, Trading Card Stores, Online

SELL
Community Events, Kiosks, Flea Markets, Collector's Events, Mail Order, Online

RESOURCES
—About.com, ✄ http://sportscards.about.com/od/sportscardglossary/Sports_Card_Glossary.htm
—BCW Supplies, ✄ bcwsupplies.com
—Beckett Publications, ✄ beckett.com
—Cards Network, ✄ cardsnetwork.com
—DSC Sports Cards, ✄ dcssportscards.com
—Homerun Cards, ✄ homeruncards.com/cardlinks.htm

Bath Products

Bath product gift baskets and gift sets are very popular. For entrepreneurs looking for a simple yet potentially profitable buy-and-sell option that can be started for less than $500, look no further than buying and selling bath products.

Purchase stand-alone products (at wholesale prices) from manufacturers and wholesalers: soaps, gels, scrubs, salts, aromatherapy oils for the bath, and after-bath creams, balms and powders. You can then bundle these products into high-priced gift baskets, or sell them as separate products. You could also hire salespeople to organize and host bath product sales parties from their homes, develop your own website for online sales, and display your products at health fairs and home shows. Another option is to rent kiosk space in malls and shopping centers around key holidays such as Christmas, Valentine's Day and Mother's Day.

BUY
Wholesalers, Manufacturers, Liquidators

SELL
Kiosks, eBay, Flea Markets, Consumer Shows, Home Parties

RESOURCES
—Bath and Body Wholesale, ☎ (888) 935-2639,
  ✆ wholesalebathproducts.com
—Cottage Soap Wholesale, ✆ cottagesoap.com
—Honey Hill Farm, ✆ honeyhillfarm.com/wholesale.htm
—Wellington Fragrance, ✆ wellingtonfragrance.com
—Wholesale Bath Supplies, ✆ hodgepodgegifts.com

Bed and Bath Linens

Every home has at least one bathroom and bedroom. Thus homeowners need to buy towels, shower curtains, area rugs, comforters, shams, sheets and curtain panels, which are just some popular bed and bath linen products you can sell at flea markets, home and garden shows, mall kiosks or in-home parties, through an e-commerce website, and on eBay, for example.

Buy from wholesalers, liquidators and manufacturers at low prices, especially for end-of-run and seconds merchandise. Grow your business by hiring contract salespeople to organize and host bed and bath linen sale parties from their own homes. Since you'll have competition, such as Wal-Mart, Target and Bed, Bath & Beyond, you might consider specializing in specific types of bed and bath linen products, such as high-end merchandise or all-natural/organic merchandise.

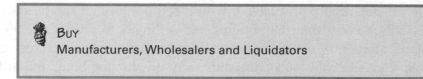

BUY
Manufacturers, Wholesalers and Liquidators

🤝 **SELL**
Kiosks, Flea Markets, eBay, Home and Gift Shows, Home Parties, E-Commerce Website

🏭 **RESOURCES**
—Hotfrog, ✄ hotfrog.com.au/Products/Linen-Wholesale-Manufacturing
—Kimlor Innovative Home Fashion Wholesale, ☎ (800) 762-0007, ✄ kimlor.com
—Royal Tradition, ✄ royaltradition.com
—Suntex, ✄ suntexindia.com/bed-linen.htm
—Towels & Linen Wholesale, ☎ (305) 624-1331, ✄ towelsandlinen.com

Belt Buckles

Belt buckles come in every imaginable design and appeal to a wide range of people. Belt buckles are in demand as gifts and as fashion accessories. They can also be purchased very cheaply and marked up by 300 to 400 percent for retail. These items are also small, easy to store and inexpensive to ship.

You'll find lucrative sales opportunities through eBay, flea markets, mall kiosks, community events and specialty shows. If you want an easy buy-and-sell enterprise that can be started for peanuts but has the potential to earn you an extra few hundred dollars per day, week or month—depending on how much time you want to commit—then you have found it.

🌰 **BUY**
Manufacturers, Wholesalers, Craftspeople

🤝 **SELL**
Kiosks, Flea Markets, eBay, Consumer Shows, Community Events

🏭 **RESOURCES**
—Buckle, ✄ buckle.com
—Hot Buckles, ✄ hotbuckles.com/wholesalebeltbuckles
—Kamp Accessories, ✄ kampaccessories.com
—The Belt Buckle Shop Wholesale, ☎ (800) 962-5003, ✄ beltbuckleshop.com
—Wholesale Belt Buckles, ✄ wholesalebeltbuckles.net

Billiard Tables

Billiards is a recreational pastime enjoyed by millions of people. Entrepreneurs with drive can easily start a buy-and-sell enterprise specializing in the sale of new and used billiard tables and accessories: cues, balls, chalk, replacement covers and overhead lights. The trick is understanding the target audience for these products, and then finding innovative ways to reach them through your advertising and marketing.

Buying secondhand tables will mean spending time searching classified ads and attending auctions. New tables and accessories can be purchased directly from manufacturers and wholesalers. Keep in mind that you might want to establish a retail financing account with a bank, credit union or leasing company so you can offer customers financing and leasing options. Doing so will greatly increase your potential market and total sales.

BUY
Manufacturers, Wholesalers, Classified Ads, Auctions

SELL
Homebased Sales, Online Marketplaces, Special Events

RESOURCES
—Cuestix International Wholesale, ☎ (303) 926-2670, ✆ cuestixint.com
—Hi Star Manufacturing, ☎ 886-5-2217692 (Taiwan), ✆ hi-star.com
—Pool Tables USA, ✆ pooltablesusa.com
—Rockwell Billiards, ✆ rockwellbilliards.com/wholesale_billiards.html

Birdhouses

Birding is a hugely popular hobby, and millions of people with porches and yards opt to install birdhouses in order to attract colorful birds to their property. As a result, millions of birdhouses are sold annually. Buy birdhouses from manufacturers who mass-produce them, or acquire more exotic birdhouses from craftspeople who build one-of-a-kind products.

Displaying birdhouses at your home in your front yard—along with bold, attention-grabbing signage—will ensure that motorists passing by will stop in and browse through your selection.

In addition to selling from home, you can also sell birdhouses on eBay and at flea markets, home and garden shows and crafts shows. Especially if you yourself enjoy birding, selling birdhouses is a great way to have some fun and subsidize your income at the same time.

BUY
Craftspeople, Manufacturers, Wholesalers

SELL
Flea Markets, Kiosks, Online Marketplaces, Homebased Sales

RESOURCES
—Best Nest Distributing, ✆ bestnest.com
—Duncraft, ✆ wildbirdfeeding.com
—Mitech Trading, ✆ mitechtrading.com/bird-feeders-wholesale-85.html
—Super Wholesaler, ✆ superwholesaler.com/merchandise/bird-feeders/
—Woodside Gardens Manufacturing, ☎ (845) 355-8412,
   ✆ abirdshome.com

Blu-Ray Players and Movies

Thanks to technological advancements and America's mandatory transition to high-definition televisions in February 2009, millions of people are investing in the latest Blu-ray players and movies to upgrade their existing DVD players and libraries. Blu-ray technology has officially beat out the HD-DVD format, so people looking to create or upgrade their home theater systems can be confident that the Blu-ray technology will remain relevant, at least for a few years.

For buy-and-sell entrepreneurs, there's currently a market for new and refurbished Blu-ray players, accessories (remote controls and cables), and new and used Blu-ray movies.

BUY
Wholesalers, Distributors, Liquidators, Flea Markets, Online Markets

SELL
Flea Markets, eBay, E-Commerce Website, Shows, Events

RESOURCES
—Brooke Distributors, ✆ http://brookedist.com
—Drop-Ship Design, ✆ dropshipdesign.com

—eBay, ✆ http://everythingelse.search.eBay/blu-ray-player_Information-Products
—Global Sources, ✆ globalsources.com/gsol/I/Blu-ray-player-manufacturers/b/2000000003844/3000000186337/23848.htm
—JM Distribution, ✆ http://jmdistribution.net
—TradeKey, ✆ tradekey.com/buyoffer_view/id/108005.htm

Board Games and Table Games

In addition to high-end editions or collectible editions of board games, such as chess, checkers, backgammon and countless others, there's also an excellent buy-and-sell business opportunity when it comes to table games suitable for family recreation rooms, offices or employee lunchrooms.

Purchase and resell both new and previously owned table games, including shuffleboard games, Ping-Pong tables, air hockey, chess/checkers tables, poker tables, foosball games and related equipment and accessories.

You can also sell your goods through sports and recreation shows and online marketplaces, such as eBay or your own e-commerce website. Because the average price of table games ranges from $250 to $1,000 or more, the profit potential is excellent. Used table games can be bought from private sellers and auction sales. New table games can be purchased directly from manufacturers, agents or distributors.

BUY
Manufacturers, Wholesalers, Classified Ads, Auctions, eBay

SELL
Homebased Sales, eBay, Home and Garden Shows, Toy Shows and Other Events

RESOURCES
—Escalade Sports Manufacturing, ☎ (800) 467-1206, ✆ escaladesports.com
—Hi Star Manufacturing, ☎ 886-5-2217692 (Taiwan), ✆ hi-star.com
—American Table Tennis, ☎ (800) 825-7664, ✆ americantabletennis.com
—Pool Tables USA, ✆ pooltablesusa.com
—Wholesale Chess, ✆ wholesalechess.com/store/chess_tables

Books (New and Used)

Thanks to Amazon.com and BN.com, plus many book liquidators and distributors, it's possible to operate a new and used book sales business from home or create a successful online-based operation. New books can be bought directly from publishers and distributors for 40 to 60 percent off their cover price and then resold for the cover price. Used books can be bought for much, much less than the book's original cover price from a variety of liquidators and other sources. Used books can be sold through Amazon.com or your own website, for example, as well as at flea markets and a wide range of other in-person selling events.

One way to differentiate your business from the competition is to specialize in specific types of books, such as mysteries, cookbooks, children's books, erotica, etc. You can market your business to avid readers and book club members.

BUY
Wholesalers, Distributors, Liquidators, Online Sources, Auctions, Collectors

SELL
Book Fairs, Online, Amazon.com, eBay, Book Clubs, Flea Markets

RESOURCES
—Bargain Books Wholesale, ✄ bargainbookswholesale.com
—Book Depot, ✄ bookdepot.com
—Book Liquidator, ✄ bookliquidator.com
—Bookmasters, ✄ bookmasters.com
—Books-A-Million, ✄ booksamillioninc.com
—Wholesale Books, ✄ http://wholesalebooks.net

Building Project Plans

The rise in popularity of do-it-yourself home renovations and woodworking projects has made selling building project plans very lucrative. When operating this type of business, you can sell building plans for a number of different projects, including house blueprints, decks, garages, arbors, gazebos and furniture.

Building and project plans can be purchased wholesale or directly from building plan publishers. Plans can be sold online, by mail order, at home and garden shows and at flea markets. You may even decide to branch out and hire architects and woodworkers to design plans for you exclusively; you'd own the copyright to sell.

BUY
Publishers, Wholesalers

SELL
Online Marketplaces, Flea Markets, Woodworking and Home and Garden Shows, Mail Order

RESOURCES
—Garlinghouse Publishing, ☎ (800) 235-5700, ✎ garlinghouse.com
—Georgia-Pacific, ✎ gp.com/BUILD/
—U-Bild Publishing, ☎ (800) 828-2453, ✎ u-bild.com
—Yankee Barn Homes, ✎ yankeebarnhomes.com

Calling Cards

While most people have cell phones these days, when they travel overseas or have a need to use a payphone in the U.S., people often use prepaid calling cards. This can also be a replacement for long-distance phone service at someone's home. Buying prepaid phone cards wholesale is a straightforward process if you work through a distributor or telephone service provider. These cards can then be resold for a profit to consumers using a variety of different selling venues.

This type of business is not as lucrative as it once was, mainly due to competition and the decrease in necessity for this type of product, but it can still be a viable business opportunity, especially if you market the prepaid calling cards to overseas travelers, students, and people looking to make inexpensive overseas calls from the United States.

Another option, which is more technologically current, is to sell Skype service and accessories (**skype.com**).

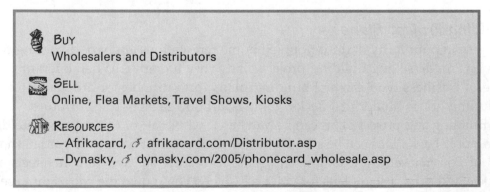

BUY
Wholesalers and Distributors

SELL
Online, Flea Markets, Travel Shows, Kiosks

RESOURCES
—Afrikacard, ✎ afrikacard.com/Distributor.asp
—Dynasky, ✎ dynasky.com/2005/phonecard_wholesale.asp

—eCall, ✆ ecallchina.com/wholesale-phone-card.asp
—PennyTalk, ✆ pennytalk.com
—Pingo, ✆ pingo.com
—Skype, ✆ skype.com

Cameras and Photo Equipment

New and previously owned film and digital cameras, along with camcorders, are great buy-and-sell products, especially for people with an interest in photography. You can offer customers new cameras, digital cameras, camcorders, vintage cameras, and accessories such as lenses, cases, tripods, darkroom equipment and film scanners.

Because there are so many types of cameras and equipment, you may want to focus on one particular specialty. Buy new cameras and equipment from wholesalers, and resell on eBay, at photography shows, flea markets and directly from a homebased showroom.

Used and antique cameras and equipment can be purchased from private sellers and online marketplaces, at auctions, and by scouring weekend flea markets and garage sales.

BUY
Wholesalers, Manufacturers, Classified Ads, Online Marketplaces

SELL
Collectors, eBay, Flea Markets, Photography Shows, Homebased Sales

RESOURCES
—AmeriCam Manufacturing, ☎ (800) 632-2824, ✆ privatelabel cameras.com
—B&H, ✆ bhphotovideo.com
—Chinavasion, ✆ chinavasion.com
—Diversified Imaging Supply, ☎ (800) 544-1609, ✆ diversifiedphoto.com
—Gamla Enterprises Wholesale, ☎ (800) 442-6526, ✆ gamlaphoto.com
—Wholesale Central, ✆ wholesalecentral.com/Cameras_Photo_ Supplies.html

Camping Equipment

Buy and sell new and used camping-related items, such as tents, stoves, water filters, sleeping bags, hiking gear, rainwear and cooking sets. New equipment can be purchased from wholesalers, importers and liquidators, and in some cases directly from manufacturers. Used equipment can be purchased from private sellers advertising in the classifieds, at auction sales and from garage sales.

Sell on eBay and other online recreation portals, at camping and recreation shows and at flea markets. Get the most for your products by ensuring that they are clean, in good condition and of high quality. Though camping gear is an enormous industry, campers belong to a tight community, so it won't take long for word to spread about your business—providing you offer great products, fair prices and top-notch customer service.

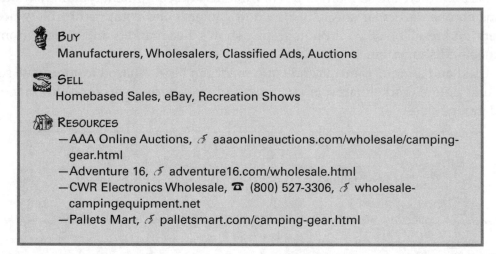

BUY
Manufacturers, Wholesalers, Classified Ads, Auctions

SELL
Homebased Sales, eBay, Recreation Shows

RESOURCES
—AAA Online Auctions, ✄ aaaonlineauctions.com/wholesale/camping-gear.html
—Adventure 16, ✄ adventure16.com/wholesale.html
—CWR Electronics Wholesale, ☎ (800) 527-3306, ✄ wholesale-campingequipment.net
—Pallets Mart, ✄ palletsmart.com/camping-gear.html

Candles

Become known as the "one stop for everything candles" by selling all kinds, including aromatherapy candles, scented jar candles, floating candles, wedding candles, novelty candles, 100 percent beeswax candles, citronella candles and decorative bowl and crock candles.

Also consider selling profitable candle accessories, such as holders and stands, snuffers, coil incense, lamp oils, candle gift baskets and candle-making supplies.

Display and sell at home and garden shows, and advertise in magazines for mail order sales. You can also sell at flea markets, at home parties and from mall kiosks at holiday times. These items can even be sold through an e-commerce website. The candle-making craft has a relatively short learning curve, so you might want to consider making your own products at home. Failing that, you can buy at deeply discounted prices from manufacturers, craftspeople, distributors and wholesalers.

Buy
Manufacturers, Wholesalers, Craftspeople, Liquidators

Sell
Online Marketplaces, Flea Markets, Kiosks, Consumer Shows, Home Parties, Homebased Sales

Resources
—Bell-A-Rama Candles, ✍ acandleco.com
—Candles 4 Less, ✍ candle4less.com
—Country Star Candles Manufacturing, ☎ (661) 269-5828, ✍ countrystarcandles.com
—Evolve Wholesale, ☎ (800) 869-9134, ✍ evolve1000.com
—National Candle Association, ✍ candles.org

Candy

Everybody loves candy, which is why it is a great product to buy wholesale and resell. You can buy candy prepackaged and resell it, or you can buy candy in bulk and repackage it into small quantities for resale. The first option is more convenient, but the second option has the potential for greater profits, because in bulk your wholesale costs are much lower than buying prepackaged. To generate a good income from candy sales, you must be able to sell in high quantities.

Candy can be sold directly from vending carts and kiosks in malls, as well as at community events, public markets, trade and consumer shows, large auction sales, sporting events, parades, carnivals, fairs, festivals and flea markets. You can also create candy-filled gift baskets and sell them to businesses, for example. Buying can be from confectioner wholesalers, or directly from any one of the numerous candy manufacturers.

BUY
Wholesalers, Manufacturers

SELL
Kiosks, Flea Markets, Community Events, Farmers' Markets, B2B

RESOURCES
—Candy Direct, ✍ candydirect.com
—Elite Distribution, ☎ (505) 797-1702, ✍ elite-distributing.com
—BulkMachine.com, ✍ gumballsupplies.com
—My Candy Supplier, ✍ mycandysupplier.com
—National Confectioners Association, ✍ candyusa.org

Cell Phones and Accessories

These days, just about everyone carries a cell phone. Thus there's a tremendous market for used cell phone equipment, as well as new accessories (cases, chargers, headsets, etc.). If you set foot in any mall, for example, you'll find at least a handful of different stores and kiosks capitalizing on this multi-billion-dollar-per-year business.

If you don't want to align yourself with a cell phone service provider, you can sell brand-new, unlocked GSM phones that can be used anywhere in the world. You can charge top dollar for these phones. You can also sell used cell phone equipment to people who lose or damage their existing phone, but can't afford to pay top dollar to buy a replacement phone from their service provider.

Plus, everyone who uses a cell phone has a need for various accessories. New equipment can be purchased through wholesalers and distributors, as well as cell phone accessory manufacturers. Look to liquidators to purchase used equipment in large quantities. Cell phones and accessories can then be sold through any of the sales venues described in Chapter 5.

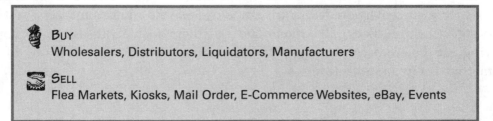

BUY
Wholesalers, Distributors, Liquidators, Manufacturers

SELL
Flea Markets, Kiosks, Mail Order, E-Commerce Websites, eBay, Events

Resources
- —Cell Pex, cellpex.com
- —Cell Phone Accessories Wholesale, http://cell-phone-accessories-wholesale.com
- —Cellular Blowout, cellular-blowout.com
- —Cellular Outfitter, cellularoutfitter.com
- —Doba, doba.com/dropship-source/b.html
- —Global Sources Direct, globalsourcesdirect.com/servlet/the-Cell-Phones/Categories
- —TradeKey, tradekey.com/ks-cell-phones
- —Wireless Galaxy, wirelessgalaxy.com/wholesale

Children's Clothing

You can buy the latest children's fashions directly from national and international apparel manufacturers, wholesalers and liquidators at deeply discounted prices, especially if you purchase end-of-season. You can then double and even triple your purchase price and resell the clothing at flea markets, from a home showroom and on eBay, for example.

Boost revenues by accepting used children's clothing trade-ins on new purchases. Offer a 20 percent rebate, and then double the price of the used clothing you acquire for resale. Obviously, your target market will be parents of young kids, so this must be an audience you know, understand, and will be able to market to effectively.

Buy
Manufacturers, Wholesalers, Liquidators

Sell
Flea Markets, Homebased Sales, Kiosks, eBay

Resources
- —1AAA Wholesale Liquidators, (800) 661-9430, 1aaawholesaleliquidators.com
- —Apparel & Textile Industry Associations, apparelsearch.com/associations.htm
- —Apparel Search, apparelsearch.com/wholesale_clothing/Childrens/wholesale_childrens.htm

—Children's Wholesale Apparel, ☎ (727) 934-1109,
  ✆ childrenswholesale.com
—Kids Resource Wholesale, ☎ (800) 552-1610, ✆ kidsresource.com
—Wholesale Fashion Square, ✆ wholesalefashionsquare.com

Christmas Trees

For many traditional families, when the Christmas holiday approaches there is no substitute for a real Christmas tree. So if you're looking for a seasonal business, selling live Christmas trees might be the perfect opportunity for you.

North American consumers spend more than $1 billion annually on live Christmas trees. Short of your having your own tree lot, you will have to rely on tree farms and wholesalers to acquire product. But be forewarned: Christmas trees sell fast. On a wholesale basis directly from tree farmers, bound trees that are ready to be shipped cost in the range of $10 to $40 each, depending on size and type of tree. Retail prices also vary greatly, depending on the type and size of tree and the area where the trees are being sold.

New Yorkers typically pay the most, on average $100. You can sell Christmas trees right from your own home if you live in a high-traffic location and won't be violating any local laws or ordinances. For most, however, a better option is to rent empty lot space starting around December 1st and counting until Christmas Eve. Good locations include grocery store parking lots, busy intersections, gas station lots and any other empty lot that is exposed to lots of passing motorists.

You will need to negotiate some sort of financial arrangement with the landlord—either a flat rental rate or perhaps a percentage of your total sales. To increase sales and help your community, align yourself with a local charity and donate a small portion of each sale, perhaps 5 percent, to the charity. Doing so enables you and your customers to help others less fortunate, which, of course, is the true meaning of Christmas. You can also sell Christmas lights and decorations to boost profits.

BUY
Growers, Wholesalers

SELL
Temporary Rental Lot, Homebased Sales

RESOURCES
—BL Christmas Trees, ☌ blchristmastrees.com
—Christmas Trees Worldwide, ☌ christmastreesww.com
—Captain Jack's Christmas Tree Farm Network, ☌ christmas-tree.com/real/wholesale
—National Christmas Tree Association, ☌ christmastree.org/wholesale.cfm

Cigars

Selling premium handmade and machine-made cigars has the potential to be very profitable. In fact, many people are earning six-figure incomes selling cigars online. However, there are a few drawbacks.

First, you will need to invest in cigar storage humidors and humidifying devices to protect your valuable inventory. Second, you will need to apply for and obtain a state tobacco tax and products license. These generally cost around $100 per year, though each state is different and has its own seller's guidelines and fee schedule.

For more details, visit the Bureau of Alcohol, Tobacco, and Firearms website located at **atf.gov/alcohol/info/faq/tobacco.htm**.

You will also need to develop a sound marketing plan, because this is a very competitive business. Buy directly from manufacturers and cigar wholesalers. Create your own website for online sales, and hire salespeople to organize and host cigar sales parties right in their own homes. You can also create a catalog listing all of your cigar brands and accessories, and then deliver the catalog to hotels, golf courses, businesses, restaurants, resorts, bars and social clubs. To boost revenues, sell cigar accessories such as clippers, cases, humidors, gift box sets, lighters and smokeless ashtrays.

BUY
Manufacturers, Wholesalers

SELL
Online Marketplaces, Direct Delivery, Kiosks, Homebased Sales

RESOURCES
—Cheap Cigars Wholesale, ☎ (813) 969-0523, ☌ cheap-cigars.com

—Cigar Aficionado Magazine, ♂ cigaraficionado.com
—Cigar Family Wholesale, ☎ (800) 477-1884, ♂ cigarfamily.com
—CigarSupply, ♂ http://cigarsupply.com
—Cuban Crafters, ♂ cubancrafters.com
—Gotham Cigars Wholesale, ☎ (888) 468-0033, ♂ gothamcigars.com
—Neptune Cigars Wholesale, ☎ (800) 655-3385, ♂ neptunecigar.com

Classic Cars

Many classic-car enthusiasts are prepared to pay top dollar to relive their youth or to finally reward themselves for years of hard work by buying the car of their dreams. Because demand is high, prices have exploded into the high five- and even six-figure range for prized classic cars.

Buying and selling classic cars is not for the faint of heart or for romantic types. You need to be educated about cars—especially about the condition, mechanical soundness and value of collector cars. Buying sources include estate sales, classified ads, auctions, classic car shows and online marketplaces.

You can sell in many of the same forums, plus direct to collectors. Keep in mind that classic car values in other countries can be different from those in the U.S., which can also provide numerous additional buying and selling opportunities. The people who will do the best in this business are those who are classic car enthusiasts themselves: people who know their product, as well as their target audience. This type of business also requires significant investment capital.

BUY
Classified Ads, Auctions, For-Sale Signs, Car Shows

SELL
Collectors, Homebased Sales, Online Marketplaces, Auctions, Swap Meets, Car Shows

RESOURCES
—NADA Guides, ☎ (800) 966-6232, ♂ nadaguides.com
—Buy Classic Cars, ♂ buyclassiccars.com
—Classic Car, ♂ classiccar.com
—Dream Car Store, ♂ dreamcarstore.net/Links.htm
—Fossil Cars, ♂ fossilcars.com/links/classiccarparts.html

Cleaning Products and Equipment

Consumers, businesses, government offices and all types of organizations spend billions annually on sanitation supplies and equipment, including cleaners, paper products, mops, brooms and disposal bags. Cashing in on this demand is probably easier than you think.

Start by securing a reliable wholesale source to buy cleaning products and equipment for low wholesale prices. These wholesalers are easy to locate in the Yellow Pages or on the internet. Next, determine how you want to sell your products: directly to businesses, or directly to consumers.

If you decide to sell directly to businesses, knock on doors and make inquiries about their current supplier, and whether or not they'd be willing to give your business a try. Offering incentives such as a special discount, free samples and guaranteed free and quick delivery will help.

If you decide to concentrate your marketing efforts toward consumers, sell through flea markets as well as trade and consumer shows. The busiest vendors at these shows are always the people who sell miracle cleaning products, chamois, dust mops and super-powerful vacuum cleaners. This marketing method works well because you can demonstrate the products live. No need to tell customers how great your cleaners are when you can show them and let them witness the fantastic results and benefits for themselves.

To help differentiate your business, consider specializing in environmentally friendly cleaning products, or another niche aspect of the overall cleaning market.

BUY
Manufacturers, Wholesalers, Liquidators

SELL
Flea Markets, Consumer Shows, B2B

RESOURCES
—Closeout Central, ♂ closeoutcentral.com/Cleaning-Supplies.html
—Dollar Days Wholesale, ☎ (877) 837-9569, ♂ dollardays.com
—Green Works Cleaners, ♂ greenworkscleaners.com
—International Sanitary Supply Association, ♂ issa.com
—ReStockIt, ♂ restockit.com/Wholesale-Cleaning-Supplies.html
—WJS, ♂ wholesalejanitorialsupply.com

Clocks

When it comes to buying and selling clocks, there are many different specialty products you can offer, including grandfather clocks, wall clocks, alarm clocks, travel clocks, mantel clocks, cuckoo clocks, carriage clocks, pendulum clocks, dial clocks, novelty clocks, toy clocks, advertising clocks, ship's clocks, calendar clocks, melody clocks, digital display clocks, Braille clocks and talking clocks.

It seems there's a clock available for every occasion, use and price point imaginable. Wholesalers, manufacturers, liquidators and importers will be your best bets for purchasing new clocks at low discount prices.

There is also money to be made in buying and selling antique clocks. The best places to look for valuable used and antique clocks include garage sales, auctions, flea markets, online marketplaces and classified ads. Antique clock price guides will prove to be an indispensable business tool for acquiring and selling. New, used or antique clocks can be sold on eBay, from a home showroom, at home shows, mall kiosks, collectible shows, and flea markets, or through an e-commerce website.

BUY
Manufacturers, Wholesalers, Auctions, Garage Sales, Classified Ads, Estate Sales

SELL
Online Marketplaces, Flea Markets, Kiosks, Consumer Shows, Collectors

RESOURCES
—CKB Products, ꝺ ckbproducts.com/index.php/cPath/36
—Dollar Days Wholesale, ☎ (877) 837-9569, ꝺ dollardays.com
—National Association of Watch and Clock Collectors, ☎ (717) 684-8261, ꝺ nawcc.org
—SZ Wholesale, ꝺ sz-wholesale.com/shenzhen_China_products/Clock-and-Watch_1.htm

Collectible Coins and Paper Money

This is a business that caters to collectors, often with specialty areas of interest, such as U.S. or foreign coins or paper money. In terms of buying, you can contact collectors directly or take advantage of garage sales, estate sales, auctions, private seller classified ads and flea markets.

Before getting started, however, you need to educate yourself not only about the value of coins and paper money, but also about how they are graded by condition for valuation from a collector's point of view. This can be accomplished by studying price guides and by reading coin and paper money collectors' publications. Timing often comes into play as well. Deals can be had when there are no other interested parties to purchase.

When selling, try eBay and other online marketplaces, as well as coin shows and other collector events. Join coin and paper money collecting clubs, and consider launching your own e-commerce website.

BUY
Auctions, Online Marketplaces, Stamp Shows, Classified Ads

SELL
Collectors, Online Marketplaces, Specialty Publications, Stamp Shows

RESOURCES
—Coin World, ♂ coinworld.com
—Heritage Coin, ♂ http://coins.ha.com/
—Kelly's Computer Shop of Coins, ♂ kcshop.com
—Krause Publications, ♂ krause.com/static/coins.htm
—U.S. Coin Values Advisor, ♂ us-coin-values-advisor.com

Collectible Toys

Just think, throughout America, Canada, and much of the world, stuffed away in dusty attics or forgotten in dark basements, are literally thousands of antique and vintage toys worth millions to toy collectors worldwide. Collectible toys can be found in every part of the country. Visit garage sales, flea markets, estate sales, junk shops and auction sales.

Unlike many buy-and-sell items, when you come across collectible toys—or any collectible in need of repairs—don't do anything to fix them! Collectors want toys in their existing condition, even if it means scratches, dents, missing parts or wear. Values tend to climb even higher if the toy still has its original packaging, advertisement or receipt.

Animals, cap pistols, construction sets, rocking horses, trains, teddy bears, banks and wagons are only a few of the bestselling and most highly prized collectible toys.

Sell at collectible auctions, to collectors via shows, through clubs, through eBay and online collectible toy marketplaces, and right from your own home.

> **BUY**
> Garage Sales, Flea Markets, Auctions, Online Marketplaces
>
> **SELL**
> Collectors, eBay, Auctions, Homebased Sales
>
> **RESOURCES**
> —3000 Toys.com, ☏ 3000toys.com
> —*A Toy Shop* Magazine, Krause Publications, ☎ (800) 942-0676,
>   ☏ collect.com
> —Antique Toys, ☏ antiquetoys.com
> —NextGen Collectible Toys, ☏ nextgentoys.com
> —The Online Collector, ☏ theonlinecollector.com/toys.html

Comic Books

Buying and selling new comic books is a snap: Buy top-name publisher brands such as DC Comics and Marvel Comics from comic book distributors and publishers, and then resell the comics online and through flea markets to avid readers and collectors.

The same, however, cannot be said for buying and selling used and vintage comic books. The industry is competitive, and you need a strong knowledge of comic book collecting to succeed. Used comic values are mainly based on rarity and condition, but, they are only worth what someone is willing to pay for them. Thus it is critical that you get them in front of the right people if you hope to get top dollar.

Comics Buyer's Guide is the longest-running magazine about comic books, available by monthly subscription from Krause Publications (800-258-0929/ **krause.com/static/comics.htm**). Monthly issues feature new comic reviews, a monthly price guide and comic convention news.

The Overstreet Comic Book Price Guide, from Gemstone Publishing (888-375-9800/**gemstonepub.com**) is considered the industry standard for rating comic-book prices and conditions. Buy your inventory at garage sales, flea markets, online marketplaces and comic book shows, and then resell in many of the same ways: to collectors, through eBay and at comic book shows.

Computer Parts (New)

A great full-time or part-time income can be earned by buying and selling new computer parts, such as CD-RW and DVD drives, hard drives, USB memory sticks, RAM, audio and video cards, processing chips and motherboards. Buy from wholesalers and sell directly to businesses for upgrade purposes. Additional revenues and profits can be earned if you have the skills and knowledge to install the parts you sell, because you can easily charge in the range of $50 to $150 per hour for this service.

Because prices for replacement PC parts have fallen dramatically in the last few years, skip buying and selling used parts. There simply is not enough profit in it, unless you can get late-model computers for next to nothing and sell them for parts.

—Shift Wholesale Computers, ☎ (303) 430-7500, ♂ skwholesale.com
—Star Tech Wholesale, ☎ (800) 265-1844, ♂ startech.com
—Tiger Direct, ♂ tigerdirect.com

Computer Peripherals

The best computer accessories to sell online and offline include inkjet printers, laser printers, scanners, DVD and CD writers, USB (external) hard drives, webcams, flat-screen and flat-panel monitors, wireless keyboards and mouse sets. Purchase new computer peripherals at deeply discounted prices from wholesalers and liquidators that offer these products by the pallet.

The best selling methods include direct-to-businesses, flea market vending, exhibiting at computer and consumer shows, and listing on eBay.

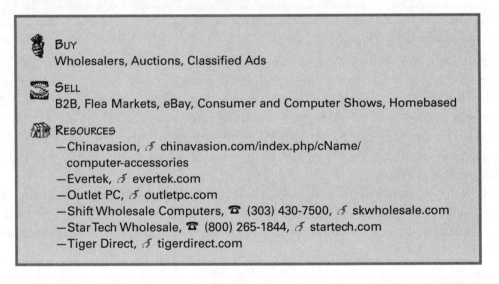

BUY
Wholesalers, Auctions, Classified Ads

SELL
B2B, Flea Markets, eBay, Consumer and Computer Shows, Homebased

RESOURCES
—Chinavasion, ♂ chinavasion.com/index.php/cName/
   computer-accessories
—Evertek, ♂ evertek.com
—Outlet PC, ♂ outletpc.com
—Shift Wholesale Computers, ☎ (303) 430-7500, ♂ skwholesale.com
—Star Tech Wholesale, ☎ (800) 265-1844, ♂ startech.com
—Tiger Direct, ♂ tigerdirect.com

Computers

Selling new and used computer systems is nowhere near as profitable as it used to be, mainly because prices have dropped and there's intense competition. Where money can be made, however, is selling computers and then offering on-site support to install, customize, network, upgrade and maintain them, plus by offering training to your customers.

New desktop and notebook computer systems can be purchased from wholesalers, liquidators and distributors, and then marked up and sold to businesses and consumers through online marketplaces such as eBay and through direct contact with business owners and customers.

To buy used computer systems, scan classified ads for bargains and attend auction sales. Many corporations, government agencies, schools and organizations replace their still-otherwise-good computer equipment on a scheduled basis. These computers can often be purchased for pennies on the dollar of the original cost at auctions or tender sales. Companies such as InterSchola (**interschola.com**) specialize in helping schools sell off their used computer equipment, which is often in excellent shape and suitable for resale.

Beware of acquiring stolen merchandise, however, especially when it comes to laptop computers. You also want to avoid used computers (hardware) that are obsolete or outdated.

Buy
Wholesalers, Auctions, Classified Ads

Sell
B2B, Flea Markets, Consumer Shows, Homebased Sales

Resources
—Bass Computers, ☎ basscomputers.com
—Buy 4 Less Electronics Wholesale, ☎ (822) 251-1391, ☎ buy4lessinc.com
—D&H Wholesale, ☎ (800) 340-1001, ☎ dandh.com
—Discount PC, ☎ discountpc.net
—Golden Surplus, ☎ goldensurplus.com
—Shift Wholesale Computers, (303) 430-7500, ☎ skwholesale.com
—USA Notebooks Used Computer Wholesale, (888) 728-9902, ☎ usanotebook.com

Cookware

Clever entrepreneurs can earn big bucks buying and selling kitchen cookware, especially if you enlist contract salespeople to organize and host cookware sales parties in their own homes. Buy cookware at low prices from wholesalers and liquidators, and directly from North American and overseas manufacturers.

In addition to in-home sales parties, brand-name cookware also can be easily sold on eBay and other online marketplaces, at flea markets and home and garden shows, through mall kiosks, and via mail order. If you specialize in commercial cookware, you can sell directly to restaurants.

Join cooking clubs in your area to network for business, and participate in online cooking forums. It is not uncommon for cookware to be marked up by 50 to 100 percent for retail sale.

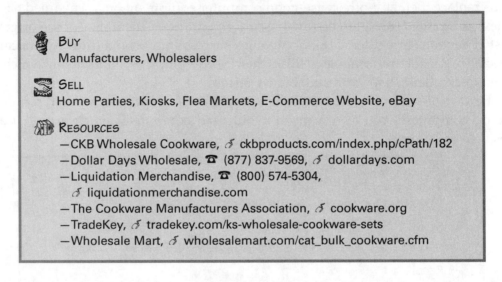

BUY
Manufacturers, Wholesalers

SELL
Home Parties, Kiosks, Flea Markets, E-Commerce Website, eBay

RESOURCES
—CKB Wholesale Cookware, ☞ ckbproducts.com/index.php/cPath/182
—Dollar Days Wholesale, ☎ (877) 837-9569, ☞ dollardays.com
—Liquidation Merchandise, ☎ (800) 574-5304,
  ☞ liquidationmerchandise.com
—The Cookware Manufacturers Association, ☞ cookware.org
—TradeKey, ☞ tradekey.com/ks-wholesale-cookware-sets
—Wholesale Mart, ☞ wholesalemart.com/cat_bulk_cookware.cfm

Cosmetics

For the innovative entrepreneur, there are numerous ways to sell cosmetics and make a bundle. You can enlist contract salespeople to organize and host home cosmetics sales parties. You can also sell cosmetics in any number of online marketplaces, including on eBay. You can rent kiosk space in malls or set up a booth at a flea market or at fashion, health or beauty shows.

The first step to getting started in cosmetics sales is to source a reliable supply of decent-quality cosmetics. One option is to create your own cosmetics brand and have it manufactured under a private labeling agreement. Or you can strike a deal with an existing cosmetics manufacturer or distributor and market that line on an exclusive or nonexclusive basis. You may also want to specialize in organic cosmetic products and market to people with skin sensitivity or allergies, for example. With this popular product category, there are many possibilities.

BUY
Wholesalers, Manufacturers

SELL
Home Parties, Direct Delivery, eBay, E-Commerce Website, Kiosks, Events

RESOURCES
—Avon, ✆ avon.com
—Independent Cosmetic Manufacturers and Distributors, ✆ icmad.org
—Liquidation Merchandise, ☎ (800) 574-5304,
    ✆ liquidationmerchandise.com
—Mary Kay Cosmetics, ✆ marykay.com
—NJ Surplus, ✆ njsurplus.com

Crystal

Waterford, Swarovski, Wedgwood, Hallmark and Fabergé are producers of some of the world's finest crystal ornaments, picture frames, toasting glasses, figurines, server sets, candleholders, bells and more. New or used crystal is always in demand and a hot seller, especially as a wedding gift item.

Buy from wholesalers and producers if you want to focus on selling new crystal, and buy at garage sales, collectibles shows, online marketplaces and auctions if you want to focus on buying and selling used and antique crystal collectibles. Sales of both can be conducted on eBay and at consumer and collectible shows, as well as through mall kiosks and flea markets.

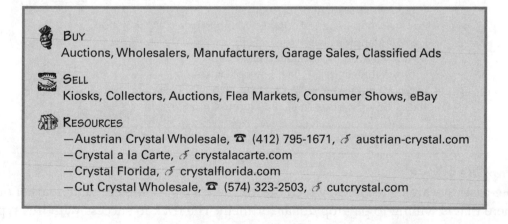

BUY
Auctions, Wholesalers, Manufacturers, Garage Sales, Classified Ads

SELL
Kiosks, Collectors, Auctions, Flea Markets, Consumer Shows, eBay

RESOURCES
—Austrian Crystal Wholesale, ☎ (412) 795-1671, ✆ austrian-crystal.com
—Crystal a la Carte, ✆ crystalacarte.com
—Crystal Florida, ✆ crystalflorida.com
—Cut Crystal Wholesale, ☎ (574) 323-2503, ✆ cutcrystal.com

Designer Fashions

Almost everyone would love to dress in expensive designer fashions, but unfortunately, economics do not afford all of us the opportunity to wear brand-new Gucci or Armani outfits that cost thousands of dollars.

There are basically two ways you can help people buy designer fashions for a fraction of the normal cost and still make a handsome profit for yourself. First, purchase new, off-brand and replica designer fashions from overseas manufacturers and wholesalers, and then resell these from a home showroom, online through eBay, or by hiring salespeople to organize and host designer fashion sales parties in their own homes.

Second, you can purchase used designer fashions from top houses such as Prada, Fendi, Nicole Miller, Armani and Ferragamo by scouring garage sales, secondhand shops, flea markets and auction sales. These garments can then be resold to consumers. To be successful in this type of business, knowledge of fashion and fashion trends is definitely required. You must also understand your target audience and be able to successfully market to these people.

BUY
Wholesalers, Manufacturers

SELL
Homebased Sales, Fashion Shows, Home Parties, eBay

RESOURCES
—1AAA Wholesale Liquidators, ☎ (800) 661-9430,
  🖉 1aaawholesaleliquidators.com
—American Apparel and Footwear Manufacturers' Association,
  🖉 apparelandfootwear.org
—Fashion Heaven, 🖉 fashionheaven.com
—Fashion Wholesaler, 🖉 fashionwholesaler.com
—Jaclyn Manufacturing, ☎ (201) 868-9400, 🖉 jaclyninc.com
—Luxury Brands Wholesale, 🖉 luxurymagazzino.com

Die-Cast Toys

Die-cast toys are collectibles, which means there's a specialized niche market out there that is willing to pay top dollar for them. The trick to success with this type of buy-and-sell enterprise is to acquire the die-cast toys that are in most demand by collectors, and then offer them at a fair price (while earning a profit at the same time). Of course, you also have to be able to identify with this specialized collector market and be able to reach your target audience effectively.

A bit of time spent scouring garage sales, flea markets and secondhand shops looking for die-cast cars and toys at rock-bottom prices to resell could be financially rewarding. Brand names such as Dinky, Corgi and Matchbox are common in the world of die-cast toys.

Though most people think of scale cars when they hear die-cast, in reality, die-cast toys represent many things—figurines, action figures, farm tractors, boats, animals, trains, planes, military equipment and soldiers—all of which can be valuable. In addition to collectible die-cast toys, the market for new die-cast toys is enormous. New products can be purchased from wholesalers, manufacturers and liquidators. Your main marketing forums will be eBay and other online marketplaces, as well as direct to collectors via auctions and shows, and vending at flea markets and community events.

BUY
Wholesalers, Online Marketplaces, Garage Sales, Flea Markets

SELL
Collectors, eBay, Flea Markets, Kiosks, Consumer Shows

RESOURCES
—Corgi, ☌ corgi-toys.com
—Empire Discount Wholesale, ☎ (914) 684-1455, ☌ empirediscount.net
—Jada Toy Manufacturing, ☎ (626) 810-8382, ☌ jadatoys.com
—Matchbox, ☌ matchbox.com

Dollar Store Items

Dollar store items are the ultimate buy-low, sell-high flea market items. (Well, within reason.) Products include hand soap, bags of marbles, paintbrushes, picture frames, flyswatters, playing cards, shampoo, ultra-cheap CDs and DVDs, and closeout greeting cards—all products that people buy on a whim. If it's cheap and useful, as almost all dollar store items are, it will sell fast and hopefully in large quantities.

The trick to buying these items for resale is to buy in bulk from wholesalers and liquidators. These products can generally be marked up 300 percent or more. Obviously, because of their low retail price, you will have to sell lots of merchandise to realize substantial profits, so make sure there's a market for the items you opt to sell.

Dollar store products are notoriously easy to store and transport. Because you pay next to nothing for your goods, offer flea market shoppers lots of great deals and reasons to buy, such as two-for-one specials, fill a bag for $20, and other promotional gimmicks that'll get your cash register ringing.

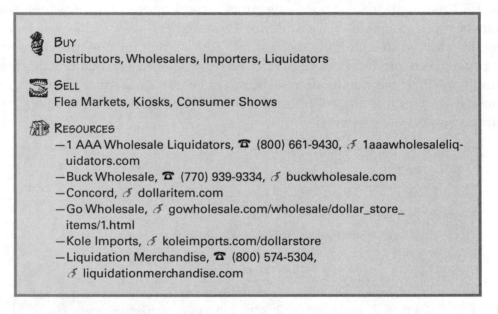

BUY
Distributors, Wholesalers, Importers, Liquidators

SELL
Flea Markets, Kiosks, Consumer Shows

RESOURCES
—1 AAA Wholesale Liquidators, ☎ (800) 661-9430, ✆ 1aaawholesaleliq-uidators.com
—Buck Wholesale, ☎ (770) 939-9334, ✆ buckwholesale.com
—Concord, ✆ dollaritem.com
—Go Wholesale, ✆ gowholesale.com/wholesale/dollar_store_items/1.html
—Kole Imports, ✆ koleimports.com/dollarstore
—Liquidation Merchandise, ☎ (800) 574-5304, ✆ liquidationmerchandise.com

Dolls and Teddy Bears

There are inexpensive dolls and teddy bears—such as the ones sold in toy stores and mass-market retailers—that are meant to be bought for kids. There are also more costly dolls and teddy bears designed for adults to be "get well," "congratulations" or "happy birthday" gifts. The doll and teddy bear market also includes a huge collectibles business, where adults pay top dollar for special edition, rare, antique or specialized dolls and teddy bears. Just one niche of this business involves collecting Barbie dolls.

If you have a passion for dolls and/or teddy bears, pick a specialty and business model and focus on it. New dolls and teddy bears can be purchased directly from manufacturers, distributors, wholesalers and liquidators. Secondhand collectibles can be obtained from flea markets, bought directly from collectors, purchased on eBay, acquired from mail order companies, or purchased at collector shows and events. These same venues are where you can achieve success selling your products.

While new dolls and teddy bears might sell for between $10 and $50, collectible dolls and teddy bears can easily sell for hundreds or even thousands of dollars.But to capitalize on this aspect of the market, you must understand the collecting business as well as the target audience, plus have access to rare, unique and quality merchandise that's in demand. Use price guides and online resources to help you determine what's currently hot in the doll and collectible marketplace.

BUY
Auctions, Flea Markets, eBay, Collector's Fairs and Events, Direct from Collectors

SELL
Flea Markets, eBay, Collector's Fairs and Events, Direct to Collectors

RESOURCES
—About.com Doll Collecting, http://collectdolls.about.com
—Bears R Gifts, bearsrgifts.com
—Burton & Burton, burtonandburton.com
—Collectible Doll Information, dollinfo.com/links.htm
—Ms. Teddy Bear, msteddybear.us
—Plush in a Rush, plushinarush.com
—Teddy Bear Buying Guide, http://pages.eBay.com/buy/guides/bears-buying-guide

DVDs

People don't enjoy just watching movies; they also enjoy collecting DVD movies and TV shows. Thanks to recent technology shifts, traditional DVD movies are priced much more affordably than ever before, allowing more people to buy DVDs as opposed to just renting them.

As a buy-and-sell business, you can opt to sell new DVDs (of movies, TV shows, concerts, how-to videos, exercise videos, self-help videos, music videos, adult videos, etc.) or you can buy and sell used DVDs.

Buy new DVDs from wholesalers, distributors and liquidators, often for prices starting at $1 each for B-movies and $15 to $25 for first-run hits. These same DVDs can be resold at flea markets, through eBay and from mall kiosks for as much as ten times your wholesale cost.

Keep in mind—with video rental stores buying, renting and selling new and used videos, plus the downloadable market (which includes iTunes)—that competition is fierce. You should seriously consider developing a specialty or niche in terms of the types of DVDs you sell. Also make sure your pricing is competitive. Stay up-to-date with the latest technologies by offering Blu-ray discs. Another option is to sell HD-DVDs, which will become increasingly harder for consumers to find now that the technology has been abandoned.

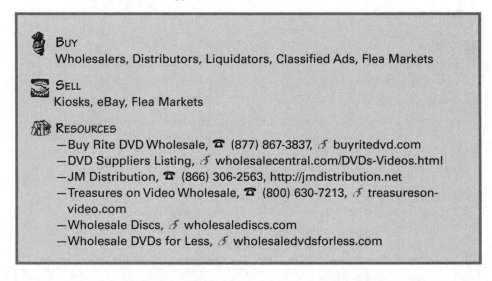

BUY
Wholesalers, Distributors, Liquidators, Classified Ads, Flea Markets

SELL
Kiosks, eBay, Flea Markets

RESOURCES
—Buy Rite DVD Wholesale, ☎ (877) 867-3837, ✍ buyritedvd.com
—DVD Suppliers Listing, ✍ wholesalecentral.com/DVDs-Videos.html
—JM Distribution, ☎ (866) 306-2563, http://jmdistribution.net
—Treasures on Video Wholesale, ☎ (800) 630-7213, ✍ treasureson-video.com
—Wholesale Discs, ✍ wholesalediscs.com
—Wholesale DVDs for Less, ✍ wholesaledvdsforless.com

Entertainment Memorabilia

Movie posters, autographed celebrity photos, authentic and replica movie props, autographed shooting scripts, and costumes from TV shows and movies are just some of the many products that are in demand by avid entertainment memorabilia collectors.

Movie and TV buffs can't get enough of everything Hollywood, which presents an incredible opportunity for a savvy and creative buy-and-sell entrepreneur. After all, if it has anything to do with the movies, television or celebrities, it is valuable and will be quickly snapped up.

Thanks to resources such as eBay, entertainment memorabilia collecting has become a passion for many more people from around the world. Your buying sources for everything Hollywood include collectors, garage sales, estate sales, Hollywood studios, internet sites and classified ads. Online marketplaces such as eBay will be your best choice for selling. Additionally, you can sell your goods at flea markets, collectible shows and memorabilia auctions.

If you're a *Star Trek* fan, you can sell *Star Trek* memorabilia at the countless conventions held around the world on any given weekend. Similar conventions are also held for other cult-favorite TV shows and movies. The trick is really understanding your target audience and getting your hands on authentic Hollywood memorabilia that will appeal to them. Another opportunity exists in buying and selling Disney memorabilia to collectors.

BUY
Garage Sales, Online Marketplaces, Auctions, Classified Ads

SELL
Collectors, Auctions, Flea Markets, Memorabilia Shows, eBay

RESOURCES
—A Big Reel Magazine, Krause Publications, ♂ collect.com
—Disney Memorabilia, ♂ http://disneymemorabilia.com
—Fantasies Come True, ♂ fantasiescometrue.com
—Film Posters, ♂ filmposters.com
—Hollywood Collectors Show, ♂ hollywoodcollectorshow.com
—Hollywood Megastore, ♂ hollywoodmegastore.com
—Hollywood Memorabilia Collector, ♂ hollywoodcollector.com
—Hollywood Souvenirs, ♂ hollywoodsouvenirs.com

Entire Household Lots

Buying partial or entire household lots is a very interesting proposition. You get lower pricing because you are buying in quantity and ultimately paying less than you would for each piece bought individually. The downside is that you may end up purchasing items you would otherwise not normally bother buying, occasionally leaving you with slow-moving inventory.

There are many reasons why a person would sell all or most of their personal belongings. Often when people are faced with liquidating belongings, it is easier to sell everything as one lot than it is to sell each item individually and have to wait for everything to sell. These types of sales are usually listed in classified ads or held through auction houses. You can also bid on entire household lots through estate sale services.

Regardless of the buying method you choose, you will need to have access to a means of transporting and storing all of the items. Because your inventory will be varied, you can sell in a number of ways, such as through flea markets or online marketplaces such as eBay, or by holding monthly or quarterly auctions to sell all inventory at one time in one place.

Significant investment capital will be needed to operate this type of business, plus you'll need plenty of storage space and the ability to sort through large numbers of items and price them accordingly so you can earn a significant profit.

Buy
Estate Sales, Classified Ads, Moving, Auctions and Storage Companies

Sell
Flea Markets, Garage Sales, eBay, Auctions, Homebased Sales

Resources
—Team Estate Sales, ☎ (901) 758-2659, ✒ teamestatesales.com
—Estate Sales Listings, ✒ estatesales.net
—The Estate Sales Company, ✒ estatesalesco.com

Fabric

Exotic fabrics from around the world are very unique products to sell to consumers including crafters, seamstresses and tailors. Spread the word by joining sewing and crafts clubs in your area, and by participating in online craft groups to network for business.

Also, create your own e-commerce website so you can sell fabrics to consumers from around the world. In the bricks-and-mortar world, you can sell your fabrics at fashion shows, home and garden shows and flea markets. You can also rent temporary space in malls and public markets. A homebased fabric boutique could also prove to be profitable.

You can purchase fabrics wholesale through domestic and international sources. However, if you can afford it, import fabrics directly from manufacturers in India and China, so you can offer the most exotic selection of merchandise that people will have difficulty obtaining elsewhere.

BUY
Manufacturers, Wholesalers, Importers, Liquidators

SELL
Kiosks, Flea Markets, Online Marketplaces, Homebased Sales, B2B

RESOURCES
—Emmaress Manufacturing, ☎ 91-22-23721232 (India),
   ✆ emmaress.com
—Narmada Manufacturing, ☎ 62-361-486-071 (Indonesia), ✆ narmada-textiles.com
—Nick of Time Textiles Wholesale, ☎ (877) 447-8370, ✆ nickoftime.net
—Textile Web, ✆ textileweb.com
—Trade India, ✆ tradeindia.com

Fad Products

Every so often, a gimmicky, trendy or fad product comes along that absolutely everyone must have, but that nobody actually needs. In the past, these products have included the pet rock, yo-yos, Beanie Babies, Crocs, charm bracelets, *The Secret*, Webkinz and licensed merchandise featuring *The Simpsons* and Pokemon. Often, but not always, these fad items are targeted to kids and teens.

As a buy-and-sell entrepreneur, tapping into the fad market can be a way to make a quick buck. After all, the typical fad only lasts between three months and three years. After that, consumers move onto the next big thing and forget all about their previous obsessions. This being the case, to get into the fad item business you'll need the following:

- A strong knowledge of pop culture and the people who follow it
- Plenty of startup capital for inventory
- The ability to sell your merchandise in high-traffic places such as mall kiosks and flea markets
- The ability to identify a trendy product, get your hands on an ample supply of inventory, and then capitalize on the popular trend while it's still popular (so you don't end up with a warehouse chock full of inventory that nobody will take off your hands when the fad ends).

The trick to earning huge profits by selling trendy or fad items is timing. You need to start selling a particular product or product category right when the fad becomes popular and then get out of the business before the popularity or trend suddenly comes to an abrupt end. These items can be purchased from wholesalers, manufacturers, distributors, importers and novelty companies.

Don't spend a fortune setting up an e-commerce website for a fad product. By the time you get up and running and drive ample traffic to your website, the fad could be over. Plus, you'll invest too much money getting the online business set up, which will ultimately need to be recouped through sales.

Buy
Wholesalers, Distributors, Importers

Sell
Flea Markets, Kiosks, Fairs and Events

Resources
—Wholesale Central, ♂ wholesalecentral.com

Figurines

There is big money to be made buying and selling both new and collectible figurines. Buy the most popular, brand-name, new figurines by Disney, Precious Moments, Cherished Teddies and Hummel wholesale, and resell these online and at flea markets, mall kiosks and gift shows. Most can be purchased for 50 percent less than retail. Off-brand figurines can be acquired for up to 80 percent off retail, making them very profitable (but these are less in demand).

Secondhand vintage and collectible figurines can be found at garage, auction and estate sales, though you'll need to do a bit of detective work to uncover the best bargains. Antique figurines can be sold to collectors via antique shows, auctions and eBay. The trick to earning profits in the secondhand collectibles market is to truly understand values, trends and the wants of avid collectors.

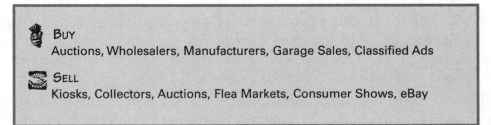

Buy
Auctions, Wholesalers, Manufacturers, Garage Sales, Classified Ads

Sell
Kiosks, Collectors, Auctions, Flea Markets, Consumer Shows, eBay

Fine Art

Like any type of high-end collectible, fine art has many subcategories and areas of specialty. Individual pieces can be bought and sold for hundreds, thousands or even millions of dollars, so it's essential that you truly understand art, as well as the mind-set of serious collectors. Inventory can be acquired through galleries, estate sales and auctions, and directly from collectors. When it comes to selling, being able to reach the collectors themselves will be your best bet for generating the highest profits possible.

When dealing in high-end art, appraisals and proof of authenticity will be important. It also helps to establish a specific area of expertise. This can be a highly competitive business, where building a positive reputation is essential.

BUY
Galleries, Estate Sales, Auctions, Collectors, Art Shows

SELL
Collectors, Art Shows

RESOURCES
—Art Exchange, ✂ art-exchange.com
—Art International, ✂ artinternationalwholesale.com
—Crown Arts, LLC, ✂ wholesale-framed-art-prints.com
—Rosenbaum Fine Art, ✂ rosenbaumfineart.com
—Wholesale World, ✂ wholesale-world.us/wholesale_fine_art.php

Fine Jewelry

The jewelry business can be an extremely lucrative one, but there are many sub-specialties you can focus on. Buy-and-sell entrepreneurs can offer one-of-a-kind handmade jewelry, antique jewelry, or new fine jewelry featuring gold, silver, platinum, diamonds and expensive jewels. Another option is to focus on lower-end costume jewelry or less expensive sterling silver jewelry, which can be purchased in bulk for low wholesale prices and then marked up at least 100 to 200 percent or more when sold at retail.

Fine jewelry can be acquired from estate sales, auctions, jewelry designers, distributors and manufacturers. For less costly jewelry, liquidators are an excellent source. Once you decide what type of jewelry to buy and sell, make sure you have the ability to reach your target audience effectively and that you have the financial resources to maintain ample inventory.

When dealing with expensive jewelry, appraisals and authenticity become extremely important.

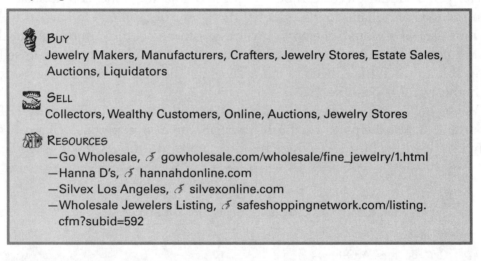

BUY
Jewelry Makers, Manufacturers, Crafters, Jewelry Stores, Estate Sales, Auctions, Liquidators

SELL
Collectors, Wealthy Customers, Online, Auctions, Jewelry Stores

RESOURCES
—Go Wholesale, ✄ gowholesale.com/wholesale/fine_jewelry/1.html
—Hanna D's, ✄ hannahdonline.com
—Silvex Los Angeles, ✄ silvexonline.com
—Wholesale Jewelers Listing, ✄ safeshoppingnetwork.com/listing.cfm?subid=592

First Aid Kits and Survival Gear

Homes, campers, hikers, businesses, factories, and schools and other public facilities all need to have first aid kits on hand. In many regions where natural disasters such as earthquakes, hurricanes or wildfires are commonplace, additional survival gear is also in demand.

Purchasing first aid kits and survival gear wholesale and reselling these items for great profits is definitely one buy-and-sell idea that could easily be overlooked because of its specialization. Yet for the right entrepreneur, this can become a lucrative business.

You have a couple of choices of how to sell first aid kits and survival gear. You can purchase preassembled first aid kits and survival gear in bulk from wholesalers, and sell them as is, with no modifications. Or you can create customized first aid kits and survival gear packs to meet the needs of specific target audiences, such as campers, small offices, or homes with kids. People have also made money selling specialized first aid kits for cat and dog owners.

When it comes to first aid kits, you'll definitely want to purchase and resell new and top-quality equipment and supplies. For survival gear, however, you can look to liquidators and army/navy surplus distributors to build your inventory. Sales of these items can be done online, B2B, at camping events and shows, and at flea markets, for example.

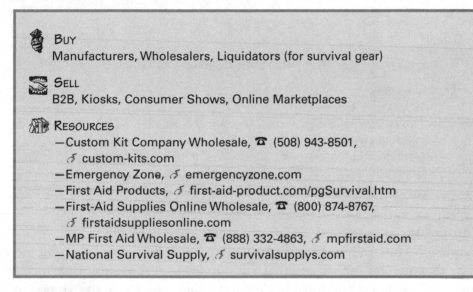

Buy
Manufacturers, Wholesalers, Liquidators (for survival gear)

Sell
B2B, Kiosks, Consumer Shows, Online Marketplaces

Resources
—Custom Kit Company Wholesale, ☎ (508) 943-8501,
      ✆ custom-kits.com
—Emergency Zone, ✆ emergencyzone.com
—First Aid Products, ✆ first-aid-product.com/pgSurvival.htm
—First-Aid Supplies Online Wholesale, ☎ (800) 874-8767,
      ✆ firstaidsuppliesonline.com
—MP First Aid Wholesale, ☎ (888) 332-4863, ✆ mpfirstaid.com
—National Survival Supply, ✆ survivalsupplys.com

Fishing Bait

A prerequisite, of course, to getting into this type of business—which caters to fishermen—is not to have an aversion to creepy-crawly things such as worms and leeches, because they will be two of your best income producers. Bait minnows, such as shiners, can be caught in rivers and creeks, using traps or a seine net. Or if you have the required space, you can install a minnow breeding pond. If you catch or raise bait, a license issued by the Department of Fisheries is generally required, so be sure to check local regulations.

Dew worms, aka nightcrawlers, are another bait. You can raise them in boxes of soil and moss or purchase them wholesale from worm farms. Leeches are yet another potentially profitable type of bait that can be raised or purchased in larger quantities and resold in smaller quantities for a profit.

To purchase the equipment necessary to store and sell fishing bait from home will require an investment of at least several thousand dollars. With that said, however, providing your home is in close proximity to popular fishing lakes or rivers, the investment can be quickly returned and rewarded with substantial profits if your business skills allow you to market your bait to local fishermen in need of your products.

BUY
Wholesalers

SELL
Homebased Sales, B2B, Fishing Shows, Tournaments and Events

RESOURCES
—Bait Net, ✆ baitnet.com
—Forked Tree Ranch Wholesale, ☎ (208) 267-2632,
   ✆ forkedtreeranch.com
—National Bait Inc., ☎ (905) 278-0180, ✆ nationalbait.com
—Shields Publications, ✆ wormbooks.com

Fishing Gear

For people who have a true passion for fishing, what better way to combine your hobby with your job than to establish a buy-and-sell business that focuses on offering all of the latest and most in-demand fishing gear to avid fishing enthusiasts such as yourself?

Fishing gear includes rods, reels, lures, knives, fish-finder electronics, waders, clipper tools, traps, line, how-to books, float tubes, vests, tackle boxes, downriggers, electric trolling motors, plus countless other highly profitable items that can be purchased from manufacturers, wholesalers and distributors.

You can then resell your products on eBay and at hunting and fishing shows, at flea markets and fishing tournaments, via mail order, or using any number of other selling venues. If you can afford to buy in volume, you will get the lowest prices purchasing factory direct from overseas manufacturers, especially in China. Also, do not overlook local fly tiers as a possible buying source for one-of-a-kind flies, as these can easily be sold for two to three times cost and will probably sell extremely well. One of the best ways to spread the word is to get out to the rivers and lakes in your area and let the fishermen know about your products.

Fitness Equipment

Fitness equipment—especially used equipment—ranks as one of the best things to buy and sell. There is always a steady supply of and demand for all types of fitness equipment. Many people purchase new fitness equipment hoping it will be their savior and put them on the path to better health, weight loss and improved fitness. Unfortunately, once they set it up at home, reality sinks in. Working out day in and day out is hard work and very time-consuming. In no time, that very expensive piece of exercise equipment becomes a very expensive clothes rack.

Finding used fitness equipment to purchase for very little money is as easy as looking on Craigslist or eBay or sifting through your local newspaper's classified ads. Flea markets are also a good source for obtaining inventory.

While used fitness equipment that's in like-new shape can be purchased cheaply, it can often be resold at a significant profit. Remember, much of the buy-and-sell game is timing, and in the case of fitness equipment, it does not take long before someone else will come along, also seeking a savior, but who wants to save money by buying used equipment.

New equipment can be bought from wholesalers and directly from manufacturers. Best sellers include treadmills, steppers, elliptical trainers, rowing machines, exercise bikes, free weights and universal multi-station machines. You can establish a homebased sales showroom or you can list your equipment for sale on any number of online marketplaces, including your own e-commerce website.

To earn a bit extra and differentiate your offerings, consider bundling your fitness equipment with fitness-oriented books and videos, or teaming up with a personal trainer who will offer their services at a discount to your customers.

BUY
Manufacturers, Wholesalers, Classified Ads, Auctions, Flea Markets

SELL
Homebased Sales, Sports and Fitness Shows, Online Marketplaces

RESOURCES
—Fit4Sale, ✆ fitnessequipmenttrader.com
—Hubie Equipment Manufacturing, ☎ 86-27-87454115 (China),
  ✆ hbcmec.com
—JIH KAO Equipment Manufacturing, ☎ 886-2-25373397 (Taiwan),
  ✆ jkexer.com.tw
—Fitness Factory Outlet, ✆ fitnessfactory.com
—American Fitness, ✆ americanfitness.net/wholesalefitnessequipment.
  html

Flags

Patriotism is at an all-time high in America. While not everyone agrees on specifics, most people and businesses want to show off their pride in America. When it comes to buying and selling flags, there is a huge variety available, including American flags, foreign country flags, state flags, provincial flags, sports flags, marine flags, gay pride flags, safety flags, historical reproduction flags, royal flags, military flags, organization flags, windsocks, auto racing flags and hand-held flags. Oh, and with flags comes the need for flagpoles or brackets to hang the flags, which means added profit potential for you.

Buy flags directly from manufacturers and wholesalers. There are numerous places to resell flags, such as online marketplaces, your own e-commerce website, and booth space in malls, flea markets, consumer shows and community events.

Additional revenues can be earned by offering a flagpole installation service, which can be subcontracted out to a local handyman on a revenue-split basis.

Buy
Manufacturers, Wholesalers

Sell
Homebased Sales, Kiosks, Online Marketplaces, Flea Markets

Resources
—American Flags Wholesale, ☎ (888) 719-9516, ✆ american-flags-wholesale.com
—National Independent Flag Dealers Association, ✆ flaginfo.com
—Patriotic Flags Wholesale, ☎ (866) 798-2803, ✆ patriotic-flags.com

Flowers

Homes and businesses use fresh cut flowers and floral arrangements as interior decoration. Flowers are also used as "Happy Birthday," "Get Well" and "Congratulations" gifts, and are sent to people mourning the death of a loved one. They're the perfect way to say "I'm sorry" or to brighten up the décor of any room.

Selling fresh cut flowers can be the perfect business for the right person. In addition to having some artistic ability to arrange flowers into attractive bouquets or arrangements, you must also be able to sell to customers and have the right combination and quantity of flowers in your inventory. After all, fresh cut flowers go bad quickly.

Unless you plan to open a retail florist shop and work full-time, you can make a part-time living selling flowers from a mall kiosk, at special events, to people hosting weddings or parties, or by setting up a small table or counter in a public area (assuming you can obtain permission to do this). This can also be the perfect holiday-only business. For example, you can sell roses around Valentine's Day.

Flowers can be purchased wholesale from distributors, growers and greenhouses. Or if you enjoy gardening, you can grow your own flowers and sell them.

Buy
Wholesalers, Distributors

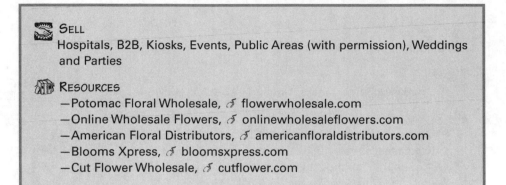

SELL
Hospitals, B2B, Kiosks, Events, Public Areas (with permission), Weddings and Parties

RESOURCES
—Potomac Floral Wholesale, ♂ flowerwholesale.com
—Online Wholesale Flowers, ♂ onlinewholesaleflowers.com
—American Floral Distributors, ♂ americanfloraldistributors.com
—Blooms Xpress, ♂ bloomsxpress.com
—Cut Flower Wholesale, ♂ cutflower.com

Furniture for Pets

People love to spoil their pets! Thus a fast-growing industry has grown around high-end pet furniture, including luxury beds that can retail for as much as $800 to $1,000. According to the book *Pampering Your Pooch: What Your Dog Wants, Needs and Loves* (Wiley Publishing, **PamperYourDogBook.com**), upscale pet furniture comes in every imaginable size, design and fabric selection. Some upscale dog bed manufacturers such as Pets At Play (**petsatplay.com**) will even customize their dog beds with special fabrics and memory foam mattresses.

Many of these high-end pet products are offered by smaller manufacturers that welcome new dealers into their distribution channels. You can then sell directly to pet owners—by attending pet shows or selling online, for example—or you can sell B2B to local pet stores. eBay is another excellent place to sell these types of items.

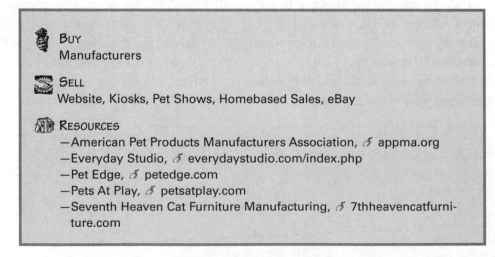

BUY
Manufacturers

SELL
Website, Kiosks, Pet Shows, Homebased Sales, eBay

RESOURCES
—American Pet Products Manufacturers Association, ♂ appma.org
—Everyday Studio, ♂ everydaystudio.com/index.php
—Pet Edge, ♂ petedge.com
—Pets At Play, ♂ petsatplay.com
—Seventh Heaven Cat Furniture Manufacturing, ♂ 7thheavencatfurniture.com

Garden Fountains

Garden fountains are a welcome addition to any garden, lawn, patio space or interior sunroom. Nothing quite matches the soothing sounds of tinkling water for relieving the day's stresses. Garden fountains and related accessories can be purchased from wholesalers, manufacturers and sometimes even local craftspeople.

Sell these products from home by displaying your fountains in the front and back yard with appropriate signage. Or exhibit and sell at home and garden shows, sell through online marketplaces (eBay), and join gardening clubs to network for new business. Additionally, sell related equipment such as replacement pump motors, underwater lights, water plants and stones. Another option is to sell directly to landscapers.

BUY
Manufacturers, Wholesalers, Crafters

SELL
Homebased Sales, Home and Garden Shows, eBay, Kiosks, Flea Markets, Landscapers (B2B)

RESOURCES
—Direct Outdoor Living, ✆ directoutdoorliving.com/fountains.aspx
—Garden Accessories & Tools Marketplace, ✆ garden-accessories-tools.com
—Garden Fountains Manufacturing, ☎ (866) 207-1674, ✆ garden-fountains.com
—Home Garden Heaven, ✆ homegardenheaven.com

Garden Ornaments

Garden statues, wall plaques and lawn ornaments are all hot sellers. Get started in this business by buying garden ornaments wholesale and reselling them to homeowners for a profit. Garden ornaments can be constructed from ceramics, wood, stone, fiberglass, plastic and a number of other materials. Display and sell right from your own front yard, or sell these products on eBay, at flea markets and at home and garden shows. You can also sell directly to landscapers.

Garden statues and ornaments can be purchased in North America and overseas from manufacturers, wholesalers and importers.

BUY
Manufacturers, Wholesalers, Craftspeople

SELL
Homebased Sales, Home and Garden Shows, eBay, Kiosks, Flea
Markets

RESOURCES
—Double D Statuary Manufacturing, ☎ (361) 364-2115, ✃ doubledstatu-
ary.com
—Home & Garden India, ✃ garden-decoratives.com/profile.html
—Kevin's Custom Crafts Manufacturing, ☎ (570) 523-0813,
✃ lighthouseman.com
—Sandstone Handicrafts, ✃ sandstone-handicrafts.com/stone-garden-
ornaments.html
—The Nurseryman, ✃ nurseryman.com/equipment-new/garden-art.html

Gift Baskets

This is the type of business that requires savvy marketing skills—not to mention plenty of creativity—since you'll make the most profits when you create your own products by combining groups of items you buy at wholesale prices. You can offer a variety of themed gift baskets incorporating small toys, plush toys, gourmet foods, candy, fruit, exotic cheeses, wine, cookies and other items.

If you decide to assemble the baskets yourself, they're surprisingly easy to assemble and all the products and baskets are readily available from wholesale sources. Simply select the items—such as specialty (gourmet) foods, flowers or personal health products—and then arrange them in attractive wicker baskets or similar containers. Wrap the basket in foil or colored plastic, add a bow and the gift basket is complete.

To earn greater profits, concentrate your marketing efforts on gaining repeat business from corporate clients, professionals, small-business owners and sales professionals such as real estate agents. Basically, focus on individuals and companies that would have reasons to regularly send out gift baskets to existing and new clients.

Promote your baskets by distributing direct mail brochures and by networking with your target audience at business and social functions in your community. You can also sell the gift baskets at community events, flea markets and public markets. With a bit of creativity and marketing savvy, the possibilities are endless, as is the profit potential.

In addition to offering your customers same-day local delivery, you'll also want to be able to ship your gift baskets via UPS, FedEx or DHL, to arrive at the recipient's destination overnight or in one to three business days.

BUY
Wholesalers, Manufacturers

SELL
B2B, Kiosks, Online Marketplaces, Community Events

RESOURCES
—Gift Basket Review Magazine Online, ✍ festivities-pub.com
—Bacon Basketware Limited, ☎ (905) 841-1525, ✍ baconbasket.com
—Burton and Burton, ✍ burtonandburton.com
—Country Baskets Imports, ☎ (703) 818-9173, ✍ basketsimports.com
—Creative Gift Packaging, ✍ creativegiftpackaging.com
—Epicurean Foods, ✍ epicureanfoods.com/ws/main.php
—Gift Basket Supplies, ✍ giftbasketsupplies.com

Golf Clubs and Equipment

Golf ranks as one of the most popular sports, hobbies and recreational pastimes in North America. You can make a bundle by selling new and used golf clubs and equipment. If you have some mechanical aptitude, you can dramatically increase profits by purchasing golf club components (heads, shafts and grips) wholesale and assembling the custom clubs at home to meet your clients' individual needs.

If you are not the handy type, you can purchase preassembled new clubs from wholesalers and manufacturers. Used golf clubs and accessories (such as bags, electric carts and pull-carts) can be bought at flea markets, garage sales, online golf websites, auctions and estate sales. New and used clubs and accessories can also be bought and sold through eBay.

To be successful at this type of business, you'll need to become a golf expert and know all about the sport as well as the equipment you'll be selling. Networking at golf clubs and regional tournaments is one way to generate additional business. Try to get local golf pros and instructors to promote your business via word-of-mouth. You can differentiate your business by selling unique or hard-to-find golf-related tools and accessories.

BUY
Wholesalers, Manufacturers, Classified Ads, Auctions

SELL
Homebased Sales, Online Marketplaces, Golf and Recreation Shows, Tournaments

RESOURCES
—Best Buy Golf Supply, ✏ bestbuygolfsupply.com
—Golf Equipment Shopping Guide, ✏ golfshoppingguide.com
—Golf Outlet USA, ✏ golfoutletsusa.com
—Golf Stuff Cheaper, ✏ http://golfstuffcheaper.com/newitems.html
—Wholesale Golf Components, ✏ https://wgcgolf.com/store

Gourmet Foods

Only the finest gourmet foods from around the globe will do for your customers if you decide to start a gourmet food buy-and-sell business. Specialize in one particular type of gourmet food, such as Canadian maple syrup, caviar or Italian olives, or in food categories, such as desserts, imported candy, gourmet chocolates, seafood or baked goods.

Buy from importers, wholesalers, producers and manufacturers, both nationally and internationally. Establish a website so people from every corner of the globe can order from you online. Also, sell at farmers' markets, public markets, and mall kiosks.

You will have to sort out storage, shipping and possibly even licensing issues, depending on the types of foods you intend to sell. However, with that said, the work is worth the effort because selling gourmet foods can be extremely profitable.

BUY
Wholesalers, Manufacturers, Growers, Producers

SELL
Mail Order, E-Commerce Website, Kiosks, Farmers' Markets

RESOURCES
—Caviar Etc. Wholesale, ☎ (800) 819-4330, ✏ caviaretc.com
—Gourmet Food Mall, ✏ gourmetfoodmall.com

—Gourmet Products, Inc., ✍ gourmetproductsinc.com
—Imperial Foods, ✍ imperial-foods.com
—Shaw Specialty Foods, ✍ shawspecialtyfoods.com
—The Gourmet Food & Accessory Trade Mart, ✍ gftm.com

Government Surplus

The U.S. federal government and many local government agencies discard unneeded or unwanted items by offering them for sale at extremely low prices. Purchasing government surplus and seized merchandise for pennies on the dollar, and then reselling to consumers at marked-up prices, can make you wealthy.

Government agencies and organizations of every sort sell off used and surplus equipment, as well as items seized for nonpayment or from criminal activity. If you get into this business, you can acquire valuable merchandise for resale from the IRS, USPS, U.S. Small Business Administration (SBA), U.S. Marshals Service, and U.S. Treasury Department, just to name a few government agencies.

There are many more government agencies at the federal, state, county and city levels that also routinely hold auctions and public sales to dispose of surplus, foreclosed and seized property. Though most of these sales are conducted like traditional auction sales, sometimes the sale can be by sealed-bid tender, which means you complete a tender form and submit the amount you are willing to pay for a specific item. Tender forms are available directly from the government agency holding the sale or the auctioneer conducting the sale.

Just some of the items that are routinely auctioned by government agencies include computers, real estate, automobiles, machinery and tools, jewelry, furniture, electronics and boats. Sell the larger items you buy from home and through eBay. Smaller items can be sold at flea markets, for example.

When acquiring inventory, it's important to know exactly what you're buying, its value, and what the demand among your potential customers will be. Otherwise, you could get stuck buying and then storing a bunch of junk.

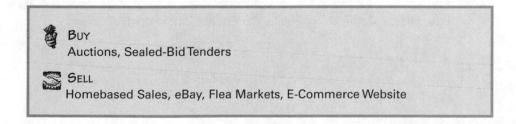

BUY
Auctions, Sealed-Bid Tenders

SELL
Homebased Sales, eBay, Flea Markets, E-Commerce Website

> **RESOURCES**
> —Government Auctions, ♂ governmentauctions.org
> —Public Works and Government Services Canada, ☎ (905) 615-2025,
>   ♂ http://crownassets.pwgsc.gc.ca/text/index-e.cfm
> —U.S. Department of the Treasury, ☎ (202) 622-2000, ♂ ustreas.gov/
>   auctions/treasury/rp
> —U.S. General Services Administration, ☎ (800) 473-7836,
>   ♂ http://gsaauctions.gov/gsaauctions/gsaauctions
> —U.S. Postal Service, ♂ usps.com/auctions

GPS (Global Positioning System) Units

Thanks to technological advancements, the price of GPS systems has dropped considerably, making these navigation devices affordable by many automobile owners, bikers, hikers, boaters and campers. With GPS systems starting in price at $200 and going up to $2,000, there's plenty of profit to be made selling these devices to individual consumers, or to businesses with fleets of cars, trucks or vans.

One reason why this market continues to grow is because of the high theft rate. Thieves specifically target cars with GPS systems. Thus the car owner who has their GPS device stolen ultimately needs to replace it. Also, as technology advances, new and more useful features are added to these units, so owners often opt to periodically purchase upgraded or more advanced models.

While there is a lot of competition, the most profit can be made selling new, higher-end GPS systems. You can acquire your inventory from wholesalers and distributors. Sales can be done in person, at car shows, consumer electronics shows, boat shows, outdoor recreation shows, and flea markets, or online using eBay or your own e-commerce website.

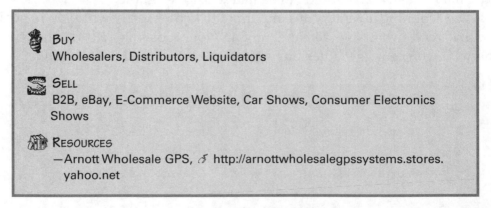

BUY
Wholesalers, Distributors, Liquidators

SELL
B2B, eBay, E-Commerce Website, Car Shows, Consumer Electronics Shows

RESOURCES
—Arnott Wholesale GPS, ♂ http://arnottwholesalegpssystems.stores.
  yahoo.net

—CWR Electronics, ✄ cwrelectronics.com/industries.html
—Go Wholesale, ✄ gowholesale.com/wholesale/gps/1.html
—GPS Discount, ✄ gpsdiscount.com/home.html
—Mega GPS, ✄ megagps.com

Greenhouses

Hobby greenhouses have become a very popular addition to many backyard and patio spaces, especially for the baby boomer generation as they slip into retirement and look for ways to keep active and enjoy life.

Hobby greenhouses are a scaled-down version of industrial greenhouses that allow people to grow their own flowers, herbs, fruits and vegetables. Retail prices range from a few hundred dollars for basic models to $5,000 or more for models with all the bells and whistles. Purchasing wholesale or direct from the manufacturer, you can expect to retain 20 to 25 percent of the retail-selling price as your profit.

Hobby greenhouses are generally sold in kit form, making them easy to ship. Many manufacturers even provide drop-shipping options direct to your customers, so you do not have to worry about storage and transportation issues.

The best ways to sell hobby greenhouses are through gardening clubs, by referral, by exhibiting at home and garden shows, and via online marketplaces such as gardening websites and eBay. If you're selling locally, you can provide full installation services. For added profits, you can also sell selections of seeds and gardening supplies to help people get started growing quickly and easily. The more you know about gardening, the easier time you'll have selling greenhouses to consumers who are gardening enthusiasts.

🏺 BUY
Manufacturers, Wholesalers

🤝 SELL
Homebased Sales, Home and Garden Shows, Online Marketplaces

🏠 RESOURCES
—BC Greenhouse Manufacturing, ☎ (888) 391-4433,
  ✄ bcgreenhouses.com
—Farm Wholesale Greenhouses, ☎ (800) 825-1925,
  ✄ farmwholesale.com

—Hobby Greenhouse Association, ✍ hobbygreenhouse.org
—National Greenhouse Manufacturers Association, ✍ ngma.com
—PharmTec Corp, ☎ (877) 833-2221, ✍ pharmteccorp.com

Greeting Cards

Every year, billions of dollars' worth of paper greeting cards are sold around the globe, thereby qualifying them as a fantastic buy-and-sell product. Service both high-end and regular greeting card markets by purchasing mass-produced greeting cards wholesale and selling them on consignment through gift shops and other retailers.

You can also sell high-end, one-of-a-kind, original greeting cards by contracting with local artists to paint original watercolor scenes to fit every occasion. Use blank greeting card stock, effectively making each card a highly collectible piece of artwork. The artists' greeting cards can be sold through retailers, direct to businesses for promotional reasons, to consumers via mall sales kiosks, eBay or your own e-commerce website, and by establishing alliances with wedding and event planners who can refer your one-of-a-kind artist cards to their clients.

Yet another option is to acquire the rights to photographs and have greeting cards printed that showcase those professionally taken photos, which can be of people, pets, nature scenes or other subjects.

BUY
Wholesalers, Publishers, Artists

SELL
B2B, Flea Markets, Kiosks, Online Marketplaces

RESOURCES
—Art Galaxy Wholesale, ☎ (905) 469-9937, ✍ artgalaxy.com
—Darren Browning Photography, ✍ darrenbrowning.com
—Dollar Days Wholesale, ☎ (877) 837-9569, 🖥 dollardays.com
—Greeting Card Association, ✍ greetingcard.org
—Sincere Sentiments, ✍ sinceresentiments.com
—SNAFU Card Designs, ☎ (651) 698-8581, ✍ snafudesigns.com
—ChuckleBerry'sWholesale Paper Cards, ✍ wholesalepapercards.com

Hammocks

Next to providing great profit potential, the best thing about selling hammocks is that they typically sell themselves. Who can resist the thought of spending a lazy summer afternoon napping in a hammock under a shady tree in their backyard or on a beach?

Purchase hammocks directly from importers, manufacturers, wholesalers and craftspeople. While the hammocks can certainly be sold through any number of online marketplaces such as eBay, do not overlook the power of demonstration. Setting up a hammock that people can try out is a very persuasive marketing tool, and one that can be effectively used at flea markets, in conjunction with rented kiosk space, at community events and at home and garden shows.

BUY
Manufacturers, Wholesalers, Craftspeople, Importers

SELL
Online Marketplaces, Consumer Shows, Flea Markets, Kiosks

RESOURCES
—Hammocks, ☞ hammocks.com/business/index.cfm
—Second May Inc., ☎ 91-120-2576746 (India), ☞ secondmay.net/hammocks.html
—Super Wholesaler, ☞ superwholesaler.com/merchandise/hammocks
—The Hammock Source Wholesale, ☎ (800) 334-1078, ☞ thehammock-source.com

Hand and Power Tools

Hand and small power tools such as hammers, screwdriver sets, socket sets, cordless drills, circular saws and wrench sets are without question some of the best and most profitable products to buy at deeply discounted prices. Simply mark up and resell these items to do-it-yourself enthusiasts.

Because used values are not terrifically high on most hand and power tools, especially on non-motorized hand tools, you are well advised to stick with selling new products, not used. Purchase from wholesalers, manufacturers, distributors and liquidators. Hand and power tools are perfect items to sell on eBay, at flea markets, at automotive and home and garden shows, and from mall kiosks.

BUY
Wholesalers, Manufacturers, Liquidators

SELL
Temporary Locations, Flea Markets, Online Marketplaces, Home Shows

RESOURCES
—Central Online Sales, ♂ centralonlinesales.com
—DCM Tools, ♂ dcmtools.com
—Drop-Shipped Products, ♂ dropshippedproducts.com
—Liquidation.com, ♂ liquidation.com
—National Wholesale Tools, ♂ nationalwholesaletools.com
—Wholesale Tool Company, ♂ wttool.com

Handcrafted Jewelry

Whether you create the jewelry yourself or contract local artists and crafters to create your inventory for you, selling high-end, one-of-a-kind, handmade jewelry can be a lucrative business. Selling opportunities include flea markets, events, craft fairs, home sales parties, online and selling B2B to jewelry stores or gift shops.

The trick to being successful with this type of business is to gather a collection of exotic, upscale and unique jewelry that women will want to buy for themselves, or that people will want to buy as gifts. You'll need to be a savvy marketer to be able to effectively reach a wide enough target audience; however, the profit potential should be significant.

Handcrafted jewelry is very different from selling costume jewelry that's inexpensive and that can be bought in bulk. It's also different from selling fine jewelry, such as what you'd find at upscale retail jewelry stores.

BUY
Crafters and Jewelry Makers

SELL
Flea Markets, B2B, Craft Shows, Home Sales Parties, Events

RESOURCES
—Austin Design, ♂ austindesignjewelry.com

—Bronte York, ✂ bronteyork.net
—Gaia, ✂ gaiaccessories.com
—Gifts Joy, ✂ giftsjoy.com
—Inca Zone, ✂ incazone.com
—Kincaid Designs, ✂ kincaidesigns.com
—ML Creations, ✂ mlcreations.net/wholesale.htm
—Olympic Gold, ✂ olympiagold.com

Hand-Knit Items

If you're a knitter or can gather together a handful of skilled knitters, there's money to be made selling handcrafted sweaters, hats, scarves, baby blankets and other knitted items. These products make perfect gifts and can be sold for top-dollar at craft shows and flea markets, online, at special events, and on consignment at certain types of retail stores.

The key to success for this type of business is to gather your inventory from crafters on a consignment basis: this means that you round up other talented knitters and they provide you with their wares in exchange for a cut of the profits. They get paid after their items are sold. As the buy-and-sell entrepreneur, it becomes your responsibility to handle marketing and sales.

This is a great part-time business for senior citizens and moms who are looking for homebased employment and who want to exploit both their creative side and business savvy.

BUY
Crafters, Knitters

SELL
Crafts Fairs, Online, Flea Markets, Special Events

RESOURCES
—Knitability, ✂ knitability.com
—A Good Yarn, ✂ agoodyarn.net/Favorite_Links.htm
—HeartStrings FiberArts, ✂ heartstringsfiberarts.com/wholesale.shtm
—Needle Nook Designs, ✂ needlenook.on.ca/product.htm

Handbags

Whether new, used, vintage or replica, the handbag marketplace is hot and a prime candidate for a profitable buy-and-sell enterprise. If you decide to sell only new handbags, stick with buying off-brand names and replicas from overseas manufacturers, as well as from liquidators for out-of-season and end-of-run handbags, or from emerging domestic handbag designers and manufacturers.

Sell at flea markets, consumer shows and fashion shows, on eBay, and from mall and public market kiosks. Street vending in a city is also a great sales venue for knock-offs and off-brand-name products. Vintage bags (which are authentic, not knock-offs) from top designers such as Fendi, Gucci, Prada, Versace, Coach, Valentino and Alviero Martini will take a little bit of detective work to uncover and buy at flea markets, garage sales, estate sales and secondhand clothing shops. These can be sold for top dollar on eBay, through collector shows and auctions, and directly to collectors—especially if they are rare and in great original condition.

Before getting into this business, make sure you fully understand the handbag marketplace and are familiar with top designers and the value of their products. It's also essential that you understand your target market and are able to cater perfectly to their wants and needs, based on your product inventory and how you do your selling.

BUY
Manufacturers, Wholesalers, Garage Sales

SELL
Kiosks, Flea Markets, eBay, Fashion Shows, Collectors, Street Vending

RESOURCES
—Bariss Enterprises, ✎ wholesaledesignerhandbags.com
—CERI Wholesale, ☎ (800) 541-1688, ✎ ceriwholesale.com
—Handbag Wholesale List, ✎ handbagwholesalelist.com
—Handbags at Wholesale, ✎ handbagsatwholesale.com
—Wholesale Purses and Jewelry, ☎ (256) 633-0168,
 ✎ wholesalepursesandjewelry.com

Hats

Among guys, baseball hats are a popular fashion accessory. Hat styles that are popular among women tend to be much more varied. Launching a buy-and-sell business based around hats, however, is a surefire way to get your head in the entrepreneurial game.

Hat types and styles include baseball hats, fashion hats, work hats, licensed sports hats, sun hats, garden hats, Panama hats, straw hats, cowboy hats, novelty hats, pillbox hats, berets, ski (winter) hats, Tiley hats, visors, fedoras, trucker hats and outdoorsmen hats.

Buy from wholesalers, liquidators and factory direct for the lowest pricing. Sell at flea markets, at consumer shows, on your own e-commerce website and on eBay. Because the retail price of many hats is relatively low, be prepared to do a volume-based business if you want to earn the big bucks. One way to make some quick cash is to purchase hats with official sports team logos from a distributor and then resell them at or near major sporting events, parades and victory celebrations.

You can also sell custom-embroidered or silkscreened hats to local sports teams (school and amateur teams), companies and other types of groups.

BUY
Manufacturers, Wholesalers, Garage Sales

SELL
Kiosks, Flea Markets, eBay, Fashion Shows, Teams and Groups, Companies

RESOURCES
—Cap Wholesalers, 🖫 capwholesalers.com
—Kraft Hat Manufacturers, ☎ (718) 620-6100, 🖫 krafthat.com
—The Hat Site, links to hat manufacturers and wholesalers,
  🖫 thehatsite.com
—TradeKey, 🖫 tradekey.com/ks-wholesale-licensed-sports-merchandise
—Village Hat Shop Wholesale, ☎ (619) 683-5533, 🖫 villagehatshop.com

Herbs and Spices

Herbs and spices not only make food taste great, but they also may be used to treat medical conditions and physiological disorders, and as an agent to help promote weight loss. You have a couple of options for buying and selling herbs and spices. First, you can purchase them directly from wholesalers, manufacturers, or even local producers whose products are prepackaged and ready for resale. Or you can purchase herbs and spices in bulk quantities and repackage them into small containers for resale. The first option is far more convenient, but the second option offers the most profit potential.

Once you have determined your buying source and packaging method, the herbs and spices can be sold directly to restaurants and at flea markets, farmers' markets and public markets. Also consider online marketplaces. To differentiate your company from your competition, look into importing exotic or unusual spices from overseas. Grenada is a great overseas source for spices.

Buy
Wholesalers, Manufacturers, Growers

Sell
Mail Order, Kiosks, Flea Market, Website, B2B, Farmers' Markets

Resources
—Atlantic Spice Company, ☎ (800) 316-7965, ✍ atlanticspice.com
—Importers.com, ✍ importers.com/Spices/trade-directory-80652-0-0-kl.html
—The Great American Spice Company, ☎ (888) 502-8058, ✍ americanspice.com
—The Spice House, ✍ thespicehouse.com

High-Definition Digital Televisions

In the United States, all of the major television networks and TV stations will begin broadcasting a digital television signal starting in February 2009. Many are already doing so. Thus traditional analog TVs will be outdated and obsolete. Millions of Americans will be buying new high-definition digital televisions, as well as special adapters for their existing TVs in order to decode the new digital signal.

While the mass-market retailers and consumer electronics superstores are already capitalizing on this fast-growing market, there's still room for the "little guy." You can buy from distributors, wholesalers and liquidators, and resell to consumers through a variety of sales venues, including eBay or your own e-commerce website.

To be successful, develop an expertise in home theater systems, so you can not only sell people their new TVs, but also help them install them in conjunction with their Tivo, Blu-ray player, digital cable box, surround sound speaker system and other high-tech gadgets.

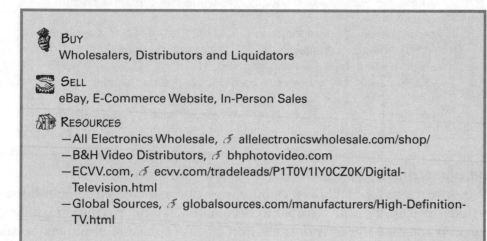

BUY
Wholesalers, Distributors and Liquidators

SELL
eBay, E-Commerce Website, In-Person Sales

RESOURCES
—All Electronics Wholesale, ♂ allelectronicswholesale.com/shop/
—B&H Video Distributors, ♂ bhphotovideo.com
—ECVV.com, ♂ ecvv.com/tradeleads/P1T0V1IY0CZ0K/Digital-Television.html
—Global Sources, ♂ globalsources.com/manufacturers/High-Definition-TV.html

Holiday Decorations

Holiday decorations are big business, especially at Christmas, Easter, New Year's Day, Thanksgiving, Halloween, Valentine's Day and Mardi Gras. You can buy and sell decorations and accessories such as lights, ornaments, costumes, masks, nativity scenes, outside yard displays, wreaths, bells and artificial Christmas trees.

One of the best aspects of buying and selling holiday decorations is that you can buy them for less than wholesale at insanely low prices by waiting to purchase out of season, hanging on to your goods until the following year, and then realizing full retail in the flurry of holiday shopping.

Sell online, at flea markets, and by renting kiosks at malls and public markets. The value of antique and vintage holiday decorations has also recently taken off, especially Christmas ornaments and figurines, so keep your eyes peeled for bargains at garage sales and auctions.

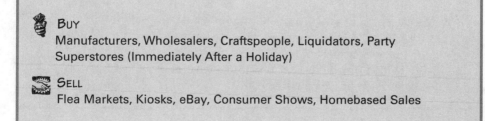

BUY
Manufacturers, Wholesalers, Craftspeople, Liquidators, Party Superstores (Immediately After a Holiday)

SELL
Flea Markets, Kiosks, eBay, Consumer Shows, Homebased Sales

RESOURCES
—Brandano Displays, ♂ brandano.com/wholesale-christmas-decorations.htm
—Four Seasons General Merchandise, ☎ (323) 582-4444, ♂ 4sgm.com
—KIP International Wholesale, ☎ (215) 289-2447, ♂ kipintl.com
—Light-Up Christmas, ♂ lightupchristmas.com
—SZ Wholesale, ♂ sz-wholesale.com/shenzhen_China_products/Holiday-Decoration_1.htm
—Wholesale Central, ♂ wholesalecentral.com/Holiday-Seasonal.html

Home Electronics

While they're not as profitable as they once were due to increased competition and lower retail prices, it's still possible to become successful buying and selling a wide variety of home and consumer electronics: DVD players, amplifiers, speaker systems, MP3 players, programmable remote controls, fax machines, wireless telephones, digital cameras, digital picture frames, headphones, home video cameras and home theater systems.

New electronics equipment can be purchased from wholesalers. To earn the highest profits possible, stay away from the used electronics business. There is, however, great money to be made selling discounted refurbished goods that come with a factory warranty. To save money and eliminate the need to maintain an inventory, consider working with a reputable drop-shipping company.

When it comes to selling your products, your own e-commerce website, eBay and flea markets are the ideal venues.

BUY
Wholesalers, Manufacturers, Liquidators

SELL
Flea Markets, eBay, Kiosks, Homebased Sales

RESOURCES
—1 AAA Wholesale Liquidators, ☎ (800) 661-9430, ♂ 1aaawholesaleliquidators.com
—B&H Video Distributors, ♂ bhphotovideo.com
—Chinavasion, ♂ chinavasion.com

—Dollar Days Wholesale, ☎ (877) 837-9569, ✍ dollardays.com
—East West Imports & Services, ✍ ewis.ca
—Mega Goods Drop-Shipper, ✍ http://megagoods.com
—Ubid.com, ✍ ubid.com/electronics

Home Medical Equipment (Used)

If you choose to buy and sell home medical equipment, you will be entering into an explosive growth industry. Just one way to operate this type of business is to convert your garage into a lavish showroom that's stocked with best-quality, previously owned home medical equipment. Bestselling products include power and manual wheelchairs, walkers, mechanical lifts and slings, scooters and bath safety products.

Use your negotiation skills to buy at low prices through online marketplaces and from private sellers advertising in classified ads, as well as at auctions and estate sales. You can utilize an e-commerce website to generate online sales, display at health fairs and also sell through eBay.

Thoroughly cleaning and tuning up all equipment, as well as providing a warranty, will greatly increase the value of your inventory. Also, be sure to build alliances with doctors, physiotherapists and chiropractors, so they can refer your business to their clients in need of home medical equipment.

BUY
Online Marketplaces, Classified Ads, Estate Sales

SELL
Homebased Showroom, E-Commerce Website, Health Fairs, eBay,
Word-of-Mouth Referrals from Medical Professionals

RESOURCES
—Med Marketplace, ✍ medmarketplace.com
—Med Matrix, ✍ classifieds.medmatrix.com
—Medical Solutions, Inc., ✍ medicalsolutionsinc.com
—Used HME, ✍ usedhme.com
—World Wide Wheelchairs, ✍ usedwheelchairs.com

Home Security Products

Like personal security products, home security products are hot sellers. These products include window security bars and roll shutters, home alarm systems, surveillance equipment, security lighting and many other devices. People from across America want to protect their families, homes and belongings. The best way to do this is to be proactive and get the security devices that get the job done.

Because there are numerous manufacturers and wholesalers of home security devices, supply at reasonable terms and prices will not be difficult to secure. Selling your products can be accomplished in a number of ways, including marketing through eBay and other online marketplaces, direct from your home, exhibiting at home and garden shows, and direct to business owners intent on protecting their shops, employees, customers and livelihoods.

This is the type of business where it's essential to become a true expert in security, so that you can properly instruct people how to use the equipment you're selling and be able to understand the individual needs of your customers. You can earn additional revenue by installing complete home security systems.

BUY
Wholesalers, Manufacturers

SELL
Homebased Sales, Consumer Shows, Kiosks, Online Marketplaces

RESOURCES
—Advance Safes, ☌ centurionsafes.com
—Cutting Edge Products, ☌ cuttingedgeproducts.net
—Homespy, www.homespy.com
—Maziuk Wholesale Distributors, ☎ (800) 777-5945, ☌ maziuk.com
—Safety Technology Wholesale, ☎ (904) 720-2188,
    ☌ safetytechnology.com

Home Theater Systems and Surround Sound

These days, people like to truly experience their TV and movie watching at home. This requires them to invest in large-screen, high-definition, digital TVs, Tivo and a Blu-ray player, pay for digital cable, and add a surround sound speaker system to their setup. The problem is, when you start adding all of these technological devices together and hope they'll work, things get very confusing.

Surround sound speaker systems and complete home theater systems can be purchased from wholesalers, distributors and liquidators and then sold directly to consumers online or through a variety of in-person sales venues. To achieve success, however, you really have to know your products, be able to address the needs of your customers, plus be able to help your customers install their equipment properly. You can change an additional fee for installation and setup services.

If you're thinking about selling home theater systems and/or surround sound systems, also look into selling the other audio/video components that people hook up to their televisions in order to generate higher profits. Because you're dealing with technology that gets out of date quickly, you're much better off selling only new equipment or factory refurbished equipment that comes with a manufacturer's warranty.

While the profit margin might not be too high with the home theater systems themselves (due to competition), there is significant profit margin in selling accessories, programmable remote controls, power surge protectors and the A/V cables needed to install and use this equipment.

Buy
Wholesalers, Distributors, Liquidators, Importers

Sell
Flea Markets, Online, Events, Homebased Sales

Resources
—All Electronics Wholesale, ✆ allelectronicswholesale.com/shop/
—B&H Video Distributors, ✆ bhphotovideo.com
—ECVV.com, ✆ ecvv.com/tradeleads/P1T0V1IY0CZ0K/Digital-Television.html
—Global Sources, ✆ globalsources.com/manufacturers/High-Definition-TV.html

Hot Tubs

Used hot tubs can be purchased for a song. The reason is simple: Even though there is a huge and growing demand for new and used hot tubs, the units themselves are generally large and heavy, and require a professional (with a truck) to install them. Obviously, these are more than sufficient reasons to scare off many would-be buyers of secondhand hot tubs.

This is where the profit equation begins, because you can put together all of these benefits: purchase used hot tubs cheaply, invest in transportation and equipment, and contract with professionals (such as handymen, electricians and plumbers) for installation. Doing so will enable you to sell secondhand hot tubs as a complete package, including the tub, the transportation, professional installation, and you can even throw in a month's worth of chemicals. If you make it easy and convenient for people to buy the things they want, they will. In the process, you will profit handsomely.

The alternative is to sell brand-new hot tubs; however, you'll probably face a lot of competition, plus the costs to enter this type of business are significantly higher. You can, however, purchase new products from wholesalers and distributors if you're so inclined. If you do well in this business, you can consider expanding your product line to include home saunas. For new equipment, look into working with drop-shippers to save yourself money and eliminate your need to maintain an inventory.

BUY
Manufacturers, Wholesalers, Classified Ads, Liquidators

SELL
Homebased Sales, Online Marketplaces, Home and Garden Shows

RESOURCES
—360 Wichita Hot Tubs, ♂ 360wichita.com/Shopping/Home/WholesaleHotTubs.html
—Association of Pool & Spa Professionals, ♂ http://apsp.org/
—North West Wholesale, ♂ http://northwestwholesale.com/
—Roberts Hot Tubs, ☎ (800) 735-5290, ♂ rhtubs.com
—Skyview Spas, ♂ sunspaces.com/spas/hottubs.htm

Houseplants

In addition to buying houseplants from wholesale nurseries or direct from growers, you can set up your own interior or exterior greenhouse(s) and grow your own plants for sale. Of course, this is provided you have a green thumb, space and available investment capital.

Regardless of whether you buy wholesale or grow your own, you can sell houseplants at home and garden shows, flea markets and mall kiosks, and directly from home.

If you decide to grow plants, you can also sell to plant wholesalers and directly to retailers (such as convenience and grocery stores) on a wholesale basis. To help boost revenues and profits, also sell plant accessories, such as pots and containers, plant stands, hanging baskets, fertilizer, soil and peat moss. There's also profit to be made selling B2B to offices that want to use plants as interior décor.

> **BUY**
> Wholesale Nurseries, Growers, Grow Your Own
>
> **SELL**
> Kiosks, Flea Markets, Homebased Sales, B2B
>
> **RESOURCES**
> —iVillage Garden Web, ✆ gardenbazaar.com/directory/cz_1J3.html
> —Specimen House, ☎ (760) 944-1193, ✆ specimen-house.com
> —The Garden Community (Wholesaler Directory),
>   ✆ gardencom.com/wtropical.html
> —The Plant Ranch, ☎ (800) 344-8733, ✆ plantranchco.com

How-To Information

How-to books, e-books (electronic and downloadable content), audio tapes, audio CDs, instructional videos/DVDs and software can retail for as much as $100 to $300 each and cost as little as a few dollars to buy wholesale or to produce yourself, making this a fantastic buy-and-sell opportunity.

Many publishers, authors and media companies sell master copies or reproduction rights to their works cheaply, which means that you can purchase and reproduce the work in various print and electronic mediums and formats to resell for a profit.

There are two kinds of rights: reprint rights and master rights. Reprint rights allow the owner of the copyrighted material to authorize a buyer (in this case, you) to reproduce the materials in print or electronic format for resale. Master rights means the copyright owner authorizes the buyer to sell the reprint rights to anyone they wish. Popular how-to and self-help information has always included subjects relating to business, sales, marketing, relationships, childrearing, home renovation, health, crafts, overcoming depression, overcoming anxiety and recovering from a tragedy, as well as diet and fitness. The best selling methods include online sales, back-of-room seminar sales, trade shows and mail order.

If you're creating your own products, focus on top-notch production quality and professional-looking packaging. If you're buying pre-created products from wholesalers, publishers or distributors, this is done for you. One business model is to team up with seminar coordinators, record their conferences and seminars, and then sell tapes, CDs, videos or DVDs to the attendees. Remember, people are willing to pay top dollar for information they perceive to be valuable to them.

BUY
Publishers, Copyright Holders (Authors), Liquidators

SELL
Website, Online Marketplaces, Mail Order, Seminars

RESOURCES
—Book Liquidator, ♂ bookliquidator.com/servlet/StoreFront
—McGraw-Hill Audio, ♂ ami-mcgraw-hillaudio.com/Wholesale-Audio-Bookst.html
—Reprint Rights, ☎ (888) 550-8855, ♂ reprint-rights.com
—Wholesale DVDs, ♂ wholesalecentral.com

Hunting Equipment

Like fishing, hunting is big business. Thus selling equipment and supplies directly to the millions of hunting enthusiasts in America (with the exception of United States Vice Presidents), can be a very viable business opportunity.

However, due to lots of red tape, regulations and a host of storage concerns, avoid selling guns and ammo, at least while you're getting your business started. Leave that to the established shops and outfitters. Instead, concentrate your efforts on other hunting equipment and supplies, such as decoys, calls, blinds, camouflage materials, scents, hearing protection, clothing, first aid kits, survival packs, portable GPS systems and instructional books and videos.

New equipment and supplies can be purchased wholesale from manufacturers and distributors, while used equipment can be bought at auctions, through classified ads, and via online marketplaces. New and used hunting equipment can be sold at sports and recreation shows, from a homebased showroom and on eBay.

🪆 **BUY**
Manufacturers, Wholesalers, Classified Ads, Auctions

🤝 **SELL**
Homebased Sales, Online Marketplaces, Recreation Shows

🏚 **RESOURCES**
—Dollar Days Wholesale, ☎ (877) 837-9569, ✒ dollardays.com
—Hunting & Fishing Gear Review, ✒ hunting-fishing-gear.com
—Valor Corporation Wholesale, ☎ (800) 899-8256, ✒ valorcorp.com
—Wholesale Buyer's Index for Hunting & Fishing, ✒ buyersindex.com/
brca/512.htm
—Wholesale Distributors Directory, ✒ wholesaledistributorsnet.com/
sporting_goods.html

Hydroponics Equipment

Hydroponics gardening is becoming increasingly popular, especially in urban centers where parks and living space are at a premium. When you consider the benefits of hydroponics gardening, it is not difficult to understand the rise in its popularity. To make things grow using this technology, no heavy soil and much less space is required. There's also less mess, but equal or greater plant production versus traditional growing methods.

In combination with nutrient-rich liquids, hydroponics equipment can be used to start and grow virtually every type of indoor and outdoor plant, which can later be transplanted directly to the garden or potting container.

For the entrepreneur who wants to operate a small, yet potentially profitable buy-and-sell enterprise, hydroponics equipment and supplies fit the bill perfectly.

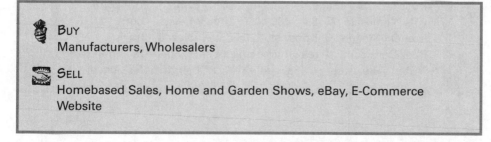

🪆 **BUY**
Manufacturers, Wholesalers

🤝 **SELL**
Homebased Sales, Home and Garden Shows, eBay, E-Commerce
Website

> 🏠 RESOURCES
> —Bloomington Wholesale Garden Supply, ☎ (800) 316-1306,
>   🖱 bwgs.com
> —Horizon Hydroponics, 🖱 hhydro.com/cgi-bin/hhydro/HYDROPONICS_
>   WHOLESALE.html
> —Hydroponics Wholesale, 🖱 hydroponicswholesale.com
> —LMC Wholesale, ☎ (866) 584-3634, 🖱 wholesale-garden.com
> —Micro Hydroponics Wholesale, ☎ (650) 968-4070, 🖱 microhydropon-
>   ics.com

Imprinted T-Shirts

Vintage T-shirts are fashionable and trendy. To get into this business, you can purchase your stock at garage sales, flea markets and used clothing stores, paying as
little as $1 per shirt, and then resell them to collectors and consumers through var-
ious online marketplaces for up to $50 each (depending on the style and rarity).

In addition to vintage T-shirts, you can sell new T-shirts emblazoned with all
sorts of designs, captions and logos. Buy from manufacturers, wholesalers and liquidators. Like vintage T-shirts, you can sell new T-shirts on eBay, at flea markets,
mall and beach kiosks and community events, and wherever people gather in
your community.

> 👜 BUY
> Wholesalers, Manufacturers, Secondhand Clothing Shops, Garage Sales
>
> 🤝 SELL
> Kiosks, Flea Markets, Community Events, eBay
>
> 🏠 RESOURCES
> —Dust Factory Vintage, 🖱 http://dustfactoryvintage.com/shirt4.htm
> —FTH Wholesale, ☎ (888) 708-1090, 🖱 fthwholesale.com
> —Iron-On Station, 🖱 irononstation.com/wholesale.htm
> —RetroDuck.com, 🖱 retroduck.com/cart/shop.cgi/page=wholesale.htm
> —T-Shirt Wholesaler, ☎ (888) 245-8141, 🖱 t-shirtwholesaler.com

Jukeboxes

If you have a passion for music and nostalgia, plus a fair amount of investment capital, you can begin buying and selling jukeboxes. Antique, new and reproduction jukeboxes are hot sellers that can earn you a fortune, especially when you consider that classic art deco Wurlitzers from the '40s command five figures, reproductions can sell for up to $10,000, and new Rowe CD models can also reach $10,000.

Because the retail value of jukeboxes is high, it is possible to make $100,000 a year and only have to buy and sell perhaps 20 to 40 units, not to mention the extra money that can be earned selling related accessories (such as new and used parts, 45 and 78 rpm records, manuals, signs and souvenirs).

Look for antique jukeboxes to buy low. Keep an eye on classified advertising, online marketplaces, collectible shows and auctions. New and reproduction jukeboxes and related accessories can be purchased directly from manufacturers and distributors.

Jukeboxes and accessories can all be sold from a homebased business, as well as through online marketplaces, such as eBay. Antique and collectible shows, auction sales and through interior designers are other potential marketplaces. Your customers might include collectors, restaurants, clubs, diners and any place that wants to create a retro ambiance.

BUY
Auctions, Wholesalers, Classified Ads

SELL
Collectors, Collectible Shows, Homebased Sales, eBay, B2B

RESOURCES
—BMI Gaming Wholesale, ☎ (561) 391-7269, ✆ bmigaming.com
—Game Room Antiques, ✆ gameroomantiques.com
—Global Sources, ✆ globalsources.com/manufacturers/Jukebox.html
—Just 4 Fun Shop, ✆ http://just4funshop.com
—The Complete Jukebox, ✆ tomszone.com

Karaoke Systems

If you are searching for a fun and unique product to buy and sell, look no further than karaoke equipment sales. Your main buying source will be from wholesalers in smaller quantities, keeping your capital investment to a minimum. You can resell the equipment through numerous online marketplaces such as eBay, at flea markets and at consumer shows. DJs, party planners, restaurants, lounges and clubs are potential B2B customers for higher-end equipment.

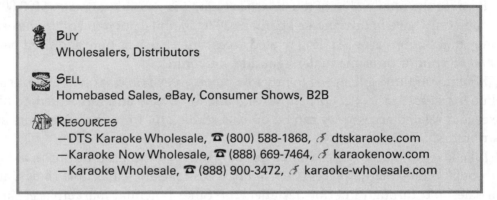

BUY
Wholesalers, Distributors

SELL
Homebased Sales, eBay, Consumer Shows, B2B

RESOURCES
—DTS Karaoke Wholesale, ☎ (800) 588-1868, ✎ dtskaraoke.com
—Karaoke Now Wholesale, ☎ (888) 669-7464, ✎ karaokenow.com
—Karaoke Wholesale, ☎ (888) 900-3472, ✎ karaoke-wholesale.com

Kites

You can get started buying and selling kites for peanuts; it only takes a few hundred dollars to establish a starting inventory and cover the cost of basic marketing materials, such as fliers, signs and business cards.

A great promotional idea is to host the occasional try-before-you-buy kite-flying event or contest. Set up at a local park or beach, and let potential customers try out a kite before they commit to the purchase. (Make sure you have a permit or permission to do this in a public place.) These kinds of events really build excitement and clearly demonstrate the end-user benefit to customers—in this case, fun.

Buying sources are plentiful. There are literally thousands of companies engaged in manufacturing, wholesaling and importing kites of every size, shape and price point. In addition to try-before-you-buy sales events, you can also sell your kites online, at sports and recreation shows, during community events, and at flea markets and public markets. To earn top dollar, consider offering hand-crafted or imported kites that are otherwise difficult to obtain. Of course, to excel in this business, you'll have to perfect your own kite-flying skills!

BUY
Manufacturers, Wholesalers

SELL
Community Events, eBay, Kiosks, Homebased Sales

RESOURCES
—American Kite Fliers Association, ✆ aka.kite.org
—Avia Sports Composites Manufacturing, ☎ (828) 345-6070, ✆ aviasport.net
—Jac's Wholesale Kites, ✆ wholesalenc.com/kites.html
—New Tech Kites Manufacturing, ☎ (512) 250-0485, ✆ newtechkites.com
—Tori Tako, ✆ toritako.com/kite.html

Knitting Supplies

Earlier in this section you discovered how you could earn profits by selling hand-crafted knitted products, such as sweaters, scarves and baby blankets. Well, another business option for knitting enthusiasts is to sell knitting supplies to other knitting hobbyists. Knitting needles and yarns from around the globe, for example, can become a lucrative, part-time business that can be operated from home.

To build your customer base, consider participating in knitting clubs, teaching knitting classes and utilizing the internet. Especially if you buy from liquidators and importers, the profit margin in knitting supplies can be substantial. To differentiate your business, consider selling all-natural, organic yarn, for example.

BUY
Wholesalers, Distributors, Liquidators, Importers

SELL
Online, Knitting Clubs, Craft Shows, Flea Markets

RESOURCES
—Fiber Gypsy Wholesale Directory, ✆ fibergypsy.com/Shopping/Knitting_Supplies_and_Patterns/
—Jagger Yarn, ✆ jaggeryarn.com
—Jimmy Beans Wool, ✆ jimmybeanswool.com
—Knitability, ✆ knitability.com
—Wholesale World, ✆ wholesale-world.us/wholesale_knitting_supplies. php

Knives

If you want to be on the cutting edge of a buy-and-sell opportunity, consider selling knives both for functional use and to collectors. Knives come in every size, and there is one for every purpose—hunting, fishing, cooking, hiking, dining, wood-carving, etc.

Antique knives and swords have long been prized collectors' items. You can sell all types of knives or opt to specialize in just one or two kinds. New knives can be purchased from wholesalers and distributors and sometimes directly from manufacturers, though they require orders in larger quantities.

Antique and collectible knives can be purchased from private sellers advertising in the classifieds, and at auction sales, online marketplaces and collectible shows. Selling can be accomplished in much the same manner, with the addition of renting kiosks in malls, vending at flea markets, and listing on eBay. As with any type of collectible, you definitely need to understand the market and your customers extremely well. If you're selling cooking knives, for example, also consider displaying your products at home shows and cooking events, contests and shows.

BUY
Wholesalers, Manufacturers, Garage Sales, Online Marketplaces

SELL
Kiosks, Collectors, eBay, Flea Markets, Consumer Shows

RESOURCES
—Buy N Save Wholesale, ☎ (909) 272-2227, ♂ buynsavedirect.com
—CKB Products, ♂ ckbproducts.com
—Cube Cart, ♂ directknifesales.com
—Hot Dandy Wholesale Superstore, ☎ (800) 875-8211, ♂ hotdandy.com
—Mitech Trading, ♂ mitechtrading.com/sports-knives-wholesale-50.html

Landscaping Supplies

Anyone with a front or back yard has a need for grass seed, fertilizers and a wide range of other products to keep their lawn lush and green. Much like the recent explosion in do-it-yourself home renovation, homeowners have also adopted a do-it-yourself approach to their landscaping as a way to save money, improve their property value and stretch their creative wings.

Many people take pride in their homes and want them to look as good on the outside as they do on the inside. The best way to accomplish this is with landscaping. This buy-and-sell enterprise necessitates that you have lots of outside storage space with proper zoning, plus a truck capable of carrying and dumping heavy loads. You also must enjoy working outdoors and interacting with people.

Providing you meet the criteria, you can purchase sand, gravel, topsoil and bark mulch by the dump truck load wholesale, and then sell it to homeowners in smaller quantities for full retail. They pick up, or you deliver for an added fee.

You can also stock and supply natural landscape products (such as driftwood and river rock). In addition to consumer sales, you can market your products to construction-related businesses and professional landscapers.

BUY
Wholesalers, Manufacturers, Free Sources, Farmers

SELL
Homebased Sales, Direct Delivery, B2B

RESOURCES
—Fusco Brothers Landscaping Supplies, ✆ fuscobrothersinc.com
—Mulch and Soil Council, ☎ (703) 257-0111, ✆ mulchandsoilcouncil.org
—National Stone, Sand, & Gravel Association, ✆ nssga.org
—Riverbend Nurseries, ✆ http://riverbendnurseries.com
—The Landscape Shop, ✆ thelandscapeshop.com

Leather Products

Leather goods and crafts, such as gloves, wallets, billfolds, jackets, business card holders, cellular telephone cases, belts, hunting sheaths and business organizers, are all fantastic items to sell for profits at weekend flea markets, on eBay, at consumer shows, and by renting kiosk space in malls and public markets.

What makes leather goods and crafts such great products for a buy-and-sell venture is they are small, easy to store and ship, always in demand for personal use and gift giving, and readily available through many manufacturing and wholesale sources.

You can mark up these items significantly and set your prices at two to three times what you paid for them. The trick is to find suppliers of quality or fine leather products that showcase good craftsmanship and nice, quality leather.

Consider buying overstock or out-of-season (genuine) name-brand items, from Coach, for example, at closeout prices, and then reselling them for higher profits on eBay or at flea markets.

BUY
Manufacturers, Wholesalers

SELL
Kiosks, Flea Markets, eBay, Consumer Shows

RESOURCES
—Costa Leather, ♂ costaleather.com
—Crazy Discounts Wholesale, ♂ crazydiscounts.com
—Indian Leather Portal, ♂ indianleatherportal.com
—Jillian Distributors, ♂ jilliandistributors.com
—SaleHoo.com, ♂ salehoo.com/articles/wholesale-coach-handbag.html
—Wholesale Central Leather Product Supplier Listing,
    ♂ wholesalecentral.com/Leather.html

Licensed Products

Well-branded, recognizable companies, professional sports teams, organizations, publishers, and even individual people often license their likenesses, logos, names, characters or mottos to other companies and manufacturers to be featured on a wide range of consumer products. These products range from T-shirts to hats to children's lunch boxes covered with Disney characters. Popular licensed goods also include sporting equipment and merchandise autographed by professional athletes. The list of potential licensed products to sell is almost endless.

Wholesalers will be your main buying source for licensed products for resale, though it is also possible to purchase directly from manufacturers that produce products with licensed images. Best sales venues will include eBay, flea markets, community events and rental kiosks in mall and public markets.

Pretty much all licensed products sell well, whether it is a bottle opener bearing a beer company logo or a hat with a sports team logo, mainly because people want to be associated with whatever the licensee represents. Whatever you do, make sure the licensed products you sell are legitimate and authorized; otherwise you could find yourself in a heap of legal problems related to copyright and trademark infringement.

Buy
Wholesalers, Manufacturers, Liquidators

Sell
Flea Markets, eBay, Kiosks, Consumer Shows, Sporting Events, Concerts

Resources
—Backstage Fashion, ✆ backstage-fashion.com
—Big Apple Card Company, ☎ (800) 883-8090, ✆ bigapplecard.com
—Four Seasons Wholesale Licensed Merchandise,
  ✆ 4sgm.com/news/wholesale-licensed-merchandise.html
—International Licensing Industry Merchandisers' Association,
  ✆ licensing.org/index.cfm

Lighters

Despite the decline in the number of people who smoke, cigarette lighters continue to be popular collectibles, gifts and handy items to have around the house. Zippo, Camel, Ronson and Scripto are all highly sought after lighter brands, in both the new and collectibles marketplace.

You can buy new lighters from wholesalers, manufacturers and distributors, and then mark up the lighters by 300 to 400 percent for resale on eBay or at flea markets, auto shows and community events.

Also, you can boost revenues and profits by investing in a simple engraving machine, enabling you to personalize your customers' lighter purchases right on location. Collectible lighters can be found by rummaging through flea markets, garage sales and online marketplaces. They can also be bought and sold on eBay and directly to collectors via clubs and associations.

Buy
Wholesalers, Manufacturers

Sell
Kiosks, Flea Markets, eBay, Collectors, Consumer Shows

Resources
—Crazy Discounts Wholesale, ✆ crazydiscounts.com
—Dollar Days Wholesale, ☎ (877) 837-9569, ✆ dollardays.com

—The Sunshine Lighter Company, ✆ sunshinewholesale.com
—Wholesale Central, ✆ wholesalecentral.com/Smoking-Products.html

Lighting

At first glance, lamps and lighting products may seem to be a strange item to buy and sell. But, when you consider the wide variety and the numerous uses of lighting products, it quickly becomes apparent why this can be a viable opportunity.

Let's shed some light on this type of opportunity and the range of products you could potentially sell. There's emergency lighting, ceiling lighting, table lamps, track lighting, rope and tube lights, patio lighting, underwater lights, fiber optics, holiday and decorative lighting, grow lighting, monorail light systems and floodlights.

There's also a huge market for antique and collectible lighting, where even a reproduction Tiffany Studio lamp sells for as much as $1,000, and the real thing from the Stickley era for ten times that amount.

If you break into this type of business, your potential customers include homeowners, architects, renovators, retailers, restaurateurs, interior designers, contractors, electrical contractors and collectors. New lighting and lamps can be purchased from wholesalers and manufacturers, while used collectible lighting fixtures and lamps can be purchased at garage sales, flea markets and auctions as well as online.

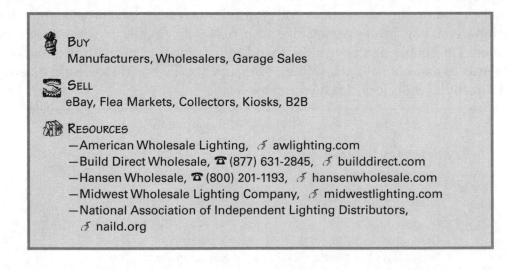

BUY
Manufacturers, Wholesalers, Garage Sales

SELL
eBay, Flea Markets, Collectors, Kiosks, B2B

RESOURCES
—American Wholesale Lighting, ✆ awlighting.com
—Build Direct Wholesale, ☎ (877) 631-2845, ✆ builddirect.com
—Hansen Wholesale, ☎ (800) 201-1193, ✆ hansenwholesale.com
—Midwest Wholesale Lighting Company, ✆ midwestlighting.com
—National Association of Independent Lighting Distributors,
   ✆ naild.org

Lingerie

Women want to look sexy for their guys, and when it comes to buying gifts, guys love to buy items that are sexy and just a wee bit naughty for their girlfriends or wives (or both, depending on the guy). Well, if you're ready to compete with Victoria's Secret, but on a much smaller scale, you could find yourself running a profitable lingerie empire buying and selling exotic lingerie from around the globe.

Lingerie can be sold through numerous online marketplaces, including eBay, and by creating your own e-commerce website. It also sells very well at home sales parties.

You can buy lingerie at deeply discounted prices from wholesalers, liquidators and manufacturers, and then sell it for big profits. This is the type of product that can be marked up by 100 to 200 percent (or more) for retail sales.

BUY
Wholesalers, Manufacturers, Liquidators

SELL
Mail Order, Kiosks, Home Parties, E-Commerce Website, Online Marketplaces, Fashion Shows

RESOURCES
—1 AAA Wholesale Liquidators, ☎ (800) 661-9430, ✍ 1aaawholesaleliquidators.com
—American Apparel and Footwear Association, ✍ apparelandfootwear. org
—Lingerie 4 Wholesale, ✍ lingerie4wholesale.com
—Sheer Fashions Wholesale, ✍ http://classywear.com
—VX Intimate Wholesale, ☎ (866) 968-4412, ✍ vxintimate.com

Liquidated Inventory

Retailers and manufacturers liquidate inventory for any number of reasons. The merchandise might be slow-moving, out of season or damaged. The company itself might be moving, merging or going out of business. Whatever the case, billions of dollars' worth of inventory becomes available every year at incredibly cheap "liquidation" prices. These are prices well below typical wholesale prices.

Savvy entrepreneurs can earn a bundle by buying this inventory and reselling it in the right places and to the right people at staggering markups. Traditionally, the best types of inventory to purchase are power and hand tools, sporting goods, music CDs and movie DVDs, toys, kitchen and bath accessories and electronics, but the possibilities are truly limitless.

When buying liquidated merchandise, stay clear of products that have a limited shelf life or have special warehousing and transportation requirements. Depending on what you're able to get your hands on, make sure it's in full working order, and consider selling your products online or at flea markets, for example.

Establish a business finding great deals when it comes to liquidation sales and then turning around and selling those products using a variety of methods. Or you can develop a buy-and-sell business that has a specialty (which is the main focus on this book) and then find merchandise that's being liquidated to help build your inventory.

BUY
Online Marketplaces, Auction Sales, Retailers, Manufacturers, Liquidators

SELL
Temporary Locations, B2B, Flea Markets, Online Marketplaces (including eBay)

RESOURCES
—Excess Technologies, ✄ excessi.com
—Liquidation Online, ✄ liquidation.com
—Liquidators.tv, ✄ http://liquidators.tv
—Merchandise USA, ✄ merchandiseusa.com
—RS Trading, ✄ rstrading.com

Luggage

Luggage is one of those little-thought-about products that has the potential to be very profitable when bought and sold by entrepreneurs with innovative marketing skills. Buy luggage cheaply from wholesalers, distributors, liquidators and importers. Sell on eBay, from a homebased showroom, through travel and leisure shows and at mall kiosks. Also build alliances with local travel agents who can refer their clients to your business for their last-minute luggage needs.

When choosing types of luggage to sell, offering quality products is essential. There's a lot of cheaply made and poorly constructed luggage available that will literally fall apart after just one use (if it survives that long). If you develop a reputation for selling junk, you'll be out of business in no time.

Quality luggage is made from durable materials, plus it has well-constructed handles and seams, as well as durable wheels. The average suitcase or piece of luggage suitable for airline travel must be able to safely hold at least 50 pounds plus be able to withstand the abuse it will receive from airport and airline personnel, hotel porters and other handlers. Be sure to request product samples from your suppliers before making a significant investment in inventory. As any frequent flier or traveler will tell you, well-known brand names when it comes to luggage manufacturers do not automatically mean quality and durable products.

BUY
Manufacturers, Wholesalers, Liquidators

SELL
Kiosks, Flea Markets, eBay, Consumer Shows

RESOURCES
—AAXIS Wholesale Luggage, ☎ (310) 719-1837,
   ✆ aaxiswholesaleluggage.com
—Al Khayam Exhibition, ☎ 971-4-2252872 (UAE),
   ✆ buyluggageonline.com
—Crazy Discounts Wholesale, ✆ crazydiscounts.com
—JD Closeouts, ✆ jdcloseouts.com/specials/luggage.html
—TradeKey, ✆ tradekey.com/ks-wholesale-luggage
—TDW Closeouts, ✆ tdwcloseouts.com

Mailboxes

Like birdhouses, mailboxes are a great buy-and-sell item. Whether you buy your inventory directly from the manufacturers, from local craftspeople, or from wholesalers, mailboxes can be purchased in many ways at low prices. You can then sell these products from home, through online marketplaces, at flea markets, and by displaying your products at home and garden shows.

Elaborate mailboxes made from specialty materials such as copper, iron and cultured stone can sell for $1,000 and more. The one drawback to selling this type of product exclusively is that you won't get too much repeat business. Most people only need one mailbox and it'll typically last them for 10 years or longer. Thus you'll constantly need to market your products to a new crop of homeowners, new home developers or people redesigning their landscaping.

If you want to increase your profits, you can also sell house number signs, name plaques, light posts or garden ornaments that match the mailboxes you sell.

BUY
Craftspeople, Manufacturers, Wholesalers

SELL
Flea Markets, Kiosks, Online Marketplaces, Homebased Sales, Home Builders (B2B)

RESOURCES
—Brandon Industries, ☎ (972) 542-3000, ✑ brandonindustries.com
—Designer Mailboxes Manufacturing, ☎ (877) 502-3548, ✑ designer-mailboxes.com
—Gaines Manufacturing, ☎ (858) 486-7100, ✑ gainesmfg.com
—The Mailbox Works, ✑ mailboxworks.com

Major Appliances

If you have the ability to inventory and transport large items, plus the bankroll to operate this type of business, selling new or used major appliances to homeowners can be a profitable business. While the new appliance business is competitive, you can purchase (and if necessary repair) used appliances and resell them for a decent profit. By teaming up with a plumber, electrician and handyman, you can also offer installation services.

At some point, every homeowner will have one or more major appliances that break and that need to be replaced. Once this happens, the customer's need becomes urgent. Yet, that same person might not be able to afford a shiny new appliance. This is where the buy-and-sell entrepreneur who offers quality used appliances can step in and save the day.

Selling used major appliances, such as refrigerators, stoves, washers and dryers is very much a game of patience, which when played correctly, can be very profitable. Buy used appliances from private sellers through classified ads, Craigslist, moving sales and auctions. There's not usually a high demand for these products, so they can typically be purchased very inexpensively. Just make sure you clean and perform minor repairs to your inventory to make sure each item is in good cosmetic shape and fully operational. Your ability to sell used appliances with a 30-day warranty greatly increases the value.

BUY
Auctions, Classified Ads, Wholesalers, Manufacturers, Liquidators

SELL
Homebased Sales (Requires heavy advertising and promotions)

RESOURCES
—ICM, ✆ interconmktg.com
—Merchandize Liquidators, ✆ merchandizeliquidators.com/
Kitchenwarecloseoutsliquidators.htm
—Universal Appliance Recycling, ✆ universalappliance.com

Marine Electronics

Boating is a popular hobby and sport, and one where the participants typically have money. Many boaters want the biggest and best accessories and tools available to make their boating experience more pleasurable.

If you have a passion for boating, consider turning it into a lucrative venture by starting a buy-and-sell business specializing in the sale of new and used marine electronics. Bestselling marine electronic items include handheld and fixed VHF radios, hailers, GPS systems, radar and autopilot systems, electronic instrument clusters, marine stereos, satellite telephone and television systems, remote spotlights, battery chargers and fish finders.

New electronics can be purchased from wholesalers, distributors and liquidators at about 40 percent off retail, while used equipment will require a little legwork to track down through classified ads in boating publications and auction sales. New and used marine electronics can be sold through eBay, and by exhibiting at boat and recreation shows. You can also team up with boat yards and yacht clubs to help generate customers and referrals. Additional money can be earned by installing the electronics you sell, provided you have the qualifications.

BUY
Wholesalers, Classified Ads

SELL
Boat Shows, eBay, Specialty Publications

RESOURCES
—CWR Electronics, ✐ cwrelectronics.com
—Marine Wholesales, ✐ marinewholesales.com
—Navigator Electronics Wholesale, ☎ (877) 462-0208,
　✐ navigatorelectronics.com
—Online Marine Supply, ✐ onlinemarine.com

Maternity Clothing

When you stop to consider that more than four million babies are born each year in the United States and Canada, you'll quickly realize the great opportunity that exists for clever entrepreneurs who buy wholesale maternity fashions and resell them to moms-to-be.

One of the better ways to sell maternity fashions is to hire contract sales representatives to organize and host at-home maternity fashion sales parties. Ideal candidates, of course, are new moms and moms-to-be. Compensation to the sales host can be by way of commission, revenue split, free product or any combination.

Establishing a homebased boutique is also a great way to sell your goods. Advertise locally and build alliances with midwives and daycare centers, which can refer their clients to your business. Also, don't overlook the possibility of selling to a global audience by creating your own e-commerce website and by selling your inventory on eBay. Weekend flea markets may also prove to be a profitable way to market and sell your products.

Maternity clothing can be bought new from wholesalers, distributors, liquidators and manufacturers. You can save money by purchasing overstock, out-of-season items and/or garments from "last season's" product line. If you're willing to launder used maternity clothes and prepare them for resale, this too can be a viable business opportunity.

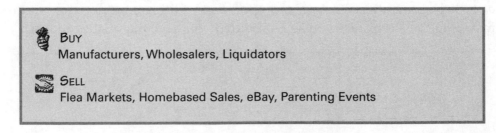

BUY
Manufacturers, Wholesalers, Liquidators

SELL
Flea Markets, Homebased Sales, eBay, Parenting Events

<span></span>

RESOURCES
—American Apparel and Footwear Association,
   ⚲ apparelandfootwear.org
—Cotlon India Manufacturing, ☎ 91-11-26431288 (India), ⚲ cotlon.com
—Liquidation Merchandise, ☎ (800) 574-5304,
   ⚲ liquidationmerchandise.com
—Maximum Mama Maternity, ☎ (415) 585-3139,
   ⚲ maximummama.com

Metaphysical Products

Metaphysical products, also known as New Age products, cover a wide range of items, including tarot cards, magnets, zodiac pendants, astrology products, crystals, candles, healing wands, fountains, meditation supplies, yoga mats, pagan products, crystal balls, pyramids, hypnosis tapes and hemp products.

To succeed selling these products, first they must be something you truly believe in. Next, you must understand the products themselves, their purpose, as well as your target audience. It makes a lot of sense to choose a specialty and start by selling a small selection of items.

Metaphysical products can be purchased directly from manufacturers and wholesalers. You may even find craftspeople who can provide inventory by making what you would like to sell, such as handcrafted Ouija boards or handcrafted crystal jewelry items that have a particular significance.

Using online marketing, as well as an e-commerce website, to sell these products will probably be your best bet, since you want to reach the broadest group of people possible with an interest in these specialty products. Join New Age chat rooms and user groups so that you can network for customers and spread the word about your products. Also, sell your goods at flea markets, consumer shows and rental kiosk space in malls.

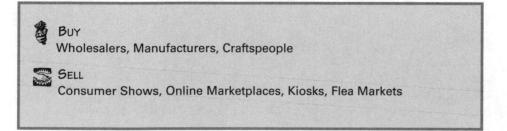

BUY
Wholesalers, Manufacturers, Craftspeople

SELL
Consumer Shows, Online Marketplaces, Kiosks, Flea Markets

> **Resources**
> —Azure Green Wholesale, ☎ (413) 623-2155, ✍ azuregreen.com
> —Gemstone Factory, ✍ gemstonefactory.com
> —Just Winging It Wholesale, ☎ (888) 430-4594, ✍ jwi.com
> —Lucky Mojo Curio Co., ✍ luckymojo.com/mojocattarot.html
> —Sanctuary Productions Wholesale, ✍ sanctuarywholesale.com/store
> —The New Age Wholesale Directory, ✍ newagereseller.com

Military Collectibles

History buffs, military veterans and people who enjoy collecting have created a tremendous market for military collectibles from the Civil War, the Mexican-American War, WWI, WWII, the Korean War, the Vietnam War and the Gulf War. Military items, such as helmets, swords, guns, uniforms, official documents, medals, knives, artillery and photographs from these and other wars from around the world are very collectible and highly sought-after. However, to be successful in this type of business, you really have to be knowledgeable about history, the specific products you're selling and your customer base. This is very specialized merchandise where the people buying it are passionate and knowledgeable about what they do.

Buying military collectibles for resale requires legwork. You will have to dig through garage sales, scour flea markets, attend auctions, surf collectibles websites, bid on items through estate sales and attend exhibits and events. You will need to know how much these items are worth when you find them. To accomplish this, invest in military collectibles price guides.

List your inventory on eBay and other collectibles websites to sell them. Other alternatives are to exhibit at collectibles shows and sell through auctions to ensure that you get the highest prices. Using eBay, however, gives you access to the broadest audience of potential buyers.

> **Buy**
> Garage Sales, Auctions, Flea Markets, Classified Ads, Army/Navy Surplus
>
> **Sell**
> Collectors, Auctions, Collectible Shows, eBay, Homebased Sales

RESOURCES
—A Military Trader Magazine, Krause Publications, ☎ (800) 942-0676, ✆ collect.com
—B2B Yellow Pages, ✆ b2byellowpages.com/directory/ popular_resources/collectibles_collecting/military_collectible/
—EzGoo!, ✆ ezgoo.com/wholesalers/wsmilitary.php
—The Online Collector, ✆ theonlinecollector.com/military.html

Model Kits

Thanks to video games, MTV, hundreds of digital cable TV channels and a wide range of other activities that kids and teens enjoy doing, the popularity of building models has decreased in recent years, but there is still a viable niche market for these products.

Building models is a popular hobby. Model kits allow people to recreate scale versions of boats, cars, trucks, buildings, planes, motorcycles, tanks and trains. These models come in many designs and are available at a wide range of price points. Wholesalers and manufacturers will be your best purchasing sources. Though you will pay a bit more for each model when you buy from wholesalers, as opposed to manufacturers, the advantage is that you will not be required to buy cases of product or container lots.

Flea market vending, exhibiting at craft shows and hobby shows, posting on eBay, renting mall kiosks and selling from a homebased showroom are all suitable retailing methods for selling model kits. Also be sure to join hobby clubs and associations to spread the word about your venture and network for customers.

Building remote-controlled (R/C) vehicles, boats and airplanes is a related hobby that has a strong following and that involves products with higher retail prices than traditional model kits, so this too is a viable business opportunity. Additional profits can be earned by selling glues, paints and other tools used by model builders.

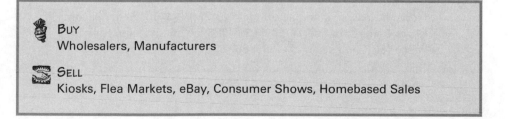

BUY
Wholesalers, Manufacturers

SELL
Kiosks, Flea Markets, eBay, Consumer Shows, Homebased Sales

> **RESOURCES**
> —Empire Discount Wholesale, ☎ (914) 684-1455, ✆ empirediscount.net
> —Hobby Surplus, ✆ hobbysurplus.com
> —Spacecraft International Manufacturing, ☎ (626) 398-4800,
>   ✆ spacecraftkits.com
> —Toy Directory, ✆ toydirectory.com
> —TradeKey, ✆ tradekey.com/ks-model-kits

Model Trains

Next to getting a job as an engineer for Amtrak, one of the best ways to cater to an interest in or passion for trains is to design, build and play with model train sets. The model trains may be small, but the industry is not. Neither is the profit potential.

Among hobbyists, scale railroading is huge. Right from home, you can sell the most popular scale model trains, train sets and accessories. Bestselling accessories include scaled scenery, trees, buildings, bridges, tunnels, people, cars, track, assembly tools, specialized paint, audio equipment and model railroading books.

Buy new trains and accessories from wholesalers and distributors. Used trains, sets and accessories can be obtained from garage sales and flea markets, as well as eBay. In addition to homebased sales, sell on eBay, through model railroading clubs, and directly to collectors for any vintage finds you stumble upon. Exhibiting at conventions is also a great way to generate sales.

> **BUY**
> Wholesalers, Online Marketplaces, Garage Sales, Flea Markets
>
> **SELL**
> Flea Markets, eBay, Collectors, Consumer Shows, Homebased Sales
>
> **RESOURCES**
> —Lionel Trains Inc. Manufacturing, ☎ (810) 949-4100, ✆ lionel.com
> —Micro Trains Line Co., ☎ (541) 535-1755, ✆ micro-trains.com
> —Pasco Toy Wholesalers, ☎ (800) 667-6121, ✆ pascotoys.com

Moving Supplies

People are always moving, whether across town, to another city or across the country. To save money, many people opt to handle their own packing and even moving. This provides a wonderful opportunity to the buy-and-sell business operator who chooses to specialize in offering moving supplies, such as boxes, packing tape, labels, bubble wrap and padding materials. These products can be bought from wholesalers and sold in a variety of ways to your customers for a hansom profit.

To help generate business, obtain referrals from mortgage brokers, real estate agents (Realtors), homeowners associations and local truck rental companies.

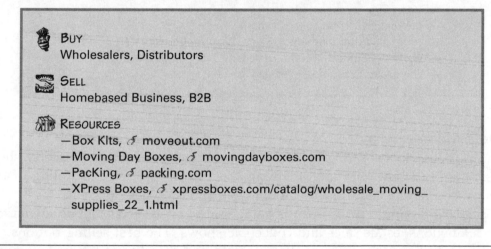

BUY
Wholesalers, Distributors

SELL
Homebased Business, B2B

RESOURCES
—Box Klts, ♂ moveout.com
—Moving Day Boxes, ♂ movingdayboxes.com
—PacKing, ♂ packing.com
—XPress Boxes, ♂ xpressboxes.com/catalog/wholesale_moving_
supplies_22_1.html

Music CDs

Thanks to online-based services, such as iTunes, the market for music CDs has dropped significantly over the past few years. However, there are still music enthusiasts who enjoy buying CDs featuring their favorite artists and building up their music libraries. Of course, when you sell new music CDs, you'll be competing head-on with music stores (retailers), as well as mass-market stores (such as Wal-Mart, K-Mart and Target).

One way to differentiate yourself in the music CD sales business is to focus on a specific type or genre of music and target your sales efforts to a niche audience, or you can buy and sell used CDs that you acquire from flea markets, garage sales, collectors and other sources.

In addition to selling your music inventory at flea markets and at mall kiosks, for example, you can also set up an e-commerce website. Highly collectible CDs can be bought and sold on eBay. To expand your offerings, you can also buy and sell vinyl albums to collectors. (See "Vintage Vinyl Records" later in this chapter.)

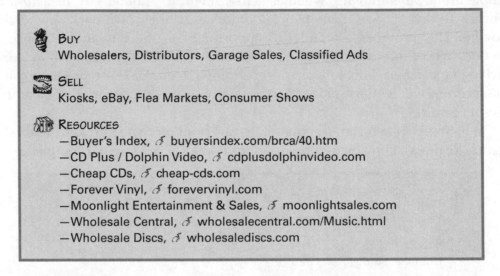

BUY
Wholesalers, Distributors, Garage Sales, Classified Ads

SELL
Kiosks, eBay, Flea Markets, Consumer Shows

RESOURCES
—Buyer's Index, ✂ buyersindex.com/brca/40.htm
—CD Plus / Dolphin Video, ✂ cdplusdolphinvideo.com
—Cheap CDs, ✂ cheap-cds.com
—Forever Vinyl, ✂ forevervinyl.com
—Moonlight Entertainment & Sales, ✂ moonlightsales.com
—Wholesale Central, ✂ wholesalecentral.com/Music.html
—Wholesale Discs, ✂ wholesalediscs.com

Music Memorabilia

Concert ticket stubs, autographs, instruments, stage clothing, posters, sheet music, handwritten lyrics and anything Woodstock are just a sampling of the music memorabilia items that are in high demand by collectors.

The best buying sources include garage sales, private sellers, online marketplaces, auctions, estate sales and collectible shows. The best selling options are similar, including eBay, auctions, flea markets, and direct to collectors by joining music memorabilia clubs and networking with members, both online and in the real world. An e-commerce website can be used to sell your merchandise to a potential worldwide audience of collectors.

Additionally, get to know concert managers and promoters, as they can be an excellent buying source for incredible, one-of-a-kind music memorabilia items. It's important to understand the music memorabilia collector's market before venturing into this business. Also, it's essential that you are passionate about music and truly understand your target audience.

BUY
Garage Sales, Online Marketplaces, Auctions, Classified Ads, Music Promoters/Managers

SELL
Collectors, Flea Markets, Memorabilia Shows, Online Marketplaces, eBay

RESOURCES
—Autographs America, 🎵 autographsamerica.com
—I Rock 'N Roll, 🎵 irocknroll.com
—Music Collectors, 🎵 musiccollectors.com
—Wolfgang's Vault, 🎵 wolfgangsvault.com/ac/store.html

Musical Instruments

Buying and selling musical instruments can be extremely lucrative, especially if you have access to top-quality new and used merchandise and have the ability to properly market your inventory to musicians. As you get started in this type of business, specializing in one type of instrument definitely helps. For example, become an expert buying and selling drums, keyboards, pianos, acoustic and electric guitars, saxophones, violins, bagpipes or harmonicas.

A valuable prerequisite is the ability to play, repair and tune the instruments you sell. This ability will also assist in buying used instruments. It is perhaps more difficult to purchase new, recognizable brand-name musical instruments on a wholesale basis for the simple reason that most manufacturers and distributors prefer to have large, authorized retailers servicing geographical areas. In spite of this, you can find smaller manufacturers and distributors prepared to sell wholesale to a small-order reseller.

Used musical instruments are no problem to buy. There is a plethora of them available in every area through classified ads, organized band sales and auctions, on eBay, and at garage sales. A homebased showroom is best suited for sales, as well as listing on eBay and exhibiting at music shows. Your target customers might be serious musicians, casual musicians or students.

BUY
Manufacturers, Wholesalers, Auctions, Classified Ads

SELL
Homebased Sales, eBay, Flea Markets, Music Shows

RESOURCES
—Echo Trade Marketing, ☎ (888) 271-4208, ✆ echotrademarketing.com
—Music Gear 4 You, ✆ musicgear4u.com
—The Shubb Company, ☎ (707) 876-3001, ✆ shubb.com/trade
—TradeKey, ✆ tradekey.com/ks-wholesale-musical-instruments
—Wholesale Hub, ✆ wholesalehub.com/wmusic1.html
—Wholesale Music Warehouse, ✆ wholesalemusicwarehouse.com/wholesale/default.asp

Nautical Charts

Most of the estimated 30 million boat and water-sports enthusiasts in North America have one thing in common: they need nautical charts to know where they are going, where they should be, or where they shouldn't be. The problem is, with GPS and electronic navigation and autopilot systems, the traditional paper-based nautical charts are quickly becoming collector's items as opposed to tools of navigation.

Start by contacting nautical chart publishers and wholesalers. Be sure to ask questions about the most popular charts. Charts are available in a wide range of styles and for a wide range of uses.

Charts can include ocean-floor maps, general waterways maps, fishing charts, dive charts and inland lake and river charts. Sell at boat-and-recreation shows, create an e-commerce website and advertise in boating magazines for mail order sales. You can also sell at boat shows. Boating enthusiasts often frame antique or localized nautical charts and display these pieces as artwork in their offices or homes, which opens up an entirely different sales opportunity.

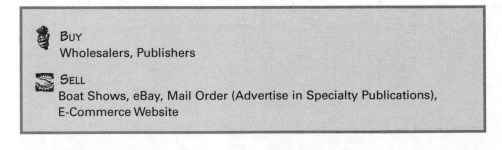

BUY
Wholesalers, Publishers

SELL
Boat Shows, eBay, Mail Order (Advertise in Specialty Publications), E-Commerce Website

Nautical Collectibles

The movie *Titanic* did more than smash all previous box-office and DVD sales records. It also ignited the marketplace for nautical collectibles, causing prices to soar. The most prized nautical collectibles include cruise liner memorabilia, model boats, brass signal lamps, sailors' sea trunks, antique sextants, glass floats, early divers' suits, ships' bells, brass cleats, portholes, wheels, propellers, barometer sets, compasses, anchors, telescopes, scrimshaw pieces and anything and everything related to the U.S. Navy.

Buying sources include private sellers, collectible shows, auctions and online marketplaces. Your selling options will be similar, and include direct to collectors, through online specialty marketplaces, eBay, an e-commerce website, boat shows, antique shows and a homebased showroom.

BUY
Classified Ads, Garage Sales, Online Marketplaces, Auctions

SELL
Collectors, Auctions, Boat Shows, eBay, Homebased Sales

RESOURCES
—Antiques & Collectibles, ∮ collectingnetwork.com/links/
   nauticalandmaritimeantiques.html
—Global Sources, ∮ globalsources.com/manufacturers/
   Wholesale-Nautical.html
—Maidhof Bros. Shipware, ∮ seajunk.com
—The Mother of All Maritime Links, ∮ boat-links.com/boatlink.html
—Wholesale Mart, ∮ wholesalemart.com/cat_nautical_decor.cfm

New Furniture

Because new furniture is a broad category, including many types, styles, construction materials and uses, you may want to specialize in one or two specific types. Do your purchasing from manufacturers, as well as distributors, wholesalers and individual craftspeople. To enter into this type of business will require significant startup capital, a warehouse (for storing inventory), at least one large truck (for deliveries), plus a comprehensive knowledge of the furniture business.

In addition to online sales, you can sell at home and garden shows. One option is to sell out of a large truck by parking it (with permission) in an empty lot or parking area and using signage to attract attention.

Yes, this is a competitive business, especially if you live in an area with a dense population, but if you offer a good selection of top-quality merchandise, fair prices, delivery service and excellent customer service, you'll quickly develop a strong reputation and positive word-of-mouth advertising.

BUY
Manufacturers, Craftspeople, Wholesalers

SELL
Consumer Shows, Homebased Sales, Temporary Locations

RESOURCES
—American Home Furnishings Alliance, ⚲ ahfa.us
—Custom Design Furniture MFG, (323) 234-6810,
 ⚲ customdesignfurniture.org
—Hansen Wholesale, (800) 365-3267, ⚲ hansenwholesale.com
—EastJava Furniture Directory, ⚲ eastjava.com/furniture
—Wholesale Furniture Brokers, ⚲ gowfb.com
—Wholesale Furniture Closeouts, ⚲ closeoutssuppliers.com

New Sporting Goods

More than any other hobby, activity, or pastime, sports (including hockey, football, racket sports, skiing, baseball, skateboarding, base jumping, rock climbing and bowling) attract the most people and participants. This creates an incredible opportunity for buying and selling new sporting goods and equipment.

Due to the sheer number of sports that people participate in around the world, you may want to specialize in one, such as rock climbing, or in a small group of related sports, such as racket sports. Your primary buying sources include wholesalers, manufacturers, liquidators, importers and distributors.

The best sales venues include flea markets, eBay, an e-commerce website, and rental kiosks in malls and public markets. You will also want to join sports clubs and associations relative to the types of equipment you deal in to network for business. Of course, being an expert on the sports you sell equipment for is essential, as is having a strong knowledge about the actual equipment and to whom it's targeted.

BUY
Wholesalers, Manufacturers, Distributors, Liquidators

SELL
Homebased Sales, Online Marketplaces, Sports and Recreation Shows, Kiosks

RESOURCES
—Atafa Sporting Goods, ⅋ atafa.com
—Jerry's Sport Center Wholesale, ⅋ jerryssportscenter.com
—Regro Sports Wholesale, ☎ (877) 384-4374, ⅋ regrosports.com
—Sporting Goods Manufacturers Association, ⅋ sgma.com
—Wholesale Central, ⅋ wholesalecentral.com/Sporting-Goods.html

New Toys

Billions of dollars' worth of toys are sold every year in the United States. You will get rock-bottom wholesale prices on toys by purchasing factory direct out of countries such as China. In fact, prices are so low, it is possible to buy items for less than $1 that retail for ten times as much in the United States.

The new toy retailing industry is super-competitive. In fact, it's one of the most competitive segments of the retail industry. Therefore, look for unusual toys or toys that are new to the U.S. marketplace. There are literally thousands of overseas companies manufacturing toys, many of which would love representation in the United States, Canada and Europe.

Buying sources will be factory direct in large quantities, and domestic wholesalers and liquidators for smaller quantities. Stick to dealing only in new toys, because the resale value of used toys is too low, except for toys of interest to collectors. The best selling options include online sales and any place a crowd gathers, such as flea markets, consumer shows, community events and mall kiosks close to any holiday.

During the 2007 Christmas holiday season, virtually every mall in America had at least one kiosk selling handheld remote-controlled helicopters, which were one of the hot toys of the year. Try to pick out hot trends and exploit them when choosing what toy products to buy and sell.

To get a preview of new toys being developed, consider attending the Toy Fair industry trade show held each year in New York City. There are also a handful of industry-oriented publications that are well worth reading if you plan on getting into the toy business.

Buy
Manufacturers, Wholesalers, Liquidators

Sell
Flea Markets, Consumer Shows, Kiosks, Online Marketplaces

Resources
—Big Lots Wholesale, ☎ (614) 278-3700, ✂ biglotswholesale.com
—Dasaq Wholesale, ✂ dasaq.com
—ESCO Imports, ☎ (210) 271-7794, ✂ escoimport.com
—Joissu Wholesale, ✂ joissu.com
—Toy Directory, ✂ toydirectory.com
—Trendtimes, ✂ trendtimes.com/wholin.html

Novelties

Novelties, magic tricks and gag products, such as key chains, whoopee cushions, yo-yos, lasers, light-up pens, gag gifts, adult-themed items and fake money, are some of the hottest and most profitable items to sell at flea markets.

You can easily double or triple your money on every sale. In addition to flea markets, you can sell novelty items from a kiosk at malls, at a public market, or during community events, such as fairs and parades.

Some novelty products, especially adult-themed toys, may also be offered via suitable online marketplaces and through print and electronic mail order catalogs. There are a great number of wholesale sources for novelty products, so be picky when it comes to choosing what types of novelty items you choose to buy and sell, based on what you believe will be popular among your customers.

> **BUY**
> Manufacturers, Wholesalers, Liquidators, Distributors
>
> **SELL**
> Online Marketplaces, Flea Markets, Kiosks, Consumer Shows, Mail Order
>
> **RESOURCES**
> —Crazy Discounts Wholesale, ✍ crazydiscounts.com
> —Empire Discount Wholesale Toys, ✍ empirediscount.net
> —Joissu Wholesale, ✍ joissu.com
> —Novelties Wholesale, ✍ noveltieswholesale.com
> —Windy City Novelties, ✍ windycitynovelties.com

Office Furniture and Equipment (Used)

Used office furniture and equipment, such as desks, chairs, photocopiers, dividers and file cabinets, can often be bought for pennies on the dollar at bankruptcy auctions, through the classifieds, and at surplus sales. Establish a homebased showroom for sales, or set up an e-commerce website listing furniture and equipment available. To generate business, join associations, such as your local chamber of commerce, so you can network.

The trick to buying and selling used office furniture and equipment is to find quality products that are in good shape and good working order. Aside from doing a bit of cleaning or polishing, for example, you don't want to purchase items that will require too much of your time or labor to transform them into resalable merchandise.

> **BUY**
> Auctions, Classified Ads, Bankruptcies, Craigslist.org, eBay
>
> **SELL**
> B2B, Homebased Showroom, Online Marketplaces
>
> **RESOURCES**
> —Furniture Wholesale Group, ✍ furniturewholesalegroup.com
> —Merchandize Liquidators, ✍ merchandizeliquidators.com/
>   american-furniure-warewhouse.htm
> —Ofousa, ✍ ofousa.com
> —Recycler's World, ✍ recycle.net/Commercial/furniture

Organic Products

People with allergies or illnesses, or who are environmentally friendly, often seek out all sorts of "organic" or "all-natural" goods, such as bedding, clothing and cleaning products. These products can all be purchased from manufacturers, wholesalers and distributors and resold for a significant profit. The good news is, few major retailers offer these types of goods, yet the market for them is growing quickly.

You can sell organic or all-natural products at flea markets, at mall kiosks, online or at home and garden shows, for example. The possibilities are endless. Because these products are in demand, but hard to find, you can typically charge top dollar for them. Doctors, allergists and other medical professionals will be able to provide you with prequalified customer referrals.

BUY
Wholesalers, Distributors, Manufacturers

SELL
Flea Markets, Online, Mall Kiosks, Home & Garden Shows

RESOURCES
—Eco Business Links, ✍ ecobusinesslinks.com/links/
 non_toxic_organic_bedding.htm
—EcoMall, ✍ ecomall.com/biz/wholes.htm
—Tikvah, ✍ tikvah.com
—Wholesale Distributors Directory, ✍ wholesaledistributorsnet.com/
 organic_products.html

Organizational Tools

Just about everyone wishes there was more time in the day, or that they could make much better use of the time they have. Some people wish they could be surrounded by less clutter or be more organized in their day-to-day lives. These people will comprise your target audience if you get into the organization tools business.

Day planners, organizers, storage units, closet organizers and a wide range of other products fall into this category. Create your own inventory of select products that can be used by everyday people to make their lives better organized, clutter-free and more productive. As you'd expect, manufacturers, distributors and wholesalers will be your key suppliers.

You can sell at seminars, through an e-commerce website, B2B, or from a mall kiosk, for example. The trick will be developing and implementing a creative marketing plan for your business that targets the right group of disorganized people.

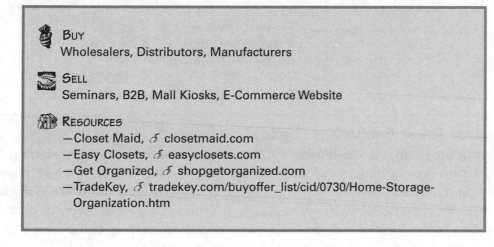

BUY
Wholesalers, Distributors, Manufacturers

SELL
Seminars, B2B, Mall Kiosks, E-Commerce Website

RESOURCES
—Closet Maid, ✄ closetmaid.com
—Easy Closets, ✄ easyclosets.com
—Get Organized, ✄ shopgetorganized.com
—TradeKey, ✄ tradekey.com/buyoffer_list/cid/0730/Home-Storage-Organization.htm

Original Artwork

Oil and watercolor paintings, ink drawings, or sculptures made from stone, wood and iron, as well as a host of other fine-art media can be the basis for a very profitable and personally rewarding buy-and-sell enterprise.

Purchase new original works of art directly from local, national or even world-renowned artists, as well as from companies that specialize in original artwork wholesaling. Previously owned original artwork can be purchased at auctions, online and through classified ads.

To make sales, establish an e-commerce website, utilize eBay and other online marketplaces, organize and host art auctions and attend plenty of art shows. When dealing in original works of fine art, you can never have enough knowledge. Buy price guides, study art books, join art clubs and network with artists and art dealers in order to learn as much as you can about the art world.

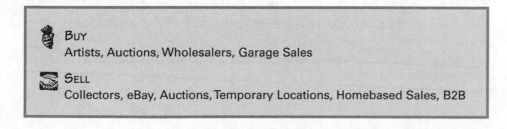

BUY
Artists, Auctions, Wholesalers, Garage Sales

SELL
Collectors, eBay, Auctions, Temporary Locations, Homebased Sales, B2B

>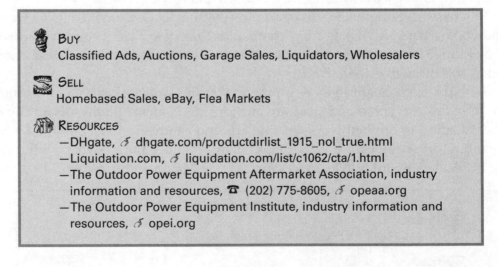
>
> **RESOURCES**
> —Davenport's Art Reference & Price Guide, Gordon's Art Sales Index,
>   ☎ (800) 892-4622, ✑ gordonsart.com
> —Art Volga Gallery, ✑ paintingofrussia.com
> —Artists Wholesale Outlet, ✑ artistswholesaleoutlet.com
> —Arts Alive, ✑ artsalive.com/wholesale.html
> —Living Drums Company, ☎ 397-9042, ✑ livingdrums.com
> —Oil Painting Wholesale, ☎ 308-0682, ✑ oilpaintingwholesale.com

Outdoor Power Equipment (Used)

Put your small-engine mechanical skills and knowledge to work by starting an outdoor power equipment buy-and-sell venture. Purchase used outdoor power equipment, such as lawn mowers, trimmers, riding mowers, chain saws, garden tillers, yard trailers, snow blowers and leaf blowers at garage sales, at auction sales and through classified ads. To get the lowest prices, buy equipment that is out of season or that needs minor repairs and a good cleaning.

You can sell outdoor power equipment from home, at flea markets, at home and garden shows or through Craigslist, for example. Close more sales and for more money by offering customers a 30-day warranty on all equipment you sell. Doing so will increase the value of each piece of equipment by 10 to 20 percent.

> **BUY**
> Classified Ads, Auctions, Garage Sales, Liquidators, Wholesalers
>
> **SELL**
> Homebased Sales, eBay, Flea Markets
>
> **RESOURCES**
> —DHgate, ✑ dhgate.com/productdirlist_1915_no1_true.html
> —Liquidation.com, ✑ liquidation.com/list/c1062/cta/1.html
> —The Outdoor Power Equipment Aftermarket Association, industry
>   information and resources, ☎ (202) 775-8605, ✑ opeaa.org
> —The Outdoor Power Equipment Institute, industry information and
>   resources, ✑ opei.org

Paintball Equipment

Paintball is becoming an incredibly popular activity among kids, teens and adults alike. It's also used as a bonding activity during corporate retreats. You can capitalize on this craze by securing the right wholesale sources to buy from, and then using a bit of clever marketing to reach the perfect target audience.

Buy from wholesalers and distributors. Once you have secured a reliable buying source, sell directly to paintball enthusiasts from a homebased business, through eBay, at flea markets and at sports and recreation shows. Join paintball clubs and associations to spread the word about your business and to network for new customers.

> **BUY**
> Wholesalers, Distributors, Manufacturers
>
> **SELL**
> eBay, Flea Markets, Recreation Shows, Homebased Sales
>
> **RESOURCES**
> —Badlands Paintball Wholesale, ☎ (416) 245-3856, ✒ badlandspaintball.com
> —National Paintball Supply, ☎ (800) 346-5615, ✒ nationalpaintball.com
> —Paintball Discounters, ✒ paintball-discounters.com
> —Xtremez, ✒ http://wholesale.paintball-online.com

Party Goods

Balloons, themed paper plates, cups, party accessories, gift bags and other types of decorations are all in demand by parents throwing birthday parties for their kids, as well as adults planning to host an anniversary party, graduation party, sweet 16, bridal shower, baby shower, Super Bowl party, office party, retirement party or party for any other type of occasion or holiday. As a buy-and-sell entrepreneur, you can become a local source for all of someone's party supply needs.

This is a great homebased business that can also take advantage of an e-commerce website. Marketing and promotions, however, will be the key to your success. Become known as the expert to turn to when someone wants to host a party in their home or office. Provide a delivery service for your local customers. You can solicit referrals through bakeries that sell birthday cakes, party performers (clowns, jugglers and magicians) in your area, local toy stores, local PTA chapters, etc.

All kinds of party supplies can be purchased at low wholesale prices from distributors and liquidators. Combine these supplies with your own creativity.

> 🤝 **BUY**
> Wholesalers, Distributors, Liquidators
>
> 🤝 **SELL**
> Homebased Business, B2B, E-Commerce, Flea Markets
>
> 🏚 **RESOURCES**
> —Bulk Party Supplies, 🖱 bulkpartysupplies.com
> —Oriental Trading Company, 🖱 orientaltrading.com
> —Party Supplies In Bulk, 🖱 http://partysuppliesinbulk.com
> —Windy City Novelties, 🖱 windycitynovelties.com

Patio Furniture

When it comes to buying and selling lawn and garden products, patio furniture has the potential to be among the most profitable. Good-quality patio furniture is available at insanely low prices from overseas suppliers, especially if you purchase by the container (in quantity). You can also buy from importers and wholesalers, though prices will be higher per unit.

Regardless of the type of patio furniture you decide to sell, great sales methods include homebased displays, direct to businesses (such as restaurants and cafes), exhibiting at home and garden shows, listing in online marketplaces and vending at flea markets. Consider concentrating on the high-end market, supplying only the best custom patio furniture, and catering to those with substantial enough budgets to make this type of purchase.

To start this type of business, you'll need significant startup capital, warehouse space and potentially a delivery truck. Another alternative is to work with drop-shippers; however, you'll still need to have product on hand or on display. In many parts of the country, this is a very seasonal business. People typically buy patio furniture in the spring or early summer.

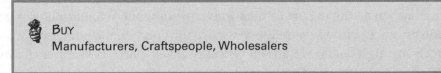

> 🤝 **BUY**
> Manufacturers, Craftspeople, Wholesalers

SELL
Homebased Showroom, Home and Garden Shows, Online Marketplaces

RESOURCES
—Best Adirondack Chair Company, ☎ (800) 418-1433,
   ✍ thebestadirondackchair.com
—DirectBuy Discount Patio Furniture, ✍ directpatiofurniture.com
—Hansen Wholesale, ☎ (800) 365-3267, ✍ hansenwholesale.com
—Patio Living & More, ✍ patiolivingandmore.com
—West Coast Patio, ✍ wcpatio.com

Pens and Fine Writing Instruments

While there's a market selling wholesale pens to offices and businesses, as well as a B2B custom-imprinted pen business opportunity (selling products that can be used as promotional giveaways), as a buy-and-sell entrepreneur looking to offer a more unique product line, consider selling extremely expensive, collectible and limited edition pens to business executives and collectors.

Companies such as Cross, Waterman and Mont Blanc, for example, offer high-end ballpoint pens, fountain pens and roller ball pens that are true works of art. There's a large collector's market for pens, especially antique and limited edition writing instruments. Sources for both buying and reselling these products include auctions, direct to and from collectors, distributors and eBay.

In addition to the collector's market, fine writing instruments make the perfect graduation gifts, as well as congratulatory gifts for business executives. A single fine writing instrument can sell for anywhere from $100 to $5,000. As with any type of collectible, it's essential that you learn about the market before trying to enter it as a businessperson. Also, watch out for counterfeit fine writing instruments that look like the real thing, but that are worthless.

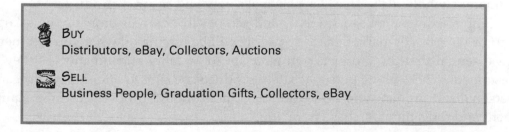

BUY
Distributors, eBay, Collectors, Auctions

SELL
Business People, Graduation Gifts, Collectors, eBay

> **RESOURCES**
> —About Time, ♂ abouttime.com/abouttime/authentic-mont-blanc-pens.invtc.html
> —Cross, ♂ http://crosspen.com/
> —Mont Blanc, ♂ montblanc.com
> —Passion4Pens, ♂ passion4pens.com
> —Waterman, ♂ waterman.com/en/
> —Wholesale Yellow, ♂ wholesaleyellow.com/stationery/writing-instruments

Personal Security Products

The time has never been better to sell personal security products, such as Mace, sirens, whistles and stun guns, to security-minded consumers. Who can blame people for being concerned about their own well-being and security, especially if they live in a big city?

Muggings, personal attacks, road rage and home invasions have people frightened to leave their own homes or to walk alone outside at night. While many people refuse to carry a gun (rightfully so), these same people are often more than willing to use personal security products that do not have such potentially lethal results.

Before launching this type of business, determine what local laws exist pertaining to the sale or possession of various types of personal protection items, such as knives, pepper spray and Mace. In many places, a special permit is required just to possess these items, not to mention sell them. There are also laws about shipping these products across state lines, so be sure you get the lowdown by doing ample research.

In addition to personal safety seminars and consumer shows, flea markets and an e-commerce website are the perfect selling venues for these products. There are numerous wholesale sources for personal safety and security products.

Single women, college students and senior citizens will probably be a large part of your target market. Because people will be relying on what you sell them, it's essential that the products you offer are top-quality and function as they're described. When selling personal safety products, be sure to offer instruction and personalized guidance on how your customers should properly use the equipment and tools they purchase from you.

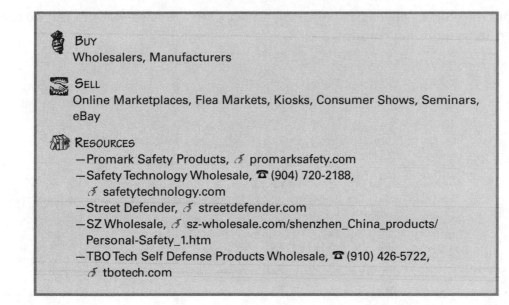

Within the box:

BUY
Wholesalers, Manufacturers

SELL
Online Marketplaces, Flea Markets, Kiosks, Consumer Shows, Seminars, eBay

RESOURCES
—Promark Safety Products, ✆ promarksafety.com
—Safety Technology Wholesale, ☎ (904) 720-2188,
  ✆ safetytechnology.com
—Street Defender, ✆ streetdefender.com
—SZ Wholesale, ✆ sz-wholesale.com/shenzhen_China_products/
  Personal-Safety_1.htm
—TBO Tech Self Defense Products Wholesale, ☎ (910) 426-5722,
  ✆ tbotech.com

Pet Food

Within millions of American homes, dogs and cats have become a loved member of the family. Thus it should come as no surprise that pet owners spend more than $5 billion annually on food to feed their cats, dogs, rabbits, birds, reptiles, fish and other domestic pets. While supermarkets and pet supply superstores sell low-cost pet food, gourmet and premium-quality pet food is typically available from smaller, independent pet stores and pet food sellers.

Simply feeding a dog a premium-quality pet food, as opposed to a supermarket brand, can increase its lifespan by as much as five years. Maintaining a healthy diet will also dramatically decrease a pet's vet bills over the course of its life. There are dozens of premium pet food manufacturers that offer top-quality brands that you can use to establish your pet food buy-and-sell enterprise.

Buy directly from manufacturers, wholesalers and distributors and sell to pet owners in person, via the internet, at flea markets, or using a mall kiosk, for example. You can increase profits by also selling premium and healthy dog treats.

One of the best sales methods is to establish a solid customer base through advertising and direct marketing, and then offer free home delivery of pet food on a regular schedule. It will take a lot of hard work and an investment of time and money to convince people to switch from their current pet food brand to yours, but the end results could be worth it. You can also sell at pet shows. Obtain customer referrals from veterinarians, dog trainers, kennels, dog walkers and doggy daycare facilities in your area.

BUY
Manufacturers, Wholesalers

SELL
Direct Delivery, Pet Shows, Online Marketplaces (E-Commerce Website)

RESOURCES
—American Pet Products Manufacturers Association, ♂ appma.org
—Metro Traders Wholesale, ☎ (877) 321-5050, ♂ wholesaleforpets.com
—Natura Pet Food, ♂ naturapet.com
—PetEdge, ♂ petedge.com
—Zuke's Pet Treats, ♂ zukes.com

Pet Products

In addition to selling gourmet or premium pet food, another pet-related buy-and-sell business venture involves offering pet products, such as accessories and toys. There are an estimated 30 million dogs and 50 million cats living in U.S. and Canadian households. Combined, that is 80 million potential customers for a buy-and-sell enterprise that specializes in pet products.

To cash in on the pet toys craze, you will first need a reliable wholesale supplier. PetEdge is a leading distributor of pet products, but this distributor also supplies pet superstores (your competition). Instead, consider selling higher-end and more unique products, such as those developed by small companies that advertise in dog enthusiast magazines, such as *Bark* and *Modern Dog*.

Marketing pet toys for profit can be accomplished in many ways, including online sales, flea markets, pet shows and vending at community events. One unique way to reach customers is to visit parks frequented by dogs and their owners. Distribute brochures or product samples to these people. On any given day, and especially on weekends, you are bound to run into 20, 30, or more pets and their owners every hour. You can also obtain customer referrals from veterinarians, dog trainers, kennels, dog walkers and doggy daycare facilities in your area.

🏺 BUY
Wholesalers and Manufacturers

🤝 SELL
Pet Shows, Kiosks, Flea Markets, E-Commerce Website

🏪 RESOURCES
—American Pet Products Manufacturers Association, ✐ appma.org
—JB Wholesale Pet Supplies, ✐ jbpet.com
—King Wholesale Pet Supplies, ☎ (800) 825-4647, ✐ kingwholesale.com
—Kong Company, ✐ kongcompany.com
—PetEdge, ✐ petedge.com
—Pets At Play, ✐ petsatplay.com
—Retail Pets, ✐ http://retailpets.com

Photo Gifts

As a buy-and-sell entrepreneur, you can become a sales agent for any number of companies that take people's traditional or digital photographs and transform them into all sorts of unique gift and novelty items, from T-shirts and mouse pads to throw blankets, puzzles and and poster-size vinyl prints.

The wholesale to retail price markup on these products can be significant, and with a few product samples in hand, they're relatively easy to sell, especially to parents and grandparents, who want to create unique items featuring photos of their kids, grandchildren or pets. One great aspect of this business opportunity is that you don't have to maintain any inventory. All you need are product samples to show customers, plus the ability to submit orders and digital or printed photos to your suppliers.

🏺 BUY
Wholesalers, Manufacturers

🤝 SELL
In-Person, Flea Markets, E-Commerce, Events, Home Shows, Gift Shows, Home Sales Parties

🏪 RESOURCES
—CafePress, ✐ cafepress.com
—Kustom Keepsakes, ✐ kustomkeepsakes.com/wholesale.htm

—Discount Photo Gifts, ♂ discountphotogifts.com/allproducts
—KeyTrade, ♂ tradekey.com/ks-photo-gifts/
—Photo Throws, ♂ blankettalk.com/jv.html
—PhotoWow, ♂ photowow.com

Portable Electronics

There are lots of people selling portable electronic devices on eBay and their own e-commerce websites, and they're making a small fortune in the process, despite the intense competition. You can sell portable CD players, DVD players, MP3 players, GPS systems, digital cameras and good old-fashioned boom boxes. There's also a huge market for noise-cancelling headphones, carrying cases and other accessories for these products.

Get started by securing one or more reliable wholesale sources for good quality portable electronics that you can buy from at rock-bottom prices. Then, when you're ready to start selling, take advantage of eBay. You can increase sales by selling at flea markets, mall kiosks and consumer shows. Sure, you'll have competition, so you'll need to differentiate yourself with your product selection, top-notch customer service and competitive pricing.

To reduce your inventory costs, consider working with a drop-shipper that's reputable and reliable and that offers quality products.

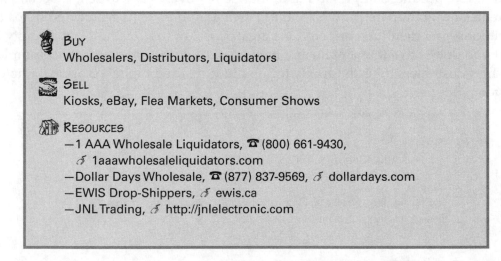

BUY
Wholesalers, Distributors, Liquidators

SELL
Kiosks, eBay, Flea Markets, Consumer Shows

RESOURCES
—1 AAA Wholesale Liquidators, ☎ (800) 661-9430,
   ♂ 1aaawholesaleliquidators.com
—Dollar Days Wholesale, ☎ (877) 837-9569, ♂ dollardays.com
—EWIS Drop-Shippers, ♂ ewis.ca
—JNL Trading, ♂ http://jnlelectronic.com

Pottery

European, Mexican, Asian, American and British pottery varies by style and quality, depending on production region. However, what does not vary is the huge demand for functional and decorative pottery, regardless of origin.

Planting pots, window boxes, picture frames, stoneware, jugs, plaques, vases, candlesticks and decorative tiles are among the products that can be made from pottery. Buying sources for new pottery include manufacturers producing mass quantities, wholesalers, liquidators and individual craftspeople. To offer the most unique and upscale products, consider using individual craftspeople as your primary suppliers.

Sell on eBay, as well as at home and garden shows, at flea markets, and right from your own home pottery showroom.

BUY
Wholesalers, Manufacturers, Craftspeople

SELL
Collectors, Flea Markets, Kiosks, Home Shows, eBay

RESOURCES
—Arizona Pottery Manufacturing, ☎ (800) 420-1808,
  ✍ arizonapottery.com
—Mexican Connexion, ✍ mexicanconnexion.com
—Pottery B2B, 🖥 potteryb2b.com
—The Polish Pottery Shop Manufacturing, ☎ (888) 254-2119,
  ✍ polishpotteryshop.com
—The Pottery Patch, ✍ thepotterypatch.com

Prints and Posters

Big money can be earned selling art prints and collectible posters. For art prints, you can scan classified ads and auctions to purchase these items secondhand from private sellers. Or buy new prints from wholesalers and directly from artists. If you decide to deal in previously owned art prints, make sure that you acquire an art print price guide for valuation purposes. It will prove to be a very valuable tool for both buying and selling.

New posters can be purchased directly from wholesalers, framed and mounted, or unframed and unmounted. Collectible posters displaying sports, advertising, theater, events, entertainment and art can be found by spending time at flea markets, online marketplaces, garage sales and auctions.

Market both new and used prints and posters by setting up a sales kiosk at consumer shows and malls, and by listing your products for sale on eBay and other online marketplaces. Market your collectible prints and posters directly to collectors by joining online and offline collectible clubs and associations. These products can also be targeted to business professionals, corporations and interior designers for home and office decorations.

BUY
Wholesalers, Auctions, Estate Sales, Garage Sales, Classified Ads, Artists

SELL
Collectors, Kiosks, eBay, Flea Markets

RESOURCES
—All Posters Wholesale, ☎ (510) 879-4700, ✎ allposters.com
—Art Lot Wholesale, ☎ (866) 422-4754, ✎ artlot.com
—Gordon's Art Sales Index, ☎ (800) 892-4622, ✎ gordonsart.com
—Lieberman's Art Prints, ✎ liebermans.net/main/home.aspx
—Poster Service, ✎ posterservice.com

Rare Books (Used)

You have the potential to hit the jackpot if you specialize in rare books, such as first editions, antique copies and author-autographed copies. There are an infinite number of used books available at rock-bottom prices; however, the truly collectible books will cost a lot, even at wholesale prices.

You can buy rare used books at garage sales, flea markets, online marketplaces, auctions, estate sales, library sales and secondhand shops. Few people who are selling their books take the time to find out their true value. Because of this, many rare and valuable books can be purchased at very low prices, and then resold at current market value to serious collectors.

Invest in rare book pricing guides, so you are armed with the resources needed to make wise purchasing decisions. Whether or not the books you sell are run-of-the mill used books for $10, or rare ones worth hundreds or thousands, the internet is your best marketing tool. List used books for sale on Amazon.com, eBay, and other used and collector book marketplaces on the web. If you plan on volume selling, to make the listing process faster, invest in barcode scanning software and a barcode reader (the cost will be under $50). With these tools, you can automatically scan all book information retrieved from the barcode on each book's back cover.

BUY
Garage Sales, Online Marketplaces, Flea Markets, Secondhand Shops

SELL
eBay, Collectors, Flea Markets, Online Marketplaces, Amazon.com

RESOURCES
—AbeBooks, ✆ abebooks.com
—Amazon.com, ✆ amazon.com (click on "Sell Items" at the bottom of the homepage)
—International Rare Book Collectors Association, ✆ rarebooks.org
—Swapbooks, textbook and used book buy-and-sell marketplace, ✆ swapbooks.com
—Used Book Central, buy-and-sell marketplace, ✆ usedbookcentral.com

Real Estate

If you have some serious money to invest and good credit, consider getting involved in buying and selling real estate, which is how countless shrewd business people have become multi-millionaires. As a rule, people looking to buy and sell real estate look for three types of buying opportunities—foreclosures, motivated sellers and fixer-uppers. These situations allow the buyer to negotiate a very low price for the purchase of the property. Once the property is yours, you can carry out minor repairs and cosmetic fix-ups, and then resell (flip) the property, often for a significant profit.

Of course, there are also plenty of things buyers should not do. For example, don't buy vacant land, because it cannot generate income until it's resold. Also, never sell for less than you have invested.

There are literally hundreds of real estate buying books, programs and training seminars available to show you how to flip properties for a profit. Some are good, while others are a waste of money. However, what does hold true is that you cannot just simply jump in with both feet and hope for the best. You must acquire the knowledge needed to make smart investments. This takes time, research and education.

Recipes

Unless you're a well known chef, chances are people won't pay top dollar for your recipes. But if you have a handful of awesome recipes that have been passed down through generations, for an award-winning apple pie, for example, you could use Microsoft Word or a desktop publishing program to create a nice printed presentation for your recipes and then sell them individually for a few dollars each, or in groups for a bit more money.

The best way to sell recipes is through classified ads or an e-commerce website, unless you invest the money to create an entire self-published recipe book, in which case the sales opportunities increase dramatically (as does the price you can charge). To learn more about self-publishing opportunities, pick up a copy of Wiley's *Self-Publishing for Dummies* book at any bookstore.

While you probably won't get rich selling recipes, you can earn a nice second income. A printed recipe is easy to ship and inventory, so your costs are extremely low. If you decide to pursue this type of business, keep in mind that you can only sell recipes you own the copyright to. You can't simply steal someone else's recipes without their written permission.

When creating your classified ads, come up with catchy headlines, such as "Grandma's Award-Winning Apple Pie Recipe" or "Three-Time State Fair Winning Apple Pie Recipe for Sale" to entice readers to spend $5 to $10 to order it from you. On your e-commerce website, you can earn additional commissions by selling existing cookbooks from major publishers. If you don't want to maintain an inventory of these books, you can become a sales affiliate through Amazon.com or the Barnes and Noble website.

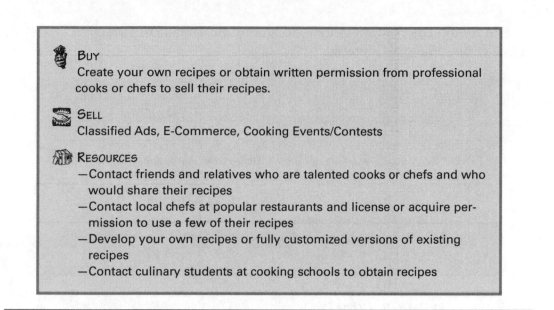

> **BUY**
> Create your own recipes or obtain written permission from professional cooks or chefs to sell their recipes.
>
> **SELL**
> Classified Ads, E-Commerce, Cooking Events/Contests
>
> **RESOURCES**
> —Contact friends and relatives who are talented cooks or chefs and who would share their recipes
> —Contact local chefs at popular restaurants and license or acquire permission to use a few of their recipes
> —Develop your own recipes or fully customized versions of existing recipes
> —Contact culinary students at cooking schools to obtain recipes

Reclaimed Building Products

Many people are emotionally fulfilled or rewarded by being earth-friendly and by recycling. One way to adapt this philosophy into a potentially profitable buy-and-sell business venture is to deal in reclaimed building products, such as bricks, lumber, kitchen cabinets, plumbing fixtures, windows, doors, hardware, ceiling tins, fireplace mantels, light fixtures, patio stones and hardwood flooring.

These materials can be purchased cheaply and resold for a profit. The value of used building products has soared in recent years as the price of new materials has skyrocketed. Especially valuable are architectural antiques, such as clear-stock casings, stained glass windows, columns and capitals, claw-foot bathtubs and cut-glass doorknobs, but the items you can obtain and resell in this product category are almost endless. Equally valuable are other reclaimed building products, such as barn board, barn timbers and split cedar-rail fencing.

Your main buying sources will include contractors specializing in renovation, flooring installers, window replacement companies, demolition companies, plumbers and homeowners doing their own renovations. Build alliances with these companies and sources so that you can get first dibs on the best and most valuable reclaimed building products as they become available. For some of your product sources, instead of paying cash upfront, you might be able to split the proceeds from the sales on a 50-50 basis and pay once you've resold the items for a profit.

Sell to homeowners, collectors, designers and architects through a variety of online and offline marketplaces.

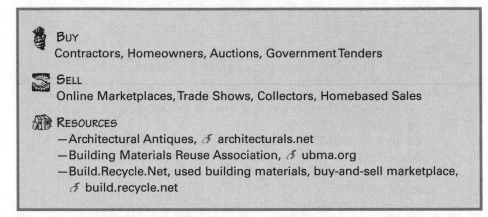

BUY
Contractors, Homeowners, Auctions, Government Tenders

SELL
Online Marketplaces, Trade Shows, Collectors, Homebased Sales

RESOURCES
—Architectural Antiques, ✆ architecturals.net
—Building Materials Reuse Association, ✆ ubma.org
—Build.Recycle.Net, used building materials, buy-and-sell marketplace,
  ✆ build.recycle.net

Recreational Vehicles (RVs)

Selling big-ticket items and products often translates into big profit potential, and in the case of buying and selling recreational vehicles, the prices and the profit potential don't come much bigger. The best buying source for RVs is from private sellers advertising with signs and through print or electronic classifieds. Distress sales will be a good starting point for finding great deals on clean, late-model RVs.

Secondary buying sources include auction sales, estate sales and bank or financier repossessions. Look for mechanically fit RVs in need of a little TLC, such as a good cleanup, minor cosmetic repairs, and the addition of items—such as generators, awnings and AC units—to boost the overall value of the vehicles.

Travel trailers of all sizes, from pop-up tent style to luxurious fifth wheels, are also great buy-and-sell items, which can be purchased and sold in the same manner as motorized RVs. You can dramatically increase your profits by selling new and used RV accessories.

Your best selling options include selling directly from home, selling via a website, eBay (eBay Motors), consignment RV lots, and exhibiting RV accessories at camping and RV shows. The RV community is a close-knit one, so the ability to network will play a huge role in your success. Generating positive word-of-mouth advertising will also be essential. Obviously, a significant amount of startup capital and a working knowledge of the RV industry will be essential to get started.

BUY
Classified Ads, Auctions, Wholesalers, Foreclosures, Estate Sales

SELL
Homebased Sales, RV Shows, Online Marketplaces, RV Brokers, Classifieds

RESOURCES
—American Recreational Equipment, ☎ (800) 640-8991,
   ✆ arewholesale.com
—RV Trader Online, ✆ rvtraderonline.com
—NADA Guides, RV price guides, ☎ (800) 966-6232,
   ✆ nadaguides.com

Religious Products

People who are deeply religious or highly spiritual typically are not afraid to spend a lot of money in order to prove it. You can tap into this market by buying and selling religious books, Bibles, Bible cases, religious bookmarks, crucifixes, plaques, rosary beads, religious jewelry, pins, religious games, "What Would Jesus Do?" bumper stickers, figurines, religious music CDs and first holy communion products, all of which can be purchased from wholesalers, distributors, liquidators and importers, and even factory direct.

Sell online, through church and Bible groups, from a homebased showroom, at flea markets and at religious-themed consumer shows and exhibitions. Follow your own faith, and concentrate your marketing efforts on the religion you know best.

BUY
Manufacturers, Wholesalers, Liquidators, Importers

SELL
Mail Order, eBay, Flea Markets, Kiosks, Consumer Shows

RESOURCES
—Dollar Days Wholesale, ☎ (877) 837-9569, ✆ dollardays.com
—Knight Light Candle & Imports, ☎ (248) 745-9035,
   ✆ knightlightcandle.com
—Parable Franchise, ✆ parablefranchise.com/HTML/franchise.html

—Roden Surplus Imports, ☎ (256) 355-4751, ♂ rodenimports.com
—Wholesale Central, ♂ wholesalecentral.com/Religious.html

Remote-Controlled (R/C) Models

Some of today's remote-controlled toys can reach speeds of 100 miles per hour and have a range of a mile. In other words, these are not necessarily kids' toys. Many are designed for serious hobbyists who pay top dollar to enjoy their favorite pastime. From a financial standpoint, remote-controlled models can sell for as much as several thousand dollars. These "toys" are available as race cars, classic cars, airplanes, helicopters, boats, motorcycles and all-terrain vehicles. They are also available at many different price points, retailing from about $20 to several thousand dollars.

R/C models can be purchased from wholesalers, from distributors, and in some instances, directly from the manufacturers or their authorized agents. Toy and hobby liquidators can also be an excellent source for buying low cost inventory.

Sell through online marketplaces, including eBay, from a homebased showroom or at consumer shows and flea markets. It does not take long for a crowd to assemble when these models start whizzing about, and even less time for the wallets to come out when people see how much fun they are to play with. Also, be sure to participate in organized R/C clubs, organizations and competitions. These all provide tremendous networking and business-generating opportunities.

As with any type of product, especially one that evolves around a hobby, don't get into this type of business unless you're truly passionate about it, you know the products, and you'll be able to successfully reach the niche target audience of R/C enthusiasts and hobbyists.

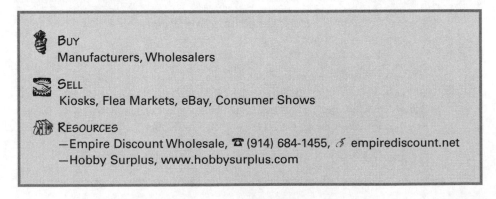

BUY
Manufacturers, Wholesalers

SELL
Kiosks, Flea Markets, eBay, Consumer Shows

RESOURCES
—Empire Discount Wholesale, ☎ (914) 684-1455, ♂ empirediscount.net
—Hobby Surplus, www.hobbysurplus.com

—Interactive Toy Concepts Manufacturing, ☎ (866) 214-2220,
  ✆ interactivetoy.com
—Megatech Manufacturing, ☎ (847) 564-9945, ✆ megatech.com
—Toy Directory, ✆ toydirectory.com

Restaurant Equipment

You don't have to be a professional chef to make money in the restaurant business. For startup restaurants and restaurants looking to expand, the cost of new restaurant equipment is often out of their price range. Thus these restaurant owners opt to purchase good-quality used equipment that meets their needs. It's this used restaurant equipment market that can become a viable buy-and-sell business opportunity for you, especially if you're able to fix up used equipment, give it a good cleaning, store it in a warehouse (until it sells) and then deliver it to your customer. To generate additional revenue, you can also offer installation services.

The secondhand restaurant equipment and fixtures you choose to buy and sell can include grills, fryers, coffee machines, tables, chairs and coolers. The formula for success is pretty simple. When a restaurant goes out of business, simply purchase the equipment and fixtures for a fraction of their original retail value. When a new restaurant, café, hotel or catering company is planning to open, resell the equipment for a handsome profit.

To buy restaurant equipment, establish working relationships with auctioneers and bankruptcy trustees who can keep you informed about restaurant closings in your area. Once you have accumulated some equipment, advertise it for sale in online marketplaces, in specialty restaurant publications, by developing your own website and by speaking directly to restaurateurs.

Another excellent source for used food service and restaurant equipment is school surplus sales and auctions. InterSchola (**interschola.com**) specializes in auctioning off used and surplus equipment from school systems throughout the country. Anyone is welcome to bid on the products being sold.

According to InterSchola's management, food service equipment is one of the most popular items typically auctioned through the service, and the prices are typically well below market value, which means for the buy-and-sell entrepreneur, generous profits can be made by reselling this type of used equipment to restaurants, cafes, catering companies, hotels, nursing homes and schools both in the U.S. and overseas. You will be able to earn top dollar selling high-end equipment to businesses in foreign countries if you have the right connections and know-how.

BUY
Auctions, Bankruptcies, Classified Ads, School Surplus Sales

SELL
Homebased Sales, B2B, Online Marketplaces, Specialty Publications

RESOURCES
—InterSchola, ⚲ interschola.com
—National Restaurant Association, ⚲ restaurant.org
—Restaurant Operator, information and resources,
   ⚲ restaurantoperator.com

Retractable Awnings

Retractable shade and rain awnings are a welcome addition to any patio space. They come in two basic mechanical designs: hand-crank models or motorized models that operate using a switch or handheld remote control. Retail prices vary greatly depending on size, model and fabric selection. They can range from a couple hundred dollars for mass-produced 8- by 10-foot awnings to $5,000 or more for large, custom-sized motorized awnings.

Homeowners seeking protection from the sun and rain will be your number-one target audience. Secondary markets include recreational vehicle owners and business owners with outdoor patio space, especially restaurants and cafés.

Buying directly from manufacturers will offer the best wholesale pricing. You can also buy from wholesalers, distributors and agents, though you will have to pay slightly higher per-unit prices.

Sell direct from home by setting up awning displays and inviting potential customers to check them out. You can also create your own website, so you can take online orders from around the globe. Awnings can also be sold through eBay, at home and garden shows and at recreational vehicle expositions.

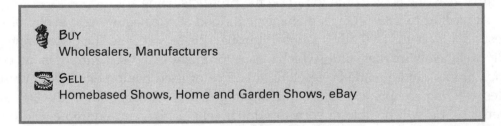

BUY
Wholesalers, Manufacturers

SELL
Homebased Shows, Home and Garden Shows, eBay

RESOURCES

—Ace Canopy Manufacturing, ☎ (888) 702-6082, ♂ acecanopy.com
—Awnings.com, ♂ awnings.com
—BST Awnings, ♂ http://bstawnings.com
—TCT&A Industries, ☎ (800) 252-1355, ♂ awning-tent.com

Rock and Gem Products

Like most products that are perfect for the buy-and-sell business model, you can purchase rocks, gems, equipment and related supplies from wholesalers, as well as directly from rock and gem hounds who spend weekends scouring the countryside for treasures hidden in the soil, riverbeds and sides of mountains.

These products can then be sold to crafters, costume jewelry makers, enthusiasts, collectors and consumers looking for unusual home and office decoration items. Your products can be sold on eBay, at industry trade shows and by renting vendor space at flea markets. This is a highly specialized business that caters to a very niche target audience. Get to know the business and your potential customers before jumping into it.

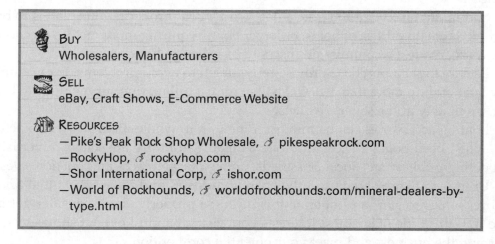

BUY
Wholesalers, Manufacturers

SELL
eBay, Craft Shows, E-Commerce Website

RESOURCES
—Pike's Peak Rock Shop Wholesale, ♂ pikespeakrock.com
—RockyHop, ♂ rockyhop.com
—Shor International Corp, ♂ ishor.com
—World of Rockhounds, ♂ worldofrockhounds.com/mineral-dealers-by-type.html

Sailboats and Motorboats (Used)

When it comes to buying and selling used boats, the trick is to find "desperation sales"—current boat owners with financial problems or a pending divorce, for example, who need to sell quickly and get whatever they can for the sale. It's also wise to purchase inventory at the end of the boating season, and to seek out used boats in need of a very good cleaning and minor repairs, if you want to find the best buying deals.

If you are going to deal in smaller, trailer boats, such as Hobbies, Lasers and Sunfish, you can sell directly from home and on eBay (or eBay Motors). Larger boats will require moorage, increasing your costs (which must then be factored into the selling price).

Used sailboats are best sold in the water rather than in dry dock, so people can take them for a test run. Out-of-water boats, which cannot be tested, always sell for less, even if they are in great shape.

Because the average 30-foot, late-model sailboat sells in the range of $40,000 to $120,000, it is also a good idea to invest in a professional survey before buying, to make sure you are not buying someone else's problems. In addition to boats, sell accessories, such as sails, life jackets, and gear and rigging, to earn additional profits.

Great profits can also be earned buying and selling powerboats of all sizes—skiffs, trawler fishing boats, cruisers and speedboats (as well as powerboat accessories). Good deals on powerboats can be found at the end of the season in the northern climates, for example. Once again, as a buyer, look for boats in need of minor repairs or a good cleaning, and boats involved in desperation sale circumstances.

You might also want to strike a deal with a boat broker if your plan is to buy and sell large quantities of boats, or larger boats requiring moorage. If you choose this route, request a commission discount based on volume.

Be sure to set a purchase proviso for yourself to avoid problems. For example, any boat costing more than $10,000 will require a full marine survey prior to buying, preferably at the seller's expense.

Boating accessories can be purchased new from wholesalers and manufacturers, while used boating accessories are available from private sellers advertising in boating publications, local classifieds, online marketplaces and auction sales.

Unless you know boats and the boating industry and have substantial financial resources to start and operate this business properly, don't consider getting into it. If this type of business interests you, visit a handful of boat shows to start learning the business and meet your potential competition.

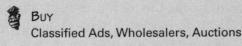

BUY
Classified Ads, Wholesalers, Auctions

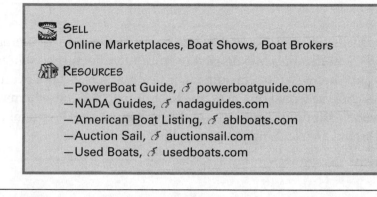

SELL
Online Marketplaces, Boat Shows, Boat Brokers

RESOURCES
—PowerBoat Guide, ✍ powerboatguide.com
—NADA Guides, ✍ nadaguides.com
—American Boat Listing, ✍ ablboats.com
—Auction Sail, ✍ auctionsail.com
—Used Boats, ✍ usedboats.com

Saunas

For people with aches and pains, athletes, or those who simply want to pamper themselves at home, in-home saunas are a fashionable, must-have item. They're the perfect companion product to a Jacuzzi or hot tub.

There are a great number of sauna manufacturers, and many offer do-it-yourself sauna kits requiring only basic hand tools and virtually no experience to assemble. Many manufacturers provide drop-shipping services. (That means you don't have to maintain any inventory, except for product samples to show your potential customers.)

You can easily sell sauna kits from home, at home and garden shows, at recreation shows, through online marketplaces and through specialty publications.

At present there is not much supply or demand for used saunas and equipment, so you're much better off selling only new equipment.

BUY
Manufacturers, Wholesalers

SELL
Homebased Sales, Online Marketplaces, Home and Garden Shows

RESOURCES
—Dolphin Pacific Manufacturing, ✍ amerisauna.com
—Sauna Fin Manufacturing, ✍ saunafin.com
—Sauna Kits Manufacturing, ✍ saunakits.com

School Supplies

Pens, paper, folders, pencils and notebooks are just some of the many different types of school supplies you can buy inexpensively from manufacturers, wholesalers and liquidators and then resell to consumers at flea markets, school events and other retail settings. As a seasonal business, the best time to sell these items is during the back-to-school shopping period, between August and September, when kids and their parents are stocking up on supplies.

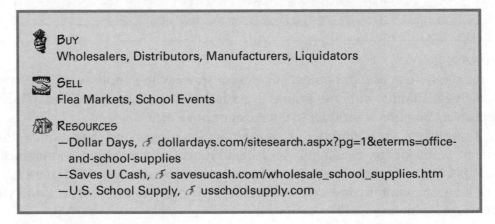

BUY
Wholesalers, Distributors, Manufacturers, Liquidators

SELL
Flea Markets, School Events

RESOURCES
—Dollar Days, ☞ dollardays.com/sitesearch.aspx?pg=1&eterms=office-and-school-supplies
—Saves U Cash, ☞ savesucash.com/wholesale_school_supplies.htm
—U.S. School Supply, ☞ usschoolsupply.com

Scuba Diving Equipment

If you scuba dive as a hobby, why not turn this passion into a cash-generating business? Sell scuba-related equipment, such as wet suits, dry suits, tanks, weights and belts, fins, masks, dive computers, first aid kits, underwater cameras and other types of scuba gear and equipment.

Buy new items from wholesalers and manufacturers, and used items from private sellers advertising in scuba publications and online portals. Convert your garage into a mini dive shop and sell right from home. It's even better if you have a pool so customers can test equipment. If not, small but adequate above-ground pools are always available in the classifieds for a few hundred dollars and sometimes for free. You can also sell at sports and recreation shows, through eBay and by word-of-mouth in the tight-knit dive community.

To be successful, you'll need to be able to market successfully to scuba divers, plus be a certified diver or dive master yourself, in order to earn credibility among potential customers.

>
> **BUY**
> Wholesalers, Manufacturers, Classified Ads
>
> **SELL**
> Homebased Sales, eBay, Sports and Recreation Shows
>
> **RESOURCES**
> —Aqua Sports Manufacturing, ☎ 82-51-6216003 (Korea), ✒ aquaz.net
> —PADI, Professional Association of Diving Instructors, ✒ padi.com
> —Joe Diver America, ✒ joediveramerica.com/?category=Wholesale
> —Diving Index, ✒ divingindex.com/diving-gear-manufacturers-
>   wholesale-distribution.html

Seashells

There are many potential customers for seashells, including tourists visiting a beach destination (if you can sell in these areas), and more globally, crafters who like to use them to create wind chimes, mosaics, costume jewelry, planters and a whole host of products.

If you determine your target audience is crafters, to sell your products, go to where the crafters are, such as craft shows, craft clubs, online craft groups and chat forums. Once again, because seashells appeal to consumers searching for nifty home and office decorations, you can also sell the shells at flea markets, public markets and community events.

If you live in an area renowned for seashells, you can collect them yourself for free, but because they do not sell for great sums, spending your time collecting them will probably prove ineffective and unprofitable. Therefore, purchasing seashells in bulk from established wholesale sources will typically be a better option.

> **BUY**
> Wholesalers
>
> **SELL**
> Craftspeople, Craft Shows, Flea Markets, Kiosks
>
> **RESOURCES**
> —APN Shell Craft Wholesale, ☎ 91-4652-246368 (India),
>   ✒ apnshells.com

—Shell Horizons Wholesale, ☎ (727) 536-3333, ✆ shellhorizons.com
—U.S. Shell Wholesale, ☎ (956) 554-4500, ✆ usshell.com
—Seashells.com, ✆ seashells.com/shells.htm

Secondhand Clothing

Secondhand clothing sales definitely rank as one of the top ten buy-and-sell items for a number of reasons. First, there is an excellent supply in every community and at rock-bottom prices. Second, previously owned and vintage clothing is now trendy to wear.

These days, people from every walk of life purchase top-quality secondhand clothing as a frugal means of getting quality, name-brand, designer-label clothing (couture) at reasonable prices. Also, many people view purchasing secondhand clothing as a way to help the planet by recycling used clothes, which otherwise would end up in landfill sites.

Buy secondhand clothing at garage sales, at estate sales and by running clothing wanted ads in the classified section of your local newspaper. There are also companies wholesaling secondhand clothing that can be purchased unsorted by the pound, sorted by the pound or sorted and pressed by the garment.

Your selling options include flea markets, online marketplaces (such as eBay) and hosting your own garage sales. Before merchandising any clothing, repair small tears, replace buttons and zippers as required, press or iron and display each garment neatly on a hanger. Doing so will double the resale value of an item.

Because secondhand clothing is available in many sizes and styles, consider having a specialty, such as designer children's clothing or designer jeans for adults. Know the hot brands, stay up-to-date on the latest fashion trends, and be creative when it comes to your marketing.

BUY
Garage Sales, Flea Markets, Wholesalers, Classified Ads

SELL
Flea Markets, Garage Sales, Online Marketplaces

RESOURCES
—Apparel Search, ✆ apparelsearch.com/wholesale_clothing/
wholesale_used_clothing.htm

—Best Used Clothing, ✂ bestusedclothing.com
—American Eagle Trade Group, ✂ eagletrade.com
—Trans-Americas Trading Co., ✂ tranclo.com

Secondhand Furniture

Breaking into the new furniture sales business requires a tremendous amount of startup capital, not to mention showroom space, warehouse space, delivery trucks and a sales team. If you're interested in selling furniture as a buy-and-sell entrepreneur, consider getting into the secondhand furniture business.

Your selling options will include a homebased showroom, flea markets, auctions and eBay (especially if you happen to purchase a rare, exotic, retro, or otherwise valuable piece of secondhand furniture you know will command top dollar when exposed to a global audience of consumers).

Buying sources for secondhand furniture include private sellers advertising in the classifieds, ads on notice boards, estate sales, garage sales, moving sales and moving and storage companies. You can also buy slightly damaged or discontinued merchandise from upscale new furniture stores at a huge discount, repair the furniture and then sell it for a profit.

To maximize your profits, thoroughly clean your merchandise before selling it. The investment made in furniture polish, small repairs and an upholstery steam-cleaning machine will be well rewarded by increased selling prices and overall profitability.

One option is to rent a large truck, load up your furniture and then find an empty lot or parking area in a public and busy area where you can sell directly from the truck (with permission, of course).

BUY
Garage Sales, Classified Ads, Auctions, Estate Sales, Moving and Storage Companies

SELL
Homebased Sales, Flea Markets

RESOURCES
—Clearance Furniture Outlet, ✂ http://clearancefurnitureoutlet.com
—Flea Market USA, www.fleausa.com

—Merchandize Liquidators, ♂ merchandizeliquidators.com/
american-furniure-warewhouse.htm
—TBW Closeouts, ♂ tdwcloseouts.com/monthly/kd_furniture.htm

Seeds and Bulbs

If you have a green thumb, enjoy gardening and would enjoy interacting with fellow gardening enthusiasts while making money at the same time, you can purchase seeds and bulbs wholesale and resell them at retail prices. Seeds and bulbs can be purchased in bulk and repackaged into smaller containers. Or you can purchase seeds and bulbs already prepackaged for individual retail sale.

You can specialize in rare and unusual plant varieties, or in run-of-the-mill vegetable, flower, herb, fruit and wildflower seeds and bulbs. Because gardening is such a broad topic appealing to millions of people, be sure to sell accessories, including how-to books and videos. Buying sources will be wholesalers, while your selling options include mail order, garden shows and online marketplaces. Many seed wholesalers offer their resellers catalogs for marketing purposes.

BUY
Wholesalers, Nurseries

SELL
Mail Order, Home and Garden Shows, Online Marketplaces, Kiosks

RESOURCES
—Bulbs Direct, ♂ bulbsdirect.com
—Easy To Grow Bulbs, ♂ easytogrowbulbs.com
—Hummert International Wholesale, ♂ hummert.com
—Park Seed Wholesale, ♂ parkwholesale.com
—Wholesale Distributors Directory, ♂ wholesaledistributorsnet.com/
garden.html

Sewing Machines

While fewer people have the time or inclination to sew, some still consider this a favorite hobby. As a buy-and-sell business, you can dabble in new and used sewing machines and accessories, such as bobbins, needles, thread, scissors and shears, pattern books, instructional videos, thread stands and sewing lamps.

Buy factory direct from manufacturers for the lowest prices, or buy smaller quantities at slightly higher prices from wholesalers and distributors. Liquidators are also a good source for acquiring inventory.

Sell on eBay and by displaying at crafts shows, fashion shows and home shows. Also, join sewing and crafts clubs in order to network with potential customers. Don't overlook buying and selling vintage sewing machines to collectors, which is a separate but equally viable business. Find vintage items at garage sales, flea markets and estate sales, and sell direct to collectors through organizations such as The International Sewing Machine Collectors' Society (**ismacs.net**).

BUY
Manufacturers, Wholesalers, Liquidators

SELL
Homebased Sales, Kiosks, Flea Markets, eBay, Fashion Shows, Craft Shows

RESOURCES
—Sewing Machines Wholesaler Directory, ✆ apparelsearch.com/wholesale_clothing/Components/Machinery/wholesale_sewing_machines.htm
—Brewer Wholesale, ✆ brewersewing.com
—Fashion Fabrics Club, ✆ fashionfabricsclub.com
—Nick-O Sewing Machine Company, ✆ nickosew.com
—Wholesale Sewing Supplies, ✆ wholesalesewingsupplies.com

Sheds and Shelters

Sheds and portable shelters can be used for any number of needs around the home, including an affordable way to add storage or workshop space, an art studio, guest accommodations, automobile protection, garden tool and patio furniture security or as a backyard playhouse for the kids.

Recently, portable carports constructed out of a basic metal frame covered by rain-resistant fabric have become a trendy alternative to building an expensive permanent garage to protect boats, automobiles, RVs and trailers.

In North America there are hundreds of companies engaged in manufacturing portable sheds and shelters made from a wide variety of materials, including plastic, wood, metal and fabric. Therefore, securing a reliable wholesale source should not be difficult. The majority of portable sheds and shelters are sold as do-it-yourself kits.

Many manufacturers provide drop-shipping services directly to your customers, cutting out the need for you to store and transport product. You can sell the sheds and shelters online and at home and garden shows, for example.

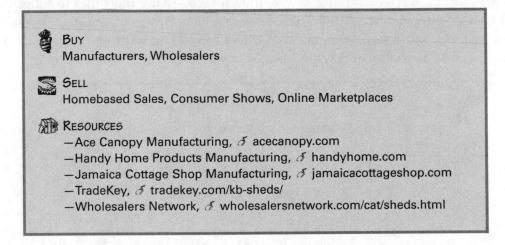

BUY
Manufacturers, Wholesalers

SELL
Homebased Sales, Consumer Shows, Online Marketplaces

RESOURCES
—Ace Canopy Manufacturing, ♪ acecanopy.com
—Handy Home Products Manufacturing, ♪ handyhome.com
—Jamaica Cottage Shop Manufacturing, ♪ jamaicacottageshop.com
—TradeKey, ♪ tradekey.com/kb-sheds/
—Wholesalers Network, ♪ wholesalersnetwork.com/cat/sheds.html

Sheet Music

There are millions of amateur and professional musicians throughout the world, and the majority of them require sheet music. All beginners, many novices and even seasoned professional musicians rely on sheet music in order to play their instruments. Sell sheet music by purchasing loose and bound sheet music from wholesalers and publishers cheaply, and then reselling it for a profit. Sell at flea markets and music shows, on eBay and through various other online marketplaces. You should also definitely consider establishing an e-commerce website that showcases all of the sheet music you stock. Because there are so many styles of music, you may want to find a niche in the market and become known as a specialist in that genre.

New music books and songbooks can be sold using Amazon.com or or the website of Barnes and Noble (**bn.com**), if you sign up to be a sales affiliate.

BUY
Publishers, Wholesalers

SELL
Online Marketplaces, Music Shows, Flea Markets

RESOURCES
—Hal Leonard Corporation, ♂ halleonard.com
—National Music Publishers Association, ♂ nmpa.org
—Southern Music Company, ♂ southernmusic.com
—Stagepass, ♂ stagepass.com/sheetmusic/songbooks

Shoes

Buying and selling new shoes has the potential to generate a significant income. You can sell a wide range of shoe styles and types, or choose an area to specialize in. A related business, also with excellent profit potential, includes buying and selling vintage shoes, especially ladies' fashion shoes. Vintage shoes can be found by scouring garage sales, flea markets and estate sales. Resell them on eBay and directly to vintage shoe collectors via collectible shows and online marketplaces.

New shoes can be purchased cheaply if you buy direct from the manufacturer, though as a general rule, you'll have to order larger quantities. For resellers with smaller budgets, buy from wholesalers and liquidators, who are a source of well-below-wholesale pricing and end-of-run and out-of-season shoes. Sell at flea markets, at fashion shows and directly to businesses (for safety and work footwear).

BUY
Manufacturers, Wholesalers, Garage Sales

SELL
Kiosks, Flea Markets, eBay, Fashion Shows, Collectors

RESOURCES
—All Footwear, ♂ allfootwear.com
—American Apparel and Footwear Association,
  ♂ apparelandfootwear.org
—Salvage Export, ♂ salvageexport.com
—ShoeNet B2B Online, ♂ shoenet.com
—Wholesale Central, ♂ wholesalecentral.com/Shoes-Footwear.html

Shop Tools

Shop tools, such as table saws, chop saws, band saws, lathes, drill presses, joiners, planners, welders, air compressors, metal breaks, metal sheers, metal presses, stamps and pipe benders are excellent buy-and-sell items, especially used shop tools, which can often be purchased for a fraction of their true value.

Buy secondhand and used tools primarily at auctions and bankruptcy sales that are liquidating the assets of woodworking shops, metal shops, glass shops, contractors and factories that have closed, that are updating equipment, or that have gone bankrupt.

Sell from home and by way of direct mail campaigns aimed at small business owners in the building, woodworking and fabrication trades. You can also sell the equipment at flea markets and on eBay. Cleaning and minor repairs, as needed, will go a long way to ensure you get the most money for every used product. Providing a 30-day warranty on all used equipment will greatly increase the value of your merchandise.

BUY
Manufacturers, Wholesalers, Auctions, Classified Ads

SELL
B2B, Online Marketplaces, Trade Shows, Homebased Sales

RESOURCES
—A Wholesale Store, ♂ awholesalestore.com
—Master Wholesale, ♂ masterwholesale.com/index/Shop-Tools.html
—Used Equipment Network, ♂ buyused.com
—Wholesale Central, ♂ wholesalecentral.com/Tools-Hardware.html
—Wiha Quality Tools Wholesale, ♂ wihatools.com

Silk Flowers

You can make a bundle selling beautiful silk flowers to consumers, crafters, event planners and party/wedding planners. Your supply source will be national and international manufacturers, wholesalers and importers of silk flowers. Or you might opt to find craftspeople in your local area to produce silk floral arrangements for you.

Set up appointments with wedding and event planners to show them your goods and explain the benefits of purchasing from your business. You can also sell at flea markets, through online marketplaces, at craft shows and by exhibiting at home and garden shows. Join crafts clubs and associations in your area to network for new business, and build alliances with other businesses that can refer your products to their clients, including interior decorators.

BUY
Manufacturers, Wholesalers, Craftspeople

SELL
Kiosks, Consumer Shows, Flea Markets, Online Marketplaces, B2B

RESOURCES
—1-888-FlowerMall, ♂ 1888flowermall.com
—Afloral, ♂ afloral.com
—Flowers By Design Wholesale, ♂ flowers-by-design.com
—King Craft Company, ♂ kingcraftco.com
—Kinkade Studios, ♂ kinkadestudios.com
—Kong Hing Silk Flower Company, ♂ silkflower.com.hk

Silverware

All things silver are fantastic buy-and-sell items, including flatware and chests, server sets, frames and ornaments made of sterling, stainless, silver plate and pewter. You can specialize in either new or used silverware, or combine the two.

New silverware can be purchased from wholesalers, distributors, manufacturers and liquidators. Great sources for used silverware include garage sales, auctions, and private sellers advertising in the classifieds.

Both new and used silverware can be sold through numerous online marketplaces, at flea markets and directly to collectors for rare products.

Like any retail venture, the keys to success will be identifying your target market, reaching your target audience and then grabbing their attention and giving them valid reason to take action and buy. Make sure that you advertise your business at online wedding sites. Establish yourself as an official wedding gift registry merchant in as many places as possible.

BUY
Auctions, Wholesalers, Manufacturers, Garage Sales, Classified Ads

SELL
Kiosks, Collectors, Auctions, Flea Markets, Consumer Shows, eBay

RESOURCES
—Belirams Silversmiths, ♂ belirams.com
—Dynasty Wholesale, ♂ dynastywholesale.com/page-16.html
—Galasource, ♂ galasource.com/landing.cfm/151,Flatware,XX
—Silverwarehouse, ♂ silverwarehouse.com

Small Appliances

Small appliances such as razors, curling irons, kitchen blenders, coffee makers, clock radios, hair dryers and air conditioners are gold mines waiting to be discovered by innovative entrepreneurs who choose to buy these products low and resell high.

As you'd expect, the best place to buy is through wholesale liquidators in pallet lots, if you can afford it. Alternately, buy wholesale in smaller quantities, but expect to pay slightly more. Buying in pallet lots can get you product for as much as 50 percent less than individual wholesale pricing—money that can wisely be used for better purposes, such as buying more valuable inventory for resale.

Flea markets and eBay are two of the best selling venues for small appliances. Other places to sell include consumer shows and mall-based kiosks. Avoid selling used small appliances, as the profit margin is very small and the demand is virtually nonexistent.

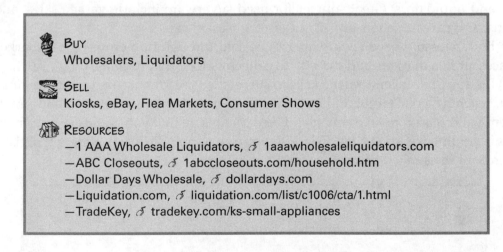

BUY
Wholesalers, Liquidators

SELL
Kiosks, eBay, Flea Markets, Consumer Shows

RESOURCES
—1 AAA Wholesale Liquidators, ♂ 1aaawholesaleliquidators.com
—ABC Closeouts, ♂ 1abccloseouts.com/household.htm
—Dollar Days Wholesale, ♂ dollardays.com
—Liquidation.com, ♂ liquidation.com/list/c1006/cta/1.html
—TradeKey, ♂ tradekey.com/ks-small-appliances

Snack Vending

People get hungry at work, at airports, in hotel lobbies, at schools and in a wide range of other public places. The snack vending business is a multibillion-dollar industry in North America and continues to grow year after year. Fortunately, claiming your piece of the very lucrative snack vending pie is easy to do.

Get started by finding the right locations before buying equipment and inventory. Do this by starting with friends and family members. Where do they work? Is there a vending machine present? If not, would the location support a vending machine? Failing this approach, explore your community and look for places that are busy with foot traffic or have a large number of employees. These locations can include car dealerships, factories, office buildings, fitness clubs and laundromats.

Once you have found the perfect location and reach an agreement with the landlord or business operator to install the vending equipment, you will be in the right position to know which type of machines to purchase and the kinds of snacks to stock. Typically, you can expect to mark up your product by 300 percent.

One of your ongoing responsibilities will be keeping the vending machines fully stocked with inventory, as well as properly maintained.

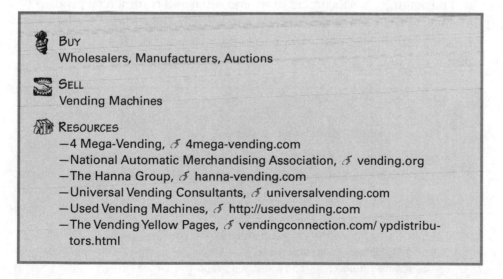

BUY
Wholesalers, Manufacturers, Auctions

SELL
Vending Machines

RESOURCES
—4 Mega-Vending, ✆ 4mega-vending.com
—National Automatic Merchandising Association, ✆ vending.org
—The Hanna Group, ✆ hanna-vending.com
—Universal Vending Consultants, ✆ universalvending.com
—Used Vending Machines, ✆ http://usedvending.com
—The Vending Yellow Pages, ✆ vendingconnection.com/ ypdistribu-tors.html

Software

There are more than 250,000 software applications currently available, including word processors, spreadsheets, accounting, productivity tools, database management, content, computer games, customer relationship management (CRM), publishing, inventory management, graphics, training, educational, communications, security and anti-virus software, to name a few popular categories.

It is safe to say that finding one or a few specialized or vertical market software categories to buy and sell should not prove difficult. Start your search on software directory websites. Buy right from developers or from wholesalers, and sell online, direct to businesses and through computer-related trade and consumer shows.

There is also a decent market for used software, especially business applications. However, when buying used, you have to make sure it is not pirated software. The best way to do that is to buy only used software that is complete with the original packaging and documentation. Buy used software at auction sales, from online marketplaces and from classified ads.

Yet another option is to hire programmers and have custom software created that you can market and sell exclusively. Or you can acquire open source software or freeware, add packaging and documentation, and sell it as a commercial product (within the guidelines of the open source or freeware software providers/publishers).

For more complicated software, you can boost your profits by offering in-person training or bundling your software with training books or videos.

🗝 BUY
Programmers, Wholesalers, Distributors, License Agents

🤝 SELL
B2B, Online Marketplaces, Consumer Shows, Flea Markets

🏚 RESOURCES
—D&H Wholesale, ✆ dandh.com
—Dirt Cheap Software, ✆ dirtcheapsoftware.com
—Soft Database, ✆ softdatabase.com
—Software Cheaper, ✆ softwarecheaper.com
—Sunnyland Software Wholesale, ✆ sunnylandsoftware.com
—The Software Network, ✆ thesoftwarenetwork.com
—TRUSTprice, ✆ trustprice.com

Solar-Powered Products

When it comes to how we power our lives, the wave of the future is without question alternative energy sources. Therefore, if you decide to start a buy-and-sell enterprise focused on the retail sales of solar-powered products, you will be engaging in a growing industry that will prove extremely profitable for years to come.

Sell solar and alternative-energy products such as solar-powered interior and exterior lights, solar-cell battery systems and chargers, wind-powered generators, rooftop solar panels and any number of other solar-cell power and storage systems for big profits.

Your buying source will be directly from manufacturers and wholesalers, mainly because it is rare to find used solar-powered and alternative-energy products for sale. Customers will include everybody who is currently or who wants to be off the grid, including remote property owners, boat owners, RV owners, campers, hikers and basically anybody else who has a need for energy to power equipment, lights and utilities where none is available.

Sell your products directly from home, as well as through consumer shows and online marketplaces catering to alternative-energy enthusiasts.

BUY
Manufacturers, Wholesalers

SELL
Online Marketplaces, Consumer Shows, Homebased Sales

RESOURCES
—Chinavasion,   chinavasion.com/index.php/cName/solar-products/
—Global Merchants,   global-merchants.com/home/solars.htm
—Solar Energy Industries Association,   seia.org
—Wholesale Solar,   wholesalesolar.com

Specialty Rugs

Specialty area rugs and runners with an international flavor are hot home décor accessories, and they allow you to make a small fortune in your spare time. Purchase Oriental, Indian and Persian rugs wholesale, direct from the factory or secondhand, and resell them for top dollar to savvy collectors, interior designers and homeowners.

If you are new to specialty carpets, make sure that you educate yourself about the products before jumping in with both feet. Specialty carpets are available in many designs, quality levels and price points. This type of business requires knowledge of the products to spot and buy great deals.

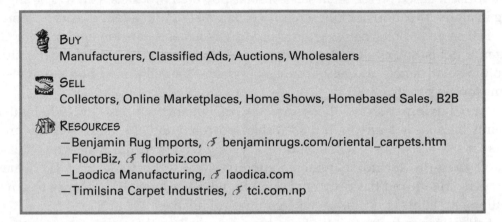

BUY
Manufacturers, Classified Ads, Auctions, Wholesalers

SELL
Collectors, Online Marketplaces, Home Shows, Homebased Sales, B2B

RESOURCES
—Benjamin Rug Imports, ☎ benjaminrugs.com/oriental_carpets.htm
—FloorBiz, ☎ floorbiz.com
—Laodica Manufacturing, ☎ laodica.com
—Timilsina Carpet Industries, ☎ tci.com.np

Specialty Soaps

With an investment of less than $500, you can be in the specialty soap business and make great money selling aromatherapy soaps, hypoallergenic soaps, dermatological soaps, novelty soaps, herbal soaps, soap-making supplies and soap gift baskets and sets.

There are just as many ways to sell soap as there are different kinds of specialty soaps. Sell from home, hire part-time salespeople to organize and host in-home soap sales parties, sell on eBay and display at home and garden shows. Selling from kiosks in malls and at flea markets is another way you can earn extra money.

Buying sources for specialty and all-natural soaps include manufacturers, wholesalers and craftspeople, or you may even decide to make your own line of specialty soaps right from home.

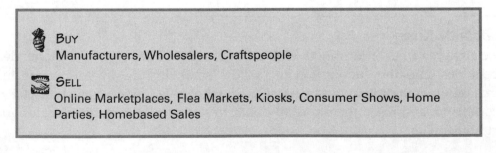

BUY
Manufacturers, Wholesalers, Craftspeople

SELL
Online Marketplaces, Flea Markets, Kiosks, Consumer Shows, Home Parties, Homebased Sales

Sports Memorabilia

If you're an avid sports fan with knowledge about popular sports, teams and players, it is time to put your knowledge of sports to good use and make a bundle of cash by buying and selling authentic sports memorabilia.

Invest the time to learn this business well before getting in too deep. Once you know what you are doing, you can buy authentic team jerseys, autographs, photographs, sports magazines, action figures, novelties, posters, ticket stubs and sports equipment at bargain-basement prices and resell to collectors and die-hard sports fans for a huge profit.

To gather inventory, devote time to rummaging through garage sales, flea markets, secondhand shops, online marketplaces and auctions to find valuable sports memorabilia items that you can buy dirt-cheap. Be sure to verify authenticity! You can also attend events where professional athletes will be appearing and collect your own autographed balls, sports cards, jerseys and photos to resell.

Sell your valuable finds directly to collectors via online sports memorabilia websites and auctions. You can also run your own e-commerce website, plus sell directly from a homebased showroom. Don't forget to invest in a handful of reliable price guides so you can identify bargains and know what you can resell items for.

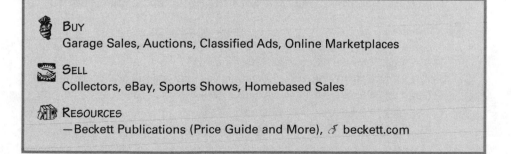

BUY
Garage Sales, Auctions, Classified Ads, Online Marketplaces

SELL
Collectors, eBay, Sports Shows, Homebased Sales

RESOURCES
—Beckett Publications (Price Guide and More), ✂ beckett.com

—Collect Sports Price Guide, ✒ collectsports.com
—It'sAlreadySigned4U, ✒ itsalreadysigned4u.com
—Leland's, ✒ lelands.com
—Pro Sports Memorabilia, ✒ prosportsmemorabilia.com
—Sports Memorabilia, ✒ sportsmemorabilia.com
—Steiner Sports Memorabilia, ✒ steinersports.com

Stamps

Collecting new and old stamps from the U.S. and abroad has long been a popular hobby. In fact, stamp collecting is one of the most popular collectible hobbies in the United States. If stamps fascinate you and you have a passion for collecting, capitalizing on your philatelic knowledge, and profiting from buying collectible stamps cheaply and reselling them for a profit, this is the business for you.

Scan classified ads, garage sales, flea markets, online marketplaces and stamp shows for inventory to purchase below market value. Then resell to collectors via auction sales, online marketplaces, stamp shows and specialty stamp publications.

You will need to be well versed in stamp grading and values, but there are numerous price guides available to help you in this endeavor. Join online and offline stamp collecting clubs so you will have the ability to sell your finds directly to other collectors, plus stay up-to-date on the latest trends related to this hobby.

To generate additional revenue, consider selling stamp collecting accessories and tools, which can easily be purchased through wholesalers.

BUY
Auctions, Online Marketplaces, Stamp Shows, Classified Ads

SELL
Collectors, Online Marketplaces, Specialty Publications, Stamp Shows

RESOURCES
—Amos Advantage Catalogs, ☎ (800) 572-6885, ✒ amosadvantage.com
—American Philatelic Society, ✒ stamps.org
—American Stamp Dealers Association, ✒ asdaonline.com/index.php
—National Stamp Dealers Association, ✒ NSDAinc.org
—Stamp Show Listing, ✒ stampshows.com
—Virtual Stamp Club, ✒ virtualstampclub.com

Store Fixtures

Retail stores in shopping centers, in malls and along Main Street, USA are constantly going out of business or relocating. These closings provide a buy-and-sell entrepreneur with the perfect opportunity to purchase used store displays and fixtures at a fraction of their actual worth, and then resell them to other retail stores planning to open or expand.

The buy-and-sell concept at work here is the same as with restaurant equipment. Seek out quality items, such as display cases, wall rack systems, light fixtures, warehouse equipment, shipping supplies, mannequins, counters, displays and signage, to sell.

You can operate from home, but also develop a website to promote and sell online to a worldwide marketplace. Of course, be sure to list items on eBay, plus sell through traditional auctions. Join business associations to network for new business. This type of venture can be very lucrative because, although it is unfortunate for the merchants who are facing financial ruin, you will be able to purchase the used store fixtures at low prices.

BUY
Auctions, Classified Ads, Bankruptcies

SELL
B2B, Homebased Showroom, Online Marketplaces

RESOURCES
—ARSI Warehouse Liquidators, ✍ storefixtureliquidator.com
—Gershal Brothers New & Used Store Fixtures, ✍ gershelbros.com
—Recycler's World, ✍ recycle.net/Commercial/store
—Retail Source, ✍ retailsource.com

Stuffed Animals (Plush Toys)

Virtually every large mall in America now has a Build-A-Bear retail store, which proves that the demand for teddy bears, plush toys and stuffed animals is not only huge, it's growing!

There are two ways to profit from buying and selling stuffed animals. First, buy new stuffed animals on a wholesale basis, and resell them for a profit. Second, purchase antique stuffed animals at auctions and estate sales, and resell them to collectors for a profit. Of course, you can combine both business models, but the buying process and your target markets will be vastly different.

If you elect to buy new stuffed animals direct from manufacturers, distributors, importers and wholesalers, they can be marked up and resold at community events, on eBay and at flea markets. If you decide to specialize in collector stuffed animals and teddy bears, you'll need to devote time to hunting them down at garage sales, flea markets, secondhand shops and auction sales.

Use reliable pricing guides so you will know how much to pay and what your purchases can be resold for. Antique stuffed animals can be sold to collectors through online clubs and marketplaces, on eBay, at flea markets, through exhibiting at collectible shows and by selling at traditional auctions. Some collectible plush toys and teddy bears sell for hundreds or even thousands of dollars.

While Beanie Babies are no longer as mega-popular as they once were, as of March 2008, Webkinz were among the most popular plush toys among kids. Capitalizing on a hot trend is one way to earn big profits, as long as you stay ahead of demand changes in the trend.

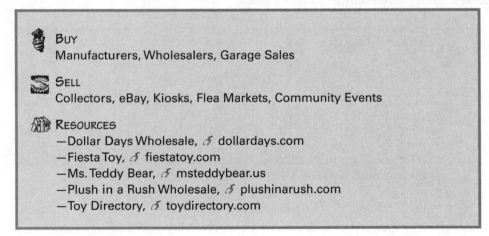

BUY
Manufacturers, Wholesalers, Garage Sales

SELL
Collectors, eBay, Kiosks, Flea Markets, Community Events

RESOURCES
—Dollar Days Wholesale, ✄ dollardays.com
—Fiesta Toy, ✄ fiestatoy.com
—Ms. Teddy Bear, ✄ msteddybear.us
—Plush in a Rush Wholesale, ✄ plushinarush.com
—Toy Directory, ✄ toydirectory.com

Sunglasses

Sunglasses are the ultimate in profitable fashion accessories for several reasons. First, styles change seasonally, which means people always want to purchase the latest models. Second, people lose or break their sunglasses and need replacements. Third, people typically own several pairs of sunglasses. Fourth, there is tremendous mark-up potential when it comes to buying wholesale and selling at retail pricing.

You can purchase good-quality sunglasses in bulk for as little as $2 each and resell the same sunglasses for $20 or more! Designer sunglasses cost a bit more, but sell for hundreds of dollars. Sunglasses are one of the best buy-and-sell items. They are cheap to buy, easy to store and transport, and even easier to sell because they are always in demand.

Sell designer sunglasses on eBay, by setting up a portable kiosk at the beach (a permit will probably be required), during community events, at car shows and at flea markets. You can also place them in retail stores on consignment and split the profits with the shop owner.

Other places you can set up temporary sales kiosks include highway rest stops, fairs and carnivals, parks, sporting events and any other type of outdoor event where lots of people gather. Be sure to obtain permission and any vending permits that are necessary.

One of the keys to your success will be your merchandising skills. Keep your selling area clean and organized, invest in attention-grabbing signage, offer many styles of sunglasses, and place mirrors all around so customers can see how great they look with the sunglasses on. While you can buy sunglasses that are junk, you'll make more money and generate a much better reputation selling higher-end, designer sunglasses.

If you get into this business, you'll need to learn all about the different types of frames and lenses and be able to explain the differences to your customers. This will require a bit of research on your part. There's a reason why virtually every mall in America has one or more sunglass stores within it. People buy sunglasses!

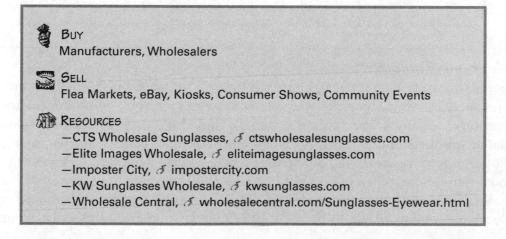

BUY
Manufacturers, Wholesalers

SELL
Flea Markets, eBay, Kiosks, Consumer Shows, Community Events

RESOURCES
—CTS Wholesale Sunglasses, ⚲ ctswholesalesunglasses.com
—Elite Images Wholesale, ⚲ eliteimagesunglasses.com
—Imposter City, ⚲ impostercity.com
—KW Sunglasses Wholesale, ⚲ kwsunglasses.com
—Wholesale Central, ⚲ wholesalecentral.com/Sunglasses-Eyewear.html

Tableware

Selling new and vintage tableware and glassware is a business that's inexpensive to get started and has great income potential. Vintage tableware from companies such as Wedgwood, Royal Doulton, Homer Loughlin and Fiestaware can be purchased at garage sales, flea markets, estate sales and auctions. Investing in glassware and tableware price guides would be wise for establishing buying and selling prices.

Once you acquire it, resell your inventory directly to collectors via the numerous online collectibles websites and on eBay. The lowest price sources for new tableware and glassware are factory direct, as well as via wholesalers and liquidators.

New tableware can be sold through eBay, at flea markets and at consumer shows. You might also consider hiring salespeople to organize and host tableware and glassware sales parties in their homes.

BUY
Manufacturers, Wholesalers, Garage Sales, Auctions

SELL
Home Parties, eBay, Kiosks, Flea Markets, E-Commerce Website

RESOURCES
—Fiesta Discounts Wholesale, ☎ (507) 427-3852, ✎ fiestadiscounts.com
—Image Tabletop, ☎ (877) 676-8222, ✎ imageimports.com
—International Housewares Association, ☎ (447) 692-0109,
　✎ housewares.org
—Vance Kitira International Wholesale, ☎ (800) 646-6360,
　✎ vancekitira.com

Telephone Equipment

People love to talk on the telephone! Buying and selling telephone equipment to consumers for their homes, as well as to businesses, can be a profitable business venture, especially if you develop a specialty and also sell a wide range of phone-related products and accessories. There are traditional corded phones, wireless phones, telephone headsets, Bluetooth phones, Skype-compatible phones, VOIP phones and many different types of business phone systems.

While there's definitely a market for new and used business telephones and telephone systems, if you'll be selling to home consumers, focus only on new equipment. You can buy from wholesalers, distributors and liquidators, and resell at flea markets, at home shows and online.

> 🪔 BUY
> Wholesalers, Distributors, Liquidators
>
> 🤝 SELL
> Flea Markets, Home Shows, Online Marketplaces, B2B
>
> 🏚 RESOURCES
> —EverTek Wholesalers, ✑ evertek.com/products.asp?cat=TEL
> —TradeKey, ✑ tradeKey.com/kb-telephone
> —Sourcing Map, ✑ sourcingmap.com/telephone-sets-c-980_1255.html
> —Wholesale Central, ✑ wholesalecentral.com/Telephone-Cellular.html

Telescopes and Binoculars

Telescopes and binoculars are great buy-and-sell items because they retail in the range of $100 to $1,000, and they're in demand by amateur astronomers and stargazers, birdwatchers, hunters, campers, nature lovers, schools and parents who want to buy a unique gift for their child.

Stick with retailing new telescopes and binoculars, and buy directly from manufacturers and through wholesale distributors. Sell online, from a homebased showroom and at consumer shows. Join astronomy clubs and associations to network for business. To boost sales and revenues, also sell accessories, such as tripod stands, replacement parts, carrying cases, night sky map software, eyepieces, filter kits, and photographic, telescopic and binocular lenses. Most of your business will come from hobbyists, so be sure you know your products and these hobbies.

> 🪔 BUY
> Manufacturers, Wholesalers
>
> 🤝 SELL
> Online Marketplaces, Homebased Sales
>
> 🏚 RESOURCES
> —Crazy Discounts Wholesale, ✑ crazydiscounts.com
> —Discount Binoculars Wholesale, ☎ (877) 523-4400,
>   ✑ discountbinoculars.com

—MerchantMonkey, ✂ merchantmonkey.com/shoppingcart/html/Wholesale-Telescopes.html
—Wholesale Photo Cafe, ✂ wholesalephoto.com/prod_telescopes.html

Temporary Tattoos

Today's peel-and-stick tattoos are nothing like the kind you used to get out of penny gumball machines 30 years ago. The ones now available rival the best authentic tattoos in terms of color and design, and can last for a week. There are two major differences between temporary tattoos and their real counterparts. Temporary tattoos are not permanent and they cost a fraction of what permanent tattoos cost. In fact, temporary tattoos can be purchased in bulk for as little as five cents apiece and resold for several dollars. The trick to this business is being able to sell large quantities to consumers—at public events, fairs, flea markets, sporting events, birthday parties, tourist attractions, mall kiosks, and anywhere else people gather and might be interested in making fun impulse purchases for themselves or their kids.

When choosing your inventory, be sure to select a wide range of styles that'll appeal to kids, teens and adults, so everyone who wants a temporary tattoo will be able to find one that's age-appropriate or suitable. While you can buy pre-created temporary tattoos, if you're an artist, you can also create your own and have them manufactured inexpensively; plus, you can generate additional revenue by offering hand-painted henna artwork.

BUY
Manufacturers, Wholesalers

SELL
Community Events, Flea Markets, Kiosks

RESOURCES
—Dune Tattoo Corporation, ✂ customtattoos.net
—Dune Temporary Tattoos Wholesale, ✂ temptats.com
—iLot Trading, ✂ wholesalestation.com
—Tattoo Manufacturing, ✂ tattoosales.com
—Temporary Tattoos, ✂ temporarytattoos.com

Tickets

By obtaining a license, you can become a licensed ticket broker in your city or state. This allows you to buy show, concert and sporting event tickets that are in demand and then resell them for prices far exceeding their face value. For example, during the Christmas holiday season in New York, tickets to a sold-out Broadway show could sell for $500 each, while tickets to a sold-out concert by a mega-popular artist may sell for $1,000 or more.

As a licensed ticket broker, you can buy bulk tickets from venues, promoters and show producers, plus buy small quantities from Ticketmaster, as well as from individual sellers on eBay, Craigslist and other online services. To make the most money, you'll want to focus on buying tickets well in advance of shows you know will ultimately sell out. Demand for your tickets will be high, allowing you to charge top dollar.

Obviously, you'll want to be careful and avoid buying counterfeit tickets. You can sell your inventory on eBay, Craigslist, and outside the show, sporting event or concert venue. There are, however, rules you'll need to adhere to. You can also place classified ads in newspapers to sell your tickets, plus generate word-of-mouth advertising.

Being a licensed ticket broker is vastly different from being a scalper, which is illegal in most areas.

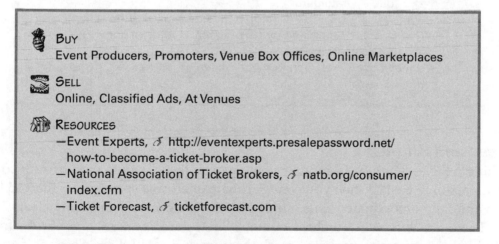

BUY
Event Producers, Promoters, Venue Box Offices, Online Marketplaces

SELL
Online, Classified Ads, At Venues

RESOURCES
—Event Experts, ♂ http://eventexperts.presalepassword.net/
    how-to-become-a-ticket-broker.asp
—National Association of Ticket Brokers, ♂ natb.org/consumer/
    index.cfm
—Ticket Forecast, ♂ ticketforecast.com

Tour and Vacation Packages

Tourism is a huge industry. People love to travel for pleasure, plus they need to travel for business. While a specialized license is required, there's money to be made selling tours and vacation packages. You can either create and host your own tours or team up with established tour and vacation package providers and serve as an authorized sales representative.

In addition to generic tours and vacation packages that'll appeal to anyone, higher profits can be generated by focusing on specific audiences. Singles, senior citizens, college students, gays, lesbians and newlyweds are all separate groups of people that seek out different types of travel or vacation experiences and are willing to pay more to experience a vacation targeted specifically to them.

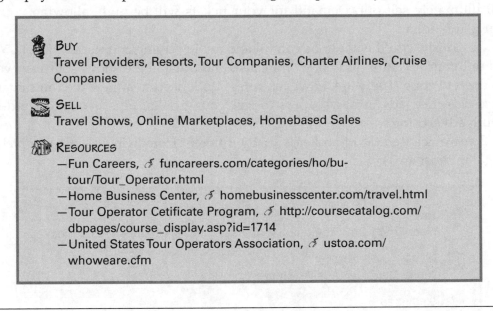

> **BUY**
> Travel Providers, Resorts, Tour Companies, Charter Airlines, Cruise Companies
>
> **SELL**
> Travel Shows, Online Marketplaces, Homebased Sales
>
> **RESOURCES**
> —Fun Careers, ✆ funcareers.com/categories/ho/bu-tour/Tour_Operator.html
> —Home Business Center, ✆ homebusinesscenter.com/travel.html
> —Tour Operator Cetificate Program, ✆ http://coursecatalog.com/dbpages/course_display.asp?id=1714
> —United States Tour Operators Association, ✆ ustoa.com/whoweare.cfm

Trees and Shrubs

Selling trees and shrubs from your home is a fantastic way to earn extra income on a part-time basis. When you consider that Americans spend more than $5 billion annually on outdoor plants, the opportunity becomes abundantly clear.

There are two main purchase options. First, purchase trees and shrubs from wholesale commercial nurseries, mark them up and resell them. Second, if space is available, grow your own trees and shrubs at home. Surprisingly, not much space is required.

For example, you can purchase a Japanese maple seedling for about 75 cents, pot or plant it in burlap, wait a season or two while it grows, and resell it for $50 to $150. A 20-foot-square garden area is large enough to support 300 of these seedlings, thus producing approximately 100 saleable trees annually when planting is alternated.

To maximize profit potential, combine both methods, buying some wholesale and growing some of your own. A green thumb and marketing skills are definitely required. In addition to selling from home, you can sell B2B to landscapers, plus sell at home and garden shows. You can also post free ads on Craigslist.

BUY
Wholesalers, Growers

SELL
Homebased Sales, Online Marketplaces, Gardener Clubs

RESOURCES
—J. Frank Schmidt & Son, ☎ (503) 663-4128, ✆ jfschmidt.com
—Lawyer Nursery, ☎ (406) 826-3881, ✆ lawyernursery.com
—Tennessee Nursery Company, ☎ (866) 526-4527,
　✆ tennesseewholesalenursery.com
—Nature Hills Nursery, ☎ (402) 934-8116, ✆ naturehills.com
—Woods Creek Wholesale Nursery, ☎ (360) 794-6823,
　✆ woodscreeknursery.com

Umbrellas

When it rains, it can pour in profits for you if you get into a buy-and-sell enterprise that sells umbrellas. Umbrellas can be resold for two to three times wholesale cost, and they are always in demand. There are numerous types of umbrellas, including standard rain umbrellas, mini carry-along umbrellas, beach umbrellas, patio umbrellas, market umbrellas and promotional umbrellas emblazoned with logos for businesses.

Umbrellas can be purchased from wholesalers, manufacturers, importers, liquidators and distributors. Flea markets, consumer shows, community events, eBay and mall kiosks are all excellent locations to sell. With a permit, on rainy days you can also target city street corners, train stations, airports, bus stations, sporting events and other locations where people typically get stuck in the rain.

Don't overlook the possibility of forming a partnership with a silkscreen printing company so you can sell umbrellas to corporations, organizations and small businesses as a promotional item bearing their name, logo and promotional message.

BUY
Manufacturers, Wholesalers

SELL
Kiosks, B2B, Home and Garden Shows, eBay, City Street Corners

RESOURCES
—Seagull International Manufacturing, ☎ (800) 666-9300, ✍ seagullintl.com
—Stromberg Brand, ✍ strombergbrand.com
—Umbrella Shop Wholesale, ✍ umbrellashop.com
—Anchor Umbrella, ✍ anchorumbrella.com

Uniforms

Most people would not consider uniforms to be one of the best products to buy and sell for a profit. But, when you consider the vast number of people who are required to wear uniforms for work or school, you quickly begin to understand the opportunity and income potential.

Think about all the people in uniforms—hospital staff, security personnel, auto mechanics, fire and police personnel, school students, amateur sports teams, food and beverage workers and airline personnel—just to name a few potential target audiences.

Establish an in-home uniform showroom for sales. Many corporations, organizations and government agencies that require a large number of uniforms usually put their purchases out to tender annually or every few years. It is important to make inquiries and be placed on the tender list. Both nationally and worldwide, there are hundreds of companies engaged in uniform apparel manufacturing, so secure reliable wholesale buying sources that offer competitive prices and a broad product selection.

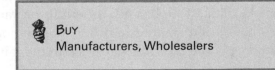

BUY
Manufacturers, Wholesalers

> **SELL**
> B2B, Trade Shows, Homebased Sales
>
> **RESOURCES**
> —B&A Uniforms, ✑ bauniforms.com
> —National Association of Uniform Manufacturers and Distributors,
> ✑ naumd.com
> —Apparel Search Company, ✑ apparelsearch.com/wholesale_clothing/
> wholesale_uniforms.htm
> —Workwear USA Wholesale, ☎ (800) 208-1662, ✑ workwear-usa.com

Used Vehicles

Not everybody can afford to spend $15,000 to $50,000 (or more) on a new car. Because of this, the market for good-quality used vehicles is very strong. This is great news for entrepreneurs who decide to buy and sell used vehicles. Keep in mind, however, that mechanical repairs are very expensive, so buying and selling used vehicles is definitely best left to people who have mechanical aptitude and who can thoroughly inspect vehicles to ensure they are in good working order before buying them.

Used vehicles can be purchased at auctions, from private sellers and from car dealers who take trade-ins. Dealers wholesale the older vehicles to other people to resell to the public. To maximize profits, try to buy off-season—SUVs in the spring and summer, and convertibles and sports cars in the fall and winter. Doing so can net you an additional 10 percent or more.

Prior to reselling a vehicle, go out of your way to clean and detail it. This could increase the sales value by 10 percent or more. Some areas of the United States and Canada have laws that prohibit non-licensed car dealers, often referred to as curbsiders, from buying and selling cars. Make sure to check into the legal issues in your area prior to getting started.

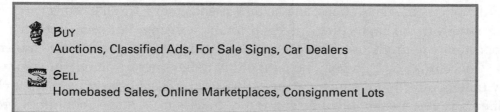

> **BUY**
> Auctions, Classified Ads, For Sale Signs, Car Dealers
>
> **SELL**
> Homebased Sales, Online Marketplaces, Consignment Lots

> 🏠 RESOURCES
> —Blackbook National Auto Research, ✂ blackbookusa.com
> —Kelley Blue Book, ✂ kbb.com
> —Trader Publications, ✂ autotrader.com
> —Used Cars, ✂ usedcars.com

Used Sporting Goods

Much like dealing in new sporting goods, great profits can also be earned buying and selling certain types of used sporting goods and equipment, especially if you specialize in high-end and name-brand gear.

Buy at garage sales, sports swap meets and auctions, and through the classifieds. Sell from a homebased showroom, at flea markets and on eBay. It's essential that you know all about the equipment you'll be selling, as well as the related sports.

> 🎖 BUY
> Classified Ads, Online Marketplaces, Auctions, Garage Sales,
> Liquidators, Craigslist.org
>
> 🤝 SELL
> Homebased Sales, eBay, Craigslist.org, Flea Markets, Sporting Goods
> Swap Meets, Recreational and Camping Shows
>
> 🏠 RESOURCES
> —U.S. Free Ads, ✂ usfreeads.com/_sports
> —Sports Recycle, ✂ backstreetinline.com/sportsrecycle
> —Ocala4Sale, ✂ http://ocala4sale.com/coolstuff/sporting-goods.php

Utility Trailers

Yard work, home renovations, and helping friends move are all reasons why owning a utility trailer has become a necessity for many people. With demand comes the opportunity to profit for entrepreneurs who decide to buy and sell utility trailers.

Concentrate on both new and used utility trailer sales by purchasing new utility trailers directly from manufacturers and used trailers from private seller classified ads and auction sales. Selling utility trailers from home should not prove difficult, provided you have the zoning permits and required space.

Advertise your trailers using classified ads, bulletin boards and attention-grabbing signage on display models. You might also want to market directly to contractors and landscape companies, or any business that needs work trailers.

Like many buy-and-sell opportunities, this one targets a niche audience and will require both significant startup capital and extensive product knowledge to get started.

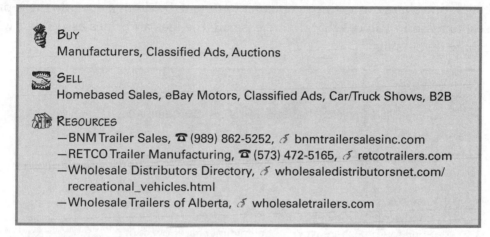

BUY
Manufacturers, Classified Ads, Auctions

SELL
Homebased Sales, eBay Motors, Classified Ads, Car/Truck Shows, B2B

RESOURCES
—BNM Trailer Sales, ☎ (989) 862-5252, ✐ bnmtrailersalesinc.com
—RETCO Trailer Manufacturing, ☎ (573) 472-5165, ✐ retcotrailers.com
—Wholesale Distributors Directory, ✐ wholesaledistributorsnet.com/
   recreational_vehicles.html
—Wholesale Trailers of Alberta, ✐ wholesaletrailers.com

Vacation Timeshares

Vacation timeshares are often sold to people visiting popular tourist destinations using extremely strong and sometimes misleading sales tactics. Thus these vacationers often purchase something they can't afford, have no long-term interest in owning, or are unable to make full use of. This creates an opportunity for the buy-and-sell entrepreneur interested in brokering vacation timeshares.

This type of business requires incredibly sharp negotiation skills, liberal use of high-pressure sales tactics and strong closing proficiency. There is no shortage of timeshares to purchase. An estimated 200,000 timeshares are for sale at any given time in the United States alone, not including developer sales of new timeshares.

It is even possible to acquire timeshares for nothing, outside of deed transfer costs, and sometimes not even that. Why? Simply because timeshares are difficult to resell, and many people want to get out from under the ongoing membership or maintenance fees charged to manage and maintain resorts, buildings and units.

When buying, there are a few key issues to keep in mind. Only buy units with prime weeks (generally December through March) and in prime areas such as Florida, California and Hawaii. The closer the property is to beaches and major tourist attractions, the better.

In terms of price negotiations, if you have to pay, drive a hard bargain and request that owners pay all transfer fees. There are a number of online timeshare marketplaces where you can buy and sell. Before getting into this business, make sure you understand all of the nuances of it as both a buyer and seller. While it's possible to make money in this business, it's also easy to lose money by making bad purchases and then being unable to resell the timeshares. Contrary to popular belief, timeshare ownership is not an investment. Seldom, if ever, do these purchases increase in value. What do increase are the fees and dues associated with timeshare ownership.

BUY
Online Marketplaces, Real Estate Brokers, Classified Ads

SELL
Websites, Online Marketplaces, Specialty Publications, Real Estate Brokers

RESOURCES
—Redweek, ✍ redweek.com
—Sell My Timeshare Now, ✍ sellmytimesharenow.com
—Timeshare Transfer, ✍ timesharetransfer.com
—The Timeshare User's Group, ✍ tug2.net
—Timeshares, ✍ timeshares.com
—The Timeshare Beat, ✍ thetimesharebeat.com

Vacuum Cleaners

New and used vacuums are terrific buy-low, sell-high items. Built-in, canister, upright, portable, workshop, backpack and cordless vacuum cleaners are available for a wide range of uses. The best buying sources for new vacuum cleaners include wholesalers and liquidators.

Used vacuum cleaners are generally available for purchase at auctions, through classified ads and at garage sales. Vacuum cleaners manufactured during the past few years, however, are typically much lower in quality than those made years ago. Thus avoid buying used junk that will have little or no resale value. It's often cheaper to buy a new vacuum cleaner than it is to have a broken late-model vacuum cleaner repaired.

Sell from a homebased showroom, on eBay, at home and garden shows and at flea markets. Residential models that tend to hold their value the best are Electrolux and Kirby.

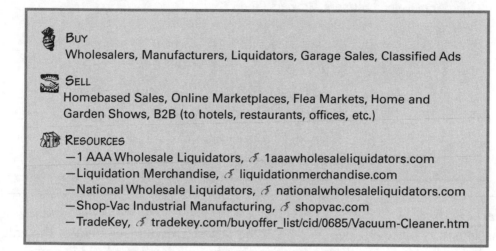

> **BUY**
> Wholesalers, Manufacturers, Liquidators, Garage Sales, Classified Ads
>
> **SELL**
> Homebased Sales, Online Marketplaces, Flea Markets, Home and Garden Shows, B2B (to hotels, restaurants, offices, etc.)
>
> **RESOURCES**
> —1 AAA Wholesale Liquidators, ✍ 1aaawholesaleliquidators.com
> —Liquidation Merchandise, ✍ liquidationmerchandise.com
> —National Wholesale Liquidators, ✍ nationalwholesaleliquidators.com
> —Shop-Vac Industrial Manufacturing, ✍ shopvac.com
> —TradeKey, ✍ tradekey.com/buyoffer_list/cid/0685/Vacuum-Cleaner.htm

Vegetable Stand / Farmers' Market Merchant

Whether it's a roadside stand, a rented booth at a farmers' market, or a portable kiosk set up at a local flea market, selling fresh, in-season fruits and vegetables can be very profitable. Like any type of retail venture, the key to success is location. With that goal in mind, excellent locations include gas stations, industrial parks, busy intersections, and along roadways leading to popular attractions such as beaches, garden centers and public parks.

The stand you work from needs to be nothing more than a basic framework covered by a tarp to keep the sun and heat off the veggies. Of greater importance, however, are the signs needed to advertise your products and presence. Signs should be large and colorful, and compel passing motorists to stop. Be sure to place your signs well ahead of your stand to give motorists ample warning, so they have time to slow down and stop.

Buy vegetables directly from farmers, farmers' cooperatives in your area or produce wholesalers. Regardless of your buying sources, sell only the highest-quality and freshest products available.

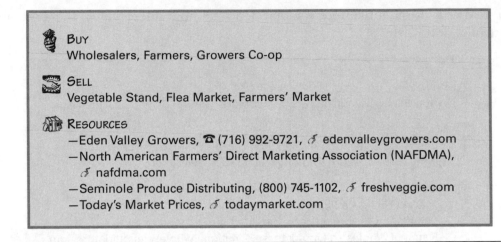

BUY
Wholesalers, Farmers, Growers Co-op

SELL
Vegetable Stand, Flea Market, Farmers' Market

RESOURCES
—Eden Valley Growers, ☎ (716) 992-9721, ✑ edenvalleygrowers.com
—North American Farmers' Direct Marketing Association (NAFDMA),
   ✑ nafdma.com
—Seminole Produce Distributing, (800) 745-1102, ✑ freshveggie.com
—Today's Market Prices, ✑ todaymarket.com

Video Games

Console and computer video gaming is the fastest-growing segment of the entertainment industry in North America. You can buy and sell used video games and new accessories, and it can be a very profitable undertaking, assuming that you deal in the most popular game titles for the gaming machines that are currently hot.

Buying from wholesalers is really your only option for obtaining new games. With so much competition, however, it's a difficult business to do well in. Used video games and equipment can be more profitable. These items can be purchased through online marketplaces, as well as at garage sales and flea markets. New or used, the best selling venues for video games and accessories are eBay, Amazon.com, mall kiosks, gaming shows and flea markets.

As of mid-2008, the most popular (current) video game systems included the Nintendo Wii, Nintendo DS, Sony PlayStation 2, Sony PlayStation 3, Sony PSP (PlayStation Portable), Microsoft Xbox and Microsoft Xbox 360. Used games for older (classic) systems will also sell well to collectors. To do well in this business, you'll want to become an avid video gamer yourself and be comfortable selling to fellow gamers who are passionate about their hobby. Profits can also be made selling used video game systems (hardware), not to mention selling new gamepads, controllers, joysticks and other accessories.

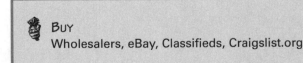

BUY
Wholesalers, eBay, Classifieds, Craigslist.org

>
>
> **SELL**
> Kiosks, eBay, Craigslist.org, Amazon.com, Flea Markets, Consumer Shows
>
> **RESOURCES**
> —D&H Wholesale, ☎ (800) 340-1001, ✂ dandh.com
> —Pacific Games Wholesale, ☎ (213) 627-7259, ✂ pacificgames.com
> —Regal Games Wholesale, ☎ (954) 455-8445, ✂ regalgames.com
> —The Gamers' Corner, ✂ thegamerscorner.com
> —Video Game Suppliers, ✂ http://videogamesuppliers.net

Vintage Clothing

While this may sound like a fancy name for buying and selling used or second-hand clothing, vintage clothing typically refers to designer fashions from 10, 20, 30 or more years ago that are still in wearable condition. Thus each garment may be worth $50 to several hundreds of dollars.

You can acquire vintage clothing from flea markets, secondhand shops, estate sales, auctions and private collectors. These are pretty much the same places you'll ultimately use to resell your goods. Focus on well-known designer names. Stay on top of current fashion trends and look for innovative ways to market your vintage clothing to savvy and fashion-oriented customers. A secondary market includes theatre groups in need of period-specific costumes.

> **BUY**
> Flea Markets, Collectors, Auctions, Estate Sales
>
> **SELL**
> Flea Markets, Online Markets, Collectors, Boutiques (B2B), Consignment Shops
>
> **RESOURCES**
> —The Attic Vintage Clothing Wholesale, ✂ atticvintage.com/whole.html
> —Dust Factory Vintage, ✂ http://dustfactoryvintage.com
> —Rusty Zipper, ✂ rustyzipper.com/featured_wholesale.cfm
> —Vintage Clothing Apparel Search, ✂ apparelsearch.com/wholesale_clothing/wholesale_vintage_clothes.htm

Vintage Jewelry

As you already know, there are many types and styles of jewelry you can sell, potentially for big profits. Vintage jewelry refers to high-end, antique jewelry you acquire from estate sales, auctions and collectors. Vintage jewelry pieces can potentially be expensive. You can specialize in handcrafted, one-of-a-kind pieces, or antique jewelry that is decades or centuries old.

To be successful buying and selling vintage jewelry, you must be extremely knowledgeable about high-end jewelry, diamonds, gold, platinum, silver, and other precious gems and jewels. You must be able to identify valuable and resalable items, negotiate the best possible purchase prices, and then know how to mark up these items so you can effectively sell them for a profit.

Work closely with a jewelry appraiser and take advantage of price guides to help you. When it comes to selling your merchandise, jewelry shows, auctions, eBay and craft shows will all serve you well.

BUY
Auctions, Estate Sales, Collectors

SELL
Online Markets, Auctions, Collectors, Jewelry Shows

RESOURCES
—About.com: Antique Jewelry, ✒ http://jewelry.about.com/od/
   antiquejewelry/Antique_and_Collectible_Jewelry.htm
—China Jewelry Factory, ✒ chinajewelryfactory.com
—The Vintage Jewelry Guide, ✒ vintagejewelryguide.com
—WholesaleWholesale, ✒ wholesalewholesale.com/vintage.html

Vintage Vinyl Records

Thanks to CDs and digital downloads, the vinyl record business has become outdated. These days, the market for these items is among collectors and disc jockeys, not everyday consumers. Yet the collectible market is significant.

Vinyl records have one of the largest followings of people who collect for hobby and listening enjoyment. Rock 'n' roll, jazz, country, blues and big band are all equally popular in 33⅓, 45 or 78 rpm formats. They can sell for big bucks, especially rare first-run vinyl in mint condition.

The best buying source is, without question, garage sales, so be prepared to spend some time hunting for vintage vinyl. Typically, you'll find boxes full at nearly every sale. Price guides will assist you in accessing value and condition.

In addition to garage sales, you can also buy from online marketplaces and from private sellers who often use classifieds to advertise the sale of their entire collection. Vintage vinyl can be sold to collectors through record collecting clubs, on eBay, at flea markets and at music and collectible shows.

BUY
Garage Sales, Online Marketplaces, Auctions, Classified Ads

SELL
Collectors, Flea Markets, Memorabilia Shows, Online Marketplaces

RESOURCES
—Record Collectors Guild, ☞ recordcollectorsguild.org
—Vinyl Web, ☞ vinylweb.com
—Forever Vinyl, ☞ forevervinyl.com

Vitamins and Nutritional Supplements

The time has never been better to cash in on the health craze by selling vitamins and nutritional supplements. Sell general vitamins and supplements, or specialize in one particular area such as diet or sports supplements. You could also offer customers a wide product selection, including vitamins, nutritional supplements, holistic products, aromatherapy and essential oils, and natural health products.

Buy direct from manufacturers and wholesalers at deeply discounted prices, and resell through any number of venues, such as mall kiosks, online sales, health fairs and mail order. Also consider seminars and home parties as two viable sales options. Organize free community health seminars focused on the benefits of vitamins and nutritional supplements, and enlist the services of health experts to speak while you sell at the back of the room.

Obviously, before getting into this business, you'll want to become a vitamin and nutritional supplements expert, so you'll be able to accurately answer your customers' questions and recommend reliable and appropriate products to achieve their health, fitness or weight loss goals. You can boost your profits by selling related health, fitness and diet books and videos.

BUY
Manufacturers, Wholesalers

SELL
Mail Order, Online Marketplaces, Kiosks, Health Fairs, Seminars, Home Parties, eBay

RESOURCES
—CA Vitamin Wholesale, ✄ cavitamin.com
—eVitamins, ✄ evitamins.com/vitamins_main.asp
—NHS Labs, ✄ nutritionmanufacturer.com
—TID Health Wholesale, ✄ tidhealth.com
—Wholesale Supplement Store, ✄ wholesalesupplementstore.com

Watches

Wristwatches and timepieces are among the most popular gifts for any number of special occasions, such as birthdays, Christmas, graduation or retirement. This makes them a terrific buy-and-sell product. Wristwatches can be purchased wholesale for as little as a few dollars each, and retailed for five to ten times as much.

There are a number of great places to sell watches, including flea markets, eBay and rental kiosks. There is also enormous demand for high-quality used watches and antique collectible watches. For instance, a secondhand stainless steel Rolex Submariner watch with an oyster face still commands in the range of $3,500 to $4,000.

If you decide to deal in collectible and secondhand fashion watches, educate yourself about brands and values. You can do this by purchasing wristwatch price guides, joining collectible watch clubs and subscribing to collectible watch publications. Your best buying sources for used watches will be flea markets, estate sales, auctions, garage sales and private sellers advertising in the classifieds.

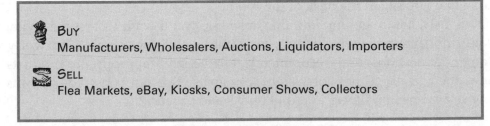

BUY
Manufacturers, Wholesalers, Auctions, Liquidators, Importers

SELL
Flea Markets, eBay, Kiosks, Consumer Shows, Collectors

RESOURCES
- A&E Watches, ✍ aandewatches.com
- Any Time Watch & Clock Wholesale, ☎ (610) 380-4518, ✍ anytimewholesale.com
- DH Gate, ✍ dhgate.com/productdirlist_201904_nol_true.html
- Global Sources Direct, ✍ globalsourcesdirect.com/servlet/Categories?keyword=Wrist+Watches
- MBK Wholesale, ☎ (770) 631-8940, ✍ mbkwholesale.com
- National Association of Watch and Clock Collectors, ☎ (717) 684-8261, ✍ nawcc.org
- Time & Gems, ✍ timeandgems.com

Water Purifiers

Selling water purification and filtering systems from home, online, and at home shows is a fantastic way to supplement your income, or even replace your current income altogether. Next to natural spring water, the best way to provide safe and clean drinking water for the family is to install a water purification system in the home.

Water purifiers can be costly inline systems or inexpensive under-counter or countertop filters. There are also portable filters for camping and the cottage, marine and RV water purifiers, and water filters for the bath, the showerhead, and even the garden hose.

Buying sources include factory direct from the manufacturer and through wholesalers and distributors. Selling methods include direct-to-businesses for commercial filter systems, exhibiting at home and garden shows for residential, a home-based showroom, and online sales via your own e-commerce website. If you have the skills and tools, extra money can be earned by installing the under-counter and inline systems, offering customers a convenient, one-stop shopping package.

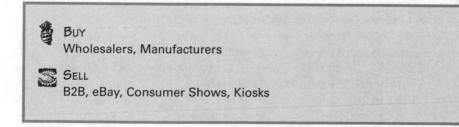

BUY
Wholesalers, Manufacturers

SELL
B2B, eBay, Consumer Shows, Kiosks

>  RESOURCES
> —Aquasana Manufacturing, ☎ (817) 536-5250, ✎ aquasana.com
> —Crystal Quest Wholesale, ☎ (888) 363-9842, ✎ crystalquest.com
> —Pure Earth Technologies, ☎ (800) 669-1376, ✎ pure-earth.com

Wedding Apparel

With more than two million weddings taking place each year in the United States alone, the prospects for a buy-and-sell venture specializing in wedding gowns, bridal dresses and accessories are incredible.

New gowns and accessories can be purchased directly from manufacturers, designers and wholesalers, while used gowns and accessories can be purchased from classified ads and online marketplaces. Set up a boutique right in your home and advertise locally, making sure to build alliances with people in the industry, such as wedding planners, invitation printers, cake bakers and photographers. All can refer your business to their clients.

Gowns also sell extremely well on eBay and other online wedding-themed marketplaces. Count on earning in the range of 20 to 30 percent of the retail selling price of new gowns and accessories, and as much as 50 percent on secondhand gowns. To do well, it's important to stay on top of the latest fashions and trends, so read all of the bridal and wedding planning magazines and books you can get your hands on!

> BUY
> Wholesalers, Manufacturers, Classified Ads, Online Marketplaces
>
> SELL
> Homebased Sales, Bridal Shows, eBay
>
> RESOURCES
> —American Apparel and Footwear Manufacturers' Association,
>   ✎ apparelandfootwear.org
> —Discount Bridal Service, ✎ workwithbrides.com
> —TB Wedding Dresses Wholesale, ✎ tbweddingdresseswholesale.com
> —Used Wedding Dresses, ☎ (972) 365-7603,
>   ✎ usedweddingdresses.com
> —Wholesale Wedding Gowns, ✎ wholesaleweddinggowns.com

Western Apparel

Anything and everything "Western" is hot. Hats, boots, shirts, jackets, belts and buckles, and any other garments with a decisively Western flavor are big sellers in Texas and elsewhere. Buy for half of retail value or less from wholesalers, liquidators and manufacturers of fine Western-themed apparel and accessories.

Selling through online marketplaces, at flea markets, at community rodeos and events, at square dances, and right from a homebased showroom will net you your highest return. Also, consider buying and selling Native American-made clothing and crafts direct from southwestern Indian tribes.

BUY
Manufacturers, Wholesalers

SELL
Flea Markets, Homebased Sales, Online Marketplaces, Consumer Shows

RESOURCES
—American Apparel and Footwear Manufacturers' Association, apparelandfootwear.org
—Cow Town Boots, cowtownboots.com
—Infomat Western Apparel Manufacturers Directory, infomat.com/guides/westernwear.html
—Western Express, (800) 245-1380, westernexpressinc.com

Wicker Products

Interior and exterior wicker furniture and decorative items are wonderful buy-and-sell products. Whether new or used, wicker is always in demand. If your budget permits, the best way to go is with new wicker products purchased from foreign manufacturers. If not, U.S. and Canadian wholesalers and importers are a good alternative for buying in smaller quantities.

Used wicker products can be purchased from private sellers advertising in the classifieds, at garage sales, and by attending auctions. Both new and used wicker merchandise can be sold via eBay, at flea markets, through a homebased showroom or by exhibiting at home and garden shows.

Buy
Manufacturers, Wholesalers, Auctions

Sell
Homebased Sales, Kiosks, Flea Markets, eBay, Home and Garden Shows

Resources
—Bali Bintang, ♂ bali-bintang-art-gallery.com
—Buhi Imports, ♂ buhiimports.com
—Cindy Rattan Manufacturing, ♂ cindyfinishing.com
—Dollar Days, ♂ dollardays.com/wholesale-baskets.html
—TradeKey, ♂ tradekey.com/ks-wicker-products

Wind Chimes

Bamboo, anodized aluminum, cast iron, glass, seashells and ceramic tiles are only a few of the materials used to construct beautiful-sounding wind chimes. They are available in every size, style and price point imaginable to suit every individual's tastes and budget. Buy direct from foreign manufacturers of mass-produced wind chimes, or enlist the services of craftspeople to custom-make the wind chimes you'll be selling.

Regardless of the route you choose, sell the chimes on eBay, at home and garden shows, at gift shows, at flea markets and by renting kiosk space in malls and public markets. Of course, if you have a few dozen displayed in your yard with For Sale signs posted, there is no doubt you will attract lots of attention and people stopping in to make a purchase.

Buy
Manufacturers, Craftspeople, Wholesalers

Sell
Flea Markets, Kiosks, eBay, Homebased Sales, Community Events, Craft Shows, Home and Garden Shows, Gift Shows

Resources
—Akron Novelty, ♂ akron-novelty.com/Scripts/
   prodList.asp?idCategory=103
—Esco Imports, ☎ (800) 445-3836, ♂ escoimports.com
—Super Wholesaler, ♂ superwholesaler.com/merchandise/wind-chimes
—WholesaleMart, ♂ wholesalemart.com/cat_windchimes.cfm

Window Treatments

Anyone who lives in a home or apartment has windows. In addition to offering privacy, window treatments and shades add a touch of style and décor to any room. As a buy-and-sell entrepreneur, you can get into the window treatments business using drop-ship suppliers, purchasing your inventory wholesale, or by crafting custom-designed window treatments for your clients.

Making custom window treatments from scratch, if you're good at crafts and sewing, will earn you the highest profits. You can sell to new homebuyers, people renovating or redecorating their homes, and professional interior designers.

In addition to curtains, window shades and blinds (which can be bought wholesale, directly from the manufacturer) are also profitable items to sell. To succeed, you must be able to market your business to its target audience, offer creative guidance to your customers, and know all about interior design and decorating. Seek out referrals from Realtors and interior designers to help generate business.

BUY
Manufacturers, Wholesalers, Distributors, Create Your Own

SELL
Homebased Showroom, Home Shows, Interior Design Shows

RESOURCES
—Blinds Wholesale, blindswholesale.com
—Factory Bargain Drapes, factorybargaindrapes.com/
  wholesale_window_treatments.asp
—Kilmor Innovative Home Fashions, kimlor.com/Window-Treatments/
  accessories.html
—Wholesale Window Treatments, wwtc.com
—Window Toppers, windowtoppers.com/wholesale.html

Wine

Millions of people enjoy a glass of fine wine with lunch or dinner. There are also collectors of fine wine and serious wine enthusiasts. It's customary to bring wine as a gift when visiting friends or loved ones for dinner or a party. Thus buying and selling wine to collectors and customers alike can be a lucrative business. That is, if you're willing to acquire the detailed knowledge necessary to be able to sell this type of product.

Because there are literally thousands of vineyards worldwide, you'll probably want to develop a specialty and offer select wines from specific regions. You can buy wine directly from vineyards, as well as from wholesalers and distributors.

In addition to selling wine online and at gourmet food shows, you can host wine tasting parties from home. Be sure to acquire any special licenses needed to buy and sell wine in your state or region. To boost profits, consider selling gourmet cheeses and other wine-related items, such as storage racks, portable wine cellars and high-end wine glasses.

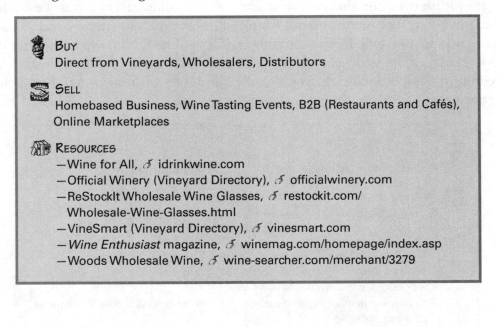

BUY
Direct from Vineyards, Wholesalers, Distributors

SELL
Homebased Business, Wine Tasting Events, B2B (Restaurants and Cafés), Online Marketplaces

RESOURCES
—Wine for All, ♂ idrinkwine.com
—Official Winery (Vineyard Directory), ♂ officialwinery.com
—ReStockIt Wholesale Wine Glasses, ♂ restockit.com/
   Wholesale-Wine-Glasses.html
—VineSmart (Vineyard Directory), ♂ vinesmart.com
—*Wine Enthusiast* magazine, ♂ winemag.com/homepage/index.asp
—Woods Wholesale Wine, ♂ wine-searcher.com/merchant/3279

INDEX